Lesbian and Gay Lifestyles

A Guide for Counseling and Education

The paper used in this publication meets the minimum requirements of
American National Standard for Information Sciences—
Permanence of Paper for Printed Library Materials,
ANSI Z39.48-1984.

Lesbian and Gay Lifestyles

A Guide for Counseling and Education

Natalie Jane Woodman, Editor
Raymond Berger
Diane Bernard
Winn Kelly Brooks
Doug Burnham
Dan Forrister
John Grace
Patricia L. Gunter
Hilda Hidalgo
Judith A. B. Lee
Harry Lenna
Dean Pierce
William D. Shattls
Michael Shernoff
Pat Terry
Carol Tully

IRVINGTON PUBLISHERS, INC.
NEW YORK

Irvington Publishers, Inc.,
Executive offices: 740 Broadway, New York, New York 10003
Customer service and warehouse in care of: Integrated Distribution
Services, 195 McGregor St, Manchester, NH 03102, (603) 669-5933

Library of Congress Cataloging-in-Publication Data

Lesbian and gay lifestyles : a guide for counseling and education /
    Natalie Jane Woodman ... [et al.].
                p.   cm.
        Includes bibliographical references and index.
        ISBN 0-8290-2472-7 : $14.95
        1. Social work with gays—United States. I. Woodman,
    Natalie Jane, 1931-   .
    HV1449.L48   1992
    362.8—dc20   92-1135
                                              CIP

First Printing 1992
1 3 5 7 9 10 8 6 4 2

Printed in the United States of America

Acknowledgements

The Editor deeply appreciates the efforts of the contributing authors in sharing their knowledge, practice expertise, and research findings. Their concern for the future of professional service to lesbian women and gay men is a tribute to social work and social work education.

Appreciation must be expressed to the CSWE Commission on Gay/Lesbian Issues for providing the initial thrust to produce this work. However, continuation, in the face of lack of support from any number of sources, would not have been possible without the on-going push from Bette Harlan.

Gratitude also is due Laura Orr at Arizona State University without whose help this manuscript could never have been coordinated on a computerized system for publication. Her assistance extended to editorial observations to make for smoother reading for students, faculty, and practioners. For hours of labor in indexing, many thanks to Janine Klabe, MSW.

Finally, appreciation must be expressed to the many lesbian and gay clients who have helped all of us recognize the importance of competent and knowledgeable service from mainstream agency resources and from all helping professionals.

Table of Contents

About the Editor and Authors

NATALIE JANE WOODMAN is a Professor Emerita at Arizona State University's School of Social Work where she continues to teach human behavior and women's issues courses. Her publications include *Counseling with Gay Men and Women* (co-author: Harry Lenna) and *Lesbian and Gay Issues: A Resource Manual for Social Workers* (co-edited with Hilda Hidalgo and Travis Peterson). Her entry on "Homosexuality: Lesbian Women" in the *Encyclopedia of Social Work*, Associate Editorship of and articles in the *Journal of Gay and Lesbian Psychotherapy* represent other scholarly accomplishments. Ms. Woodman was co-chair of the CSWE Commission on Gay/Lesbian Issues for several years and has been active with state and national NASW committees on lesbian and gay issues.

RAYMOND BERGER, is the author of *Gay and Gray: The Older Homosexual Man* published by the University of Illinois Press in 1982 and reprinted by Alyson Press in 1984. Dr. Berger received his MSW and Ph.D. degrees from the University of Wisconsin-Madison in 1973 and 1976. A widely published and nationally recognized expert in gay and lesbian aging, Dr. Berger is a recipient of the Dade County Coalition for Human Rights (1979) and the Evelyn Hooker Research Award presented by the Gay Academic Union (1982). He is listed in the *International Authors and Writers of Who's Who* (Tenth Edition) and has worked as a social work educator, researcher, consultant, and psychotherapist.

DIANE BERNARD, holder of the Belle Apafford Chair for Women at the University of Utah, has a distinguished history in academia and social work practice. Her listings in Who's Who includes those related to American Women, Women in

Education, in America and in the World. Dr. Bernard's expertise in her field has been recognized by inclusion of scholarly entries in the *Encyclopedia of Social Work*, academic and administrative positions in academia, and her participation on various Commissions of the Council on Social Work Education.

WINN KELLY BROOKS, now on the faculty of Northeastern State University in Tahlequah, Oklahoma also has served in various academic capacities at other institutions, most notably stimulating and challenging her students in the areas of human growth and development and research. She obtained her D.S.W. from the University of California at Berkeley and, from her doctoral research, proceeded to write a seminal work, *Minority Stress and Lesbian Women*. Brooks also has enjoyed opportunities to work directly with persons seeking help, integrating her feminist ideology with her persistent search for human justice.

DOUG BURNHAM is a Professor of Social Work at Eastern Kentucky University. Prof. Burnham received his MSW from the University of Alabama. Among the related experiences he brings to the article on Community Organization are: Chair of Primary Health Care Governing Council; Chair of Foster Care Review Board; Board Chair of Syncopated, Inc. (a community dance organization); Past President of Lexington Gay/Lesbian Services Organization; and President of Kentucky Association of Social Work Educators.

DAN FORRISTER was a member of the faculty at Texas Women's University, where he taught human behavior, social welfare and direct practice courses. Dr. Forrister received his MSW from the University of Michigan and his Ph.D. from the University of Texas at Austin. In addition to teaching, he had been a consultant for an agency which provides group services for sexually abused children. Dr. Forrister also was a volunteer group worker for the Fort Worth Counseling Center AIDS Project, facilitating self-help groups for persons with AIDS. He began his career as a group worker in the Army where he worked with groups of soldiers returning from Vietnam with substance abuse problems.

JOHN GRACE, MSW, ACSW, currently practicing and residing in Florida, has written and presented various articles sensitively describing coming out in a homophobic environment. He has been coordinator of the Gay and Lesbian Counseling Program at Family and Children's Service in Minneapolis, Minnesota, an agency notable for establishing the first such program in a "mainstream" setting. In addition to practice, Grace has been a member of the NASW National Committee on Lesbian and Gay Issues, NASW Editorial Advisory Committee for *Lesbian and Gay Issues: A Resource Manual for Social Workers* (to which he was a contributor), and the Editorial Board of the *Journal of Gay and Lesbian Psychotherapy*.

PATRICIA L. GUNTER will be remembered by her colleagues as an involved social worker concerned with Native American as well as gay and lesbian issues, both in clinical settings and as an educator. She wrote and published numerous articles and presented nationally and internationally on gay and lesbian topics. Dr. Gunter's professional services included: membership on NASW's National Committee on Lesbian and Gay Issues as well as CSWE's Commission on Lesbian and Gay Issues and, for many years, serving as co-chair of the Association of Social Workers Concerned with Lesbian and Gay Issues. At the time of her death, she was serving as a faculty member of the University of Tennessee, Nashville.

HILDA HIDALGO, Professor of Public Administration and Social Work at Rutgers University is the author of numerous articles on adult education, Third World concerns and oppression, and lesbian and gay issues. Public recognition honors for distinguished service and contributions to women's causes span two decades including an honorary degree in Humane Letters from Marymount Manhattan College. Her leadership in social work efforts to confront homophobia has been notable in the history of the profession's associations. As co-editor of *Lesbian and Gay Issues: A Resource Manual*, Dr. Hidalgo provided yet another major contribution to the knowledge base for those who practice with lesbian women and gay men.

JUDITH A. B. LEE received her MSW from Columbia University and a DSW from Wurzweiler School of Social Work. She is currently a Professor at the University of Connecticut School of Social Work, following experience in other social work programs and in the field of child welfare/work with oppressed groups. Dr. Lee has written extensively in a range of journals and books stressing the theme of primary groups ties as a healing force and as a vehicle for social action and social change. She also has served as President of the Association for the Advancement of Social Work with Groups. One of her most recent publications is the very complete *An Annotated Bibliography of Gay and Lesbian Readings*.

HARRY LENNA was awarded his MSW degree from the State University of New York at Buffalo and received his Ph.D. from the University of Denver. Presently, he divides his clinical social work endeavors between general private practice and consultation to persons with AIDS in the Phoenix area. Dr. Lenna also taught various aspects of social work practice at Arizona State University over a period of eleven years. He is co-author of *Counseling with Gay Men and Women*, has presented papers related to group work with gay/lesbian youth and is currently a member of the Board of the *Journal of Lesbian and Gay Psychotherapy*.

DEAN PIERCE completed his MSW studies at West Virginia University and received his Ph.D. from the University of California at Berkeley. Currently Director of the School of Social Work and Professor at University of Nevada, Reno, he also has been a social work faculty member in Minnesota, California, New York, Louisiana, and Delaware teaching policy, practice, and human behavior courses as well as coordinating field education. Dr. Pierce has been active in CSWE working as a Board Member, consultant and site visitor, presenting at Annual Program Meetings, and co-chairing the Council's Commission on Gay/Lesbian Issues. His research and writing in the area of policy and practice include *Policy for the Social Work Practioner* and *Social Work and Society: An Introduction*.

WILLIAM D. SHATTLS, CSW, ACSW, was well respected and loved by colleagues and those whom he served during his years as a psychotherapist in private practice in New York City. During his doctoral studies at Hunter College School of Social Work, CUNY, he focussed his dissertation studies on AIDS prevention. He continued both practice and research at Gay Men's Health Crisis relative to safer sex education. At GMHC, Mr. Shattls also had served as Assistant Project Coordinator for the "800 Men" safer sex education project, was a consultant in both the Education and Clinical Services Departments, and had been a Field Instructor for social work students. In a volunteer capacity, he supervised and trained crisis workers and was a member of the GMHC speaker's Bureau. Mr. Shattls also was co-author of "AIDS, Sexuality, and Sexual Control."

MICHAEL SHERNOFF, CSW, ACSW, a psychotherapist in private practice in Manhattan, received his MSW from State University of New York at Stony Brook. He was co-coordinator of the First International Lesbian/Gay Health Conference and Third AIDS Forum. His numerous publications include: co-editor of the First Edition of the *Sourcebook on Lesbian/Gay Health Care*; co-author of "When a Friend Has AIDS..." and the *Facilitator's Guide to Eroticizing Safer Sex: A Psychoeducational Workshop.* Mr. Shernoff is a volunteer at Gay Men's Health Crisis and an adjunct faculty member in their Department of Education, president of the Board of Directors of Hyacinth Foundation, and a member of the NASW National Committee on Lesbian and Gay Issues.

PAT TERRY has her MSW from Arizona State University, a Ph.D. in Health and Human Services from Columbia Pacific University, and holds NASW Diplomate status. From unit supervisor to Acting Director at Arizona State Hospital, she has moved to the position of Chief of Resource Development for the Mental Health Division of Washington State. Dr. Terry brings both practice and administrative experience to her writing. In addition to contributing to *Lesbian and Gay Issues: A Resource Manual for Social Workers*, she has presented papers on related topics at state and national conferences.

CAROL TULLY is presently Assistant Professor at the University of Georgia following her tenure as Executive Director of the Georgia Council on Aging where her primary responsibility was that of legislative advocacy. Prior to assuming these positions, she had been on the faculty of West Virginia University's School of Social Work. Dr. Tully received her MSW and PhD degrees from Virginia Commonwealth University where she was active in the academic setting following her contributions to the profession in the area of public welfare. As a regular contributor to professional journals, her knowledge of gerontology and women's issues is well documented.

Introduction

Purpose

This book has been written for educators, agency field internship instructors, students, and practioners in the helping professions. It is intended to provide a broad spectrum of knowledge related to lesbian and gay populations. For educators, it demonstrates how this content can be integrated into curricula. Field instructors will be able to see new linkages between classroom learning and activities students may encounter in social service settings. For professional workers, the articles challenge learning from prior years which neglected or distorted inclusion of content relative to lesbian women and gay men in almost every area of study. Additionally, each unit includes practice examples of social work, social action, and research with this oppressed minority.

The 1983 Council on Social Work Education Curriculum Policy Statement included sexual orientation among the areas which schools of social work should address. This mandate was included in a grouping of populations about which social work education and practice should be concerned because lesbian women and gay men represent at least 10% of all persons regardless of ethnicity, rural or urban residence, or area of the country. Including significant others of lesbians and gays, the population under concern increases to more than 40%. Prior to and since this mandate, some papers have been presented at various professional meetings describing how content relative to lesbian and gay issues could be integrated into the curriculum of programs educating helping professionals. However, the material presented hardly has trickled into the classroom or agency setting. Part of the rationale for continued inaction has been lack of knowledge about how to "fit" material into existing courses. *Lesbian and Gay Lifestyles: A Guide for Counseling and Education* shows how the Curriculum Policy Statement can be implemented.

This book supplements other works which deal with counseling lesbian women and gay men or which are concerned with assessment of issues related to diverse life styles. Also, the authors provide updated research and examples of how and where social work and other helping professions can move into the vanguard of action with this population. This is particularly the case as we look at emerging roles in coping with the AIDS crisis. The book, therefore, represents a collection of new materials which will guide educators, students, and practioners as they explore various avenues of theory and practice relative to lesbian and gay issues.

Format

Lesbian and Gay Lifestyles: A Guide for Counseling and Education is divided into the traditional six areas of curricula in schools of social work. However, there obviously are linkages and interrelationships among the sections. For example, the practice or field instruction articles are supported by human behavior, policy, and research issues and examples. Learning and teaching at the bachelor's and master's levels are considered in each area.

The first chapter in each part of the book introduces ideas and material for inclusion of lesbian and gay content in the required courses of the curriculum. This provides for integration of material for learning and practice throughout the educational process which may or may not be supplemented by elective classes. Just as educators in the area of ethnic minority studies have demonstrated, electives very often speak to the "already converted," not to those most needy of gaining new insights.

To supplement the core material for learning and growth, each part of the book also includes supplementary articles which provide examples of application in working with lesbian and gay populations. These articles were selected to cover the breadth of age groupings (for example, youth, families, and eldering), pertinent problem areas encountered by lesbian and gay client groups or communities (exemplified in the articles related to AIDS, families in rural areas, and affirmative action issues), and research needs related to lesbian and gay issues. It has been well documented that oppression is a major contributor to the life stresses encountered by lesbian women and gay men. However, minimal attention is given to using and applying conceptual knowledge about stigmatization in intervention with this population. The authors provide models for practice and advocacy which can be implemented by direct practioners, policy developers, administrators, and community practioners.

Although much of the focus is on knowledge and practice, all authors emphasize the relevance of attending to attitudes and values. All of the helping professions continue to reflect varying degrees of homophobia in education of students as well as in practice with clients. Several of the authors in *Lesbian and Gay Lifestyles: A Guide for Counseling and Education* provide role playing examples and other techniques for confronting this pernicious form of oppression.

In its totality, it is hoped that this book will take us one step further in assuring that the rights and need of *all* persons, regardless of sexual orientation, are addressed. This must include a solid body of knowledge, professional skills, and a value base which adheres to the ethics requiring advocacy, care, and elimination of oppression and inequality for lesbian women and gay men.

PART I

HUMAN BEHAVIOR IN THE SOCIAL ENVIRONMENT

Introduction

It is axiomatic that understanding the human condition and the effects of environmental forces on behavior is a prerequisite for any intervention with clients or social institutions. Additionally, recognition is usually given to the fact that unique experiences and developmental processes should be understood by all practitioners. However, many educators blatantly ignore content related to lesbian and gay development, frequently with the rationalization that it is not possible to include all variations in life styles.

Lee introduces the educator to some fundamental ways in which human behavior content indeed can be structured to include knowledge about lesbians and gays while covering necessary information for social work practice. The author begins by placing such teaching in the context of theoretical orientations and provides a rationale for using an ecological approach in these courses. She then examines the literature with regard to identity formation/ coming out and the impacts of stigmatization. Lee provides outlines demonstrating the ways in which addition of lesbian/gay content can be included without artificiality (but with "goodness of fit"). From suggested references and curriculum design, the author moves to teaching methodology and suggestions for integrating knowledge, values and skill. Her replete citation of references is an added plus for educators, students, students, and practitioners.

Bernard's article complements Lee's presentation in that it also begins by examining theory bases - in this instance, by illustrating the fallacy of reductionism when attempts are made to identify "causation" relative to homosexuality. The author then proceeds to differentiate between behaviors and orientation, a distinction frequently overlooked by practitioners and client groups. Other issues are identified, with the author describing societal pressures which compound bias and stigma. Differences between gay and lesbian development are specified as are the influences of difference in orientation on self-perception. Of note is Bernard's emphasis on the great potential for developing personal resources for coping with a homophobic society and "growing in spite of oppression."

Grace completes this section by describing the impact of homophobia on development of a positive sense of self. He gives attention to development of competence by lesbian women and gay men in spite of internalization of socially induced fears. Using the conceptual model of private and public selves, Grace then elaborates on defensive patterns which evolve in the face of feelings of shame encountered at various points in identity development. Attention to understanding the importance of "developmental lag" is part of the author's thesis. In further support of previous and subsequent chapters, Grace concludes with suggestions for intervention so as to enable gay and lesbian clients to develop identity which is self affirming and "characterized by variety, choice, and responsibility."

1

Teaching Content Related to Lesbian and Gay Identity Formation

Judith A.B. Lee, Ph.D.

Social work education has a commitment to developing and teaching content related to serving oppressed populations. Because of homophobia and taboos existing around sexuality, little attention is paid to substantive issues for lesbian women and gay men. A critical issue is lesbian and gay identity formation, also known as "the coming-out process." This content reflects a complex transactional phenomena which can appropriately be taught in all curriculum areas. However, the focus of this chapter will be the teaching and integration of this content in the basic Human Behavior in the Social Environment courses.

Identity formation is an individual lifelong process which takes place in transaction with the environment from birth to death. The positive outcomes of this process are a sense of self-esteem, relatedness, autonomy, and competence. Negative outcomes include self-hatred, isolation, and alienation.

Two critical questions must be addressed in integrating this or any other content related to oppressed statuses into a curriculum. First, does the existing curriculum have a philosophical and knowledge base that appreciates difference and emphasizes person:environment transactions instead of labelling differences as deviance, deficit, or pathology? And, what content shall we choose to integrate into appropriate existing curricula? There is a wealth of content related to gay/lesbian concerns. What are the essential bottom line additions?

This writer suggests that courses based on an ecological perspective (Germain, 1979) create a climate naturally hospitable to current thinking related to all oppressed minorities. Content related to the lesbian/gay identity formation process is an essential addition to HBSE courses because of its central concern in the lives of gay individuals and its applications to non-gay individuals dealing with a range of stigmatized statuses. The content addresses itself to a process of becoming and coping with difference and its effects on growth.

Social work practitioners have a mandate and purpose which "arises from a dual, simultaneous concern for the adaptive potential of people and the nutritive qualities of their environments" (Germain, 1979, p. 17). Human Behavior courses which embrace any linear theory tend to reduce understanding of all phenomena within the bounds of that theory. Linear theories often take us on a vain search for explanation or causality rather than understanding and appreciating differences in transactional terms. Sometimes such theories also measure whole groups of people against yardsticks of development or continua which imply normalcy at one end and pathology on the other (Perman, 1963; Klaich, 1974; Masterson, 1976, p. 43). This kind of thinking adds to the oppression of people who are outside of the dominant group's norms.

The Ecological Perspective— Goodness of Fit

The ecological perspective, on the other hand, provides us with a view of human behavior in the social environment which deals with the complexities of social living. Ecology, as described by Germain (1979), is a form of general systems theory which is:

> "concerned with the relations among living entities and between entities and other aspects of their environment . . . This perspective is concerned with the growth, development, and potentialities of human beings and with the properties of environments that support or fail to support the expression of human potential . . . In an ecological view; practice is directed toward improving the transactions between people and environments in order to enhance adaptive capacities and improve environments

The outcome of this process is a "goodness of fit" between people and environments. This dual focus provides a knowledge base capable of integrating content related to oppressed groups.

The central concept of this perspective is the reciprocal active process of adaptation. To attain goodness of fit, people use adaptive behaviors which may involve changing the environment, changing themselves, or leaving the environment. Disturbances in the adaptive balance between people and environments cause stress which may produce problems in living in three spheres of life, the life transitional, interpersonal, and environmental spheres (Germain & Gitterman, 1980). There are three sets of concepts and subconcepts on which this life model rests.

1. Transactions between people and environments— stress, coping, adaptation, reciprocity, mutuality, and goodness-of-fit;
2. Human attributes achieved in growth and development through transaction with environments - a sense of identity, competence, autonomy and relatedness; and
3. Environmental qualities - physical, social, nutritive environments, layers, pollution, time, space, textures, and so on.

A course outline for a HBSE course based on the ecological perspective is presented briefly here as it operationalizes the abstractions presented thus far (Germain, 1985). The course is conceived of as a year long course. Its design is as follows:

The HBSE Course

"Concepts from biology, evolutionary theory, and the behavioral sciences are used for an ecological perspective on development and tasks within the context of a rapidly changing, urbanized, bureaucratic society. The focus is on maturational, emotional, cognitive, sensory perceptual, and social factors within the individual; systemic factors in collective life; physical and social environmental conditions that support or inhibit development and functioning; and the variations arising from culture, ethnicity, social class, gender, sexual preference, physical or mental disabilities, and rural-urban differences - particularly as these variations pose exceptional tasks for individuals and collectivities. Implications for social work are considered throughout" (Germain, 1985).

The course objectives are achieved with the following structure which utilizes a notion of cog wheeling. That is, the needs of systems and individuals are juxtaposed to each other. Infancy is therefore considered in tandem with young adult parents and in relation to the effects of poverty on maternal care; adulthood with adolescent children, work, income and equity issues, and aging parents; children in families, with nutritive, sexist, or racist communities, schools and peer groups; and so on. The educator has the burden of moving in more than a sequential way - of making bridges between what may have been seen as discrete categories. It is a process of weaving in concepts which are also in transaction and not of considering in sequence the "life cycle from birth to death."

FIGURE 1
THE COURSE OUTLINE
(Abbreviated Form)

**Adding Gay Content
Dealing With**

I. Theoretical Orientation - the Ecological Perspective Emphasis on Transactions.	I. Stigma, homophobia, the exceptional tasks of oppressed groups.
II. The Community as Context for Groups, Families, and Individuals.	II. Community attitudes toward gays; religious, ethnic and class variables; the gay community.
III. Family Structures, Functions and Tasks	III. Alternate family forms including the gay couple or family; family acceptance of gay members.
IV. Young Adulthood and the New Family in its Community and Culture	IV. Choosing a gay identity and lifestyle; the coming out process; gay parenting; concepts of gender identity and sex role expectations from birth onward.
V. The Family and the School Age Child: The Environment and Culture	V. Gay families; children of gay parents; blended families; androgyny; sex role responses of school and environment.
VI. Middle Adulthood: The Family, the Adolescent, and the Environment	VI. Gay couples, gay adolescents and identity struggles; oppression; concepts of sexual orientation and sexual preference; marginality; dealing with difference; maintaining and ending relationships; the work place.
VII. The Aging Process: The Environment and Culture	VII. Gay Aging; Social networks; resources

Gay/Lesbian Content

The outline presented in Figure 1 includes gay and lesbian content under each of the headings. The emphasis on the exceptional tasks of oppressed groups begins with the theoretical orientation and continues throughout the course. The following areas are inter-woven in course content and readings: the often poor fit between gays, communities and other groups; the isolation and alienation of the stigmatized; the importance of knowing and building the resources of the gay community including self help groups and a range of services; the painful struggles of gays and families, the need for role models for gay/lesbian youth, and for couples; the special problems of gay/lesbian parents; and gay aging. The concept of homophobia, both that held by non-gays and internalized and held by gays as well is a central thread running through all of this material. The special tasks of belonging to this highly stigmatized group are highlighted throughout but can perhaps be best brought together with emphasis on knowledge about the gay identity formation process known as "coming out."

Substantial material on this process can be included in Section IV, "Young Adulthood and . . ." In teaching, this author adds "and the choice to come out (define one's self) as a gay person who probably won't marry and may not develop a biological family, and who will choose a different lifestyle as an adult." It is placed here because "intimacy vs. isolation" and the beginnings of laying foundations in love and work are appropriate tasks for young adults, and because the traditional view that maturity means marriage and family (Golan, 1981) is a very narrow one. It must be stressed however, that gay men and lesbian women come out (self define) at all stages of life. For many it is life long, an identity issue not resolved in adolescence nor completed by old age.

Review of the Literature: Identity Formation The Coming Out Process

Familiarity with two types of literature is important:

literature on the coming out process and literature on how identity formation occurs. Several texts related to the course outline are used. The one that covers a variety of gay/lesbian concerns is Moses' and Hawkins' *Counseling Lesbian Women and Gay Men* (1982). To provide the level of intervention to knowledge about the coming out process, Lewis' (1984) article is essential. She focuses on integrating lesbian identity into a healthy self-concept. She presents a model of this process, stressing how the various stages of the process look in actual life and practice and what clinical interventions may be helpful. Her continuum of stages involves: dealing with being different; experiencing dissonance and inner turmoil as related to the age in the life span when this is taking place; building relationships, dealing with issues of separatism, dealing with family; forming a stable lesbian identity and integrating that with a whole life and healthy self concept (Lewis, 1984). Lewis also cites other descriptions of coming out. Included are Cass' (1979) six stage model from identity confusion to identity synthesis, Lehman's (1978) five stage process including the stages of coming out publicly and politically, as well as Grace's competence model (1979) for gay men. Grace delineates clinical issues for the stages, and stresses that there is no value judgement placed at being in earlier or later stages. His chapter in Hildalgo, Peterson & Woodman (1985) *Lesbian and Gay Issues: A Resource Manual* also is excellent on the issues of "Coming Out in Social Work." Grace's definition of "coming out" is important: "Identifying and respecting one's homosexuality and disclosing this positive identity to others." His five stage model ends with "the continuing establishment of a positive and proactive self-concept . . ." (Grace, 1985:130-131). Hildalgo, et al. is also essential reading for those who want to be aware of the variety of gay/lesbian issues including individuals facing triple oppression, minorities of color, age, and the differently able as well.

Berger (1983) stresses the continua of sexuality and of homosexuality, presenting a helpful table of two dimensions, time and tasks. He discusses an early problem of the coming out process as "identity confusion" which represents an incongruence between overt behavior and covert behavior in relation to self-image and self acceptance. Passing, or posturing oneself as heterosexual, was noted as a difficult way of coping in that those who passed were more likely to score high on indicators of depression, interpersonal awkwardness, and anxiety about their gayness. He noted that gay people were increasingly dealing with identity management by coming out and that the effectiveness of this relates to the social environment and the way in which the individual shares this once private information. For many, this ability to share was a major step toward self-acceptance, although this process may take several months or several decades. The importance of peer support was also noted (Morson & McKinnis, 1983; Berger, 1983).

Where Berger spoke of the process for gay males, Moses's doctoral dissertation on *Identity Management in Lesbian Women* (1978) illuminates the coming out process for lesbian women as a way of managing an identity socially labelled as deviant. She redefines the problem from linear searching for causality to "how does one manage a deviant identity?" Moses notes that, due to social stresses and the rewards of passing, everyone indulges to some degree in this behavior. Yet "this requires a great deal of management, e.g. vigilance, resourcefulness, stamina, sustained motivation, pre-planning, sharpness, wit, knowledge, making explanations and the avoidance of situations." As Sancier said, "Imagine life as a lie. A lie that must be carefully protected and nurtured every day . . ." (1984, p. 3).

However, as a result of stringent research analysis based on a sample of 82 self identified lesbians, Moses concluded: "management is a problem but not a trauma or a chronic state of affairs . . . They are not miserable and desperate, they are not consumed by their deviance, they do not bemoan their fate. Some are angry, few are entirely satisfied, but most feel that being lesbian is their choice and that the choice is a good one for all its inevitable difficulties . . ." (Moses, 1978). She further suggests that more lesbians may now be coping less with how to pass and more with how to live as someone who has come out. Moses was also urged by many respondents who felt they had fewer problems than when they were straight, "not to focus her study on the problems of being a lesbian but to remember the joy, the love and happiness" (Moses, 1978:85). This is critical for the educator to keep in mind.

Stages of coming out also involve a variation on the stages of grieving (Kubler-Ross, 1969) and depression and loss must also be faced. Some feel that the "loss is never resolved due to environmental and political contingencies" and that one has to "keep dealing with breaking the taboo and its repercussions" throughout life (Massiah, 1985). Massiah also presents nineteen stages of the grieving process which moves from shock and guilt to hope, to an identity crisis, and reaffirmation and reintegration. She questions rightly why important works on grieving like Bertha Simos' *A Time to Grieve* say nothing about the lesbian/gay struggle with this process (Massiah, 1985). This may relate to adapting a concept to a situation where there is no death or "object loss." The fourth stage of grieving "Acceptance" (Kubler-Ross, 1963, p. 113) is not therefore "devoid of feelings" but filled with feelings of the joy of self affirmation and self actualization. Emphasis on these positive outcomes, and research like Moses' study, are crucial for lesbians/gays and all students to know.

The general literature on identity formation is better known by educators hence selective highlights are noted here. Goffman's classic work on Stigma (1963) forms a foundation on which concepts relating to the coming out process may be built. He categorizes three types of identity: *social identity*, the ways in which society defines a person, (usually negative definitions for lesbians/gays); *personal identity*, identity pegs which differentiate an individual from all others, the outstanding social and biographical facts; and *ego identity*, the felt, subjective sense of one's own situation, continuity and character obtained as a result of social experiences, the fashioning of one's self from social and personal realities. Because of stigma and difficult social experiences, gays/lesbians often internalize hatred and ambivalence and experience alienation from the self and others. These are the problems that get worked out as part of the coming out process. Goffman defines stigma as a "deeply discrediting attribute - a relational concept between self and others." An identity that carries stigma is either discredited by the dominant group or discreditable if the stigma is not a visible one (Goffman, 1963). Hence, management behaviors including passing, which leaves one open to later discrediting, are necessary. Goffman further makes the point that the nature of a "good adjustment" requires that the "stigmatized individual cheerfully and unselfishly accept himself as essentially the same as normals, while at the same time he voluntarily withholds himself from some situations in which normals find it difficult to give lip service to their singular acceptance of him" (1963, p. 121). The cost to the stigmatized who are generous enough to relieve normals of a burden of threat or contamination is, at the very least, many awkward moments.

Erikson's formulation on the consolidation of ego identity occurring at the end of adolescence and the readiness of the young adult male for intimacy is a now classic work on identity. It is to be noted that Erikson's is a male model and that he stresses heterosexuality as the only valid expression of the ability to love (Erikson, 1963:261-266). Gilligan adds the female perspective as she notes that for women identity formation and intimacy occur simultaneously throughout the life span. The woman "comes to know herself as she is known, through her relationship with others" (1984:12) while men are known and may learn to know themselves more in relation to the world of objects. Whether gay men represent the "average range" of men or differ on this variable is not known. However, it seems quite logical that a key part of the self-identity process for lesbian women is the advent of the first intimate (sexual and emotional) relationship. Many of *The Coming Out Stories* (Stanley & Wolfe, 1980) and anecdotes in Berzon's *Positively Gay* (1979) attest to an identification of the "love that has no name" in relation to an important intimate experience. The educator can use these stories also to illustrate the stages of the process formulated in Figure 2.

FIGURE 2
HOW IS IDENTITY FORMED?

A Sense of Identity Is:	A Sense of Gay and Lesbian Identity Is:
Gradual synthesis of biological givens and innate needs and drives with acquired interests and capacities and significant identification with family members and others. It arises from sound continuity between past and aspirations for future.	The gradual ability to integrate one's sexual and emotional orientation with what one can do, wants to do and is becoming with being a member of a given family, cultural, ethnic and class group, and with membership in the gay community. The affirmation of one's past and all one is with one's future hopes, as a complete, non-segmented person.

An Individual
   tribal   )
   familial   ) conception
It arises out of interaction with others and their perceptions and expectations
	Individual-unique for each person. Often in conflict with the perceptions and expectations of the straight world, hence requires extra tasks at synthesis, and interaction with people who are positive about gayness.

Arising out of human relatedness and influences the nature of relationships	Arising out of human relatedness, it is often felt as disruptive in relationships of basic importance-especially family, and friendship-as they struggle with accepting a gay member. A task of gay people in synthesizing identity is, where possible, to help heal those disruptions in external systems and in the self.
Arising out of experiences of autonomy and competence and in turn affects them	The same, though opportunities for autonomy and competence may meet with severe external oppression and limitation of social roles and, due also to internalized homophobia and low self-esteem for some, may be curtailed unless a more positive gay identity is formed.
Needful nutritive properties of the environment to support it.	Like all minority identities, often fails to find support in the wider environment. Therefore needs to develop its nurturing and support systems and to be politically active, when able, to effect change.

Teaching Methods

It is helpful when teaching these concepts to broaden the discussion to a variety of people dealing with stigma. From the author's teaching records (1986):

> In my recent class, as I reached for such student experiences, one student shared the plight of his obese client; others shared the struggle of being Jewish in a New England town; of being an "oddball Christian" in the university community; of having a disfiguring birthmark; of being a tall woman; of being a recovering alcoholic; of being a newly arrived Hispanic woman; and of being black. It was a very moving experience. The students said that it helped them learn and empathize to make connections on the experiential level and that my own coming out, done several sessions before in a discussion on community, had set the tone in the class for them to do this. Then, in a manner quick to get his piece in before we ended class, a gay man was able to "come out" and to make the applications to his own life. There was the usual silence. He knew I supported him, and felt support from him, but I too was overwhelmed by his courage at the moment and also knew the pain of the other gay/lesbian students who did not feel able to do this. I recognized the moment non-verbally but missed the opportunity to offer verbal support to him and relieve the tension for other gay and non-gay members of the class. After class, he and I hugged and several students reached out to him.
>
> In the next class (the one in which I presented the coming out process,) I did bring us back to those moments and focus the class on our silence. Again, it was a moving experience as the taboos of this stigma were brought out and aired, and both he and I shared how it was always hard to share this because of those taboos and those silences! As we then worked on the following material I encouraged continued connections.

To address the question of how identity is formed I juxtapose Germain's broadening of Erikson's definition of identity (Germain, 1979) to the formation of a gay identity. This is opened for class discussion.

Coming Out and the Search for Authenticity

As identity formation is discussed, the problem of finding one's authentic self in a broader sense may be introduced. For example, Sheehy (1974) provides us with a wonderful description of the forties as "the deadline decade" for finding authenticity. Classes particularly enjoy the following excerpt of how one arrives at a real self and are able to identity with the search for "realness" as a kind of coming out process for everyone.

> The consensus of current research is that the transition into middle life is as critical as adolescence and in some ways more harrowing. Can it possibly be worth it to ride with this chaos and see it all? Is it worth it to become real?
>
> I'm rather partial to the answer given in a children's book, *The Velveteen Rabbit*. One day the young rabbit asks the Skin Horse, who has been around the nursery quite some time, what is real? And does it hurt?
>
> "Sometimes," said the Skin Horse, for he was always truthful. "When you are REAL you don't mind being hurt."
>
> "Does it happen all at once, like being wound up," he asked, "or bit by bit?"
>
> "It doesn't happen all at once," said the Skin Horse. "You become. It takes a long time, That's why it doesn't often happen to people who break easily, or have sharp edges, or who have to be carefully kept. Generally, by the time you are REAL, most of your hair has been loved off, and your eyes drop out and you get loose in the joints and very shabby. But these things don't matter at all, because once you are REAL

you can't be ugly, except to people who don't understand."

"Yes . . ."

To reach the clearing beyond, we must stay with the weightless journey through uncertainty. Whatever counterfeit safety we hold from over-investments in people and institutions must be given up. The inner custodian must be unseated from the controls. No foreign power can direct our journey from now on. It is for each of us to find a course that is valid by our own reckoning. And for each of us there is the opportunity to emerge reborn, *authentically* unique, with an enlarged capacity to love ourselves and embrace others. (1974, pp. 361-364)

Identifying with the more general struggle for authenticity enables the students to experience the coming-out process as their own and their clients' as well as that specifically experienced by gay people.

The following outline identifies and synthesizes the stages of the coming out process.

FIGURE 3
COMING-OUT: AN IDENTITY PROCESS

Note: This is not a linear process; one may go through the phases simultaneously and more than once when under stress. Environmental response is a critical factor in this process.

Developmental/Transitional and Interpersonal
Level of Identity Struggle

I.   Coming Out to Oneself (Emerging)

    A.   "General sense of being different," denial may be paramount-there may be identity confusion, there may be a vagueness in communication. E.g. "I saw 'this person' Sunday night," a feeling of alienation from the true self.

B. The Dissonance Phase - feels in conflict with self and world. Going through the stages of grieving the "lost self" and mourning the losses associated, real and imagined; the lost status of socially accepted identity -of heterosexual privilege - to having to manage a socially stigmatized identity. Moving toward affirming a positive identity - a process over time - one must mourn the losses realistically to own the gains affirmatively.

C. Phases of Grieving Through Affirming:

1. Denial and Isolation

"I can't name what I'm feeling."
"It was only a kiss, once during college."
"I still date men."
"I'm married-bisexual."
"I'm the only one like this."

Defensive withdrawal and avoidance of others and of situations which are uncomfortable.

2. Anger - sometimes direct, often disguised and repressed.

"Why me?"
"How can they (my loved ones and others) be so mean to me? They're all ignorant."
"I'll hate them before they hate me."
"It's their fault!"

3. Bargaining

"If it has only been one woman I can't be a lesbian."
"If I'm married, I can't be . . ." (and so on)
"It doesn't matter who I love, it doesn't mean if it's not a man, I'm a lesbian."

Passing behavior may be apparent here "If I look and talk "normal" they'll accept me."

4. Depression

This is the mourning process proper - It may be tacked on more general areas of life and diffused, or quite open and specific:

"I'm just feeling so blue."
"My life is going nowhere."
"I'm nothing, no good." - self hatred/ lowering of self esteem.
"Nothing is challenging or exciting to me."

Or more openly -

"There's a lot to lose in being gay. My parents have disowned me. They consider me dead. They mourn the loss of grandchildren. I mourn the loss of children. My friends have become superficially nice. At work I can't even have a normal conversation without disguising the pronouns. I can't even hold hands in public with my partner. I'm scared all the time, it makes me sad! I thought this (gay relationship) would be perfect!"

5. Acceptance (acknowledgement)

Here we depart from Kubler-Ross' Stages of dying or grief for acceptance of death and profound loss is not a happy stage, it is almost "void of feeling." But the transition to a new status where one is comfortable and accepting of the joys, pleasures, gains, self affirmation, and new life with a different status is a potentially positive and affirming stage. Once a positive identity is affirmed, identity management issues can be attended to.

II.   Coming Out Sexually/Emotionally in a Relationship

For some, this may precede earlier struggles and for some come later. Yet this is usually a turning point in the coming out process. This can cause emotional turmoil as well as the positive feelings of joy, love, closeness, relief and authenticity. Finding and maintaining a partner relationship is a critical search and life task for many gay men and lesbian women.

III.   The Wider Relational Level Phase

A.   Coming Out to Family and Friends

Being "in love" may also be a time the client "wants to tell the world" - family and friends etc. — or hide it from the world feeling shame. Reclaiming family and friend relationships are very important for self acceptance and self esteem. Yet this may be the hardest task gay individuals face due to painful homophobic responses received and anticipated.

B.   Coming Out in the Lesbian/Gay Community

Finding special interest groups is a beginning leading to finding a comfortable niche in the wider community.

IV.   The Wider Word Phase

A.   Coming Out Publicly

This is a stage in which most people in the individual's life know about the self identity of "gay."

Individuals carefully determine how and what to share, but are comfortable sharing a positive gay identity in a range of circumstances.

B.   Coming Out Politically

Taking political positions and becoming part of groups, the gay movement etc. This may be a militant passing phase for some, and a phase of more mature "world concern" for others. These stages may well follow phase V.

V.   Self Acceptance, Identity Integration
(stable lesbian/gay identity, identity synthesis, self definition, reintegration)

All are terms connoting the attainment and continuing "establishment of a positive and pro-active self-concept, one that. . . explores the synthesis and integration of gay and lesbian identification with all other aspects of an individual's life (Grace, 1985). There is an externalization of the feelings of oppression. There is a sense of settling down, being one's full self, having a community of friends and chosen family and a special committed loyal relationship. Being gay is one key part of life, but not all of it. All of life goes on.

Discussing the Phases

Students have found that the preceding outline ties together much of the class content and this outline is particularly useful in conjunction with case material. The author has used the vignette below to help students make connections to the outline. The situation is that Nora, a 24 year old out of state beginning graduate student, approaches a college social work counselor, Jenny, with the presenting problem that "she can't concentrate and fears she will drop out."

Nora said, "I just can't get into it. Everything is so new here. Everyone is so new. This is such a big city but I stick out like a sore thumb. I think I'm homesick." "Yes," said Jenny. "You made a big change coming here, its hard to be the new kid on the block." "Yeah, I feel like a greenhorn. Everyone is so sophisticated . . ." Jenny asked Nora about home. Nora told a little about her family, stating she lived away for four years of college and she didn't miss them too much. She elaborated.

Jenny then asked if she missed her friends. She looked at the worker extra long and said yes. Jenny said that was very hard. "Was there any special friend she missed?" "Yes, there was this person . . . this person she loved. They missed each other, had lived together two years after college. My . . . uh . . . friend couldn't get into this school. It was so hard for me to leave." Jenny said softly, "You really miss your friend a lot." "Yes," Nora said firmly. "I think I want to leave school and go home . . ."

Jenny asked, "Will you get to go home and see your friend soon, maybe iron some things out?" "Yes," Nora said. "This weekend. I guess I'm afraid I won't come back after seeing this person, that I couldn't leave." "It's that bad, huh?" "Yes, we're in love." She looked away. Jenny said gently, "Nora, you say this 'person' and 'friend,' is the person you love a woman?"

Nora looked at Jenny and tears ran down her face. "Yes, oh yes - how did you know?"

Jenny said, "Many gay women omit the pronouns, it's o.k. to say 'her' here, and it's o.k. to miss her. It's very hard to miss the one you love, even if you were having troubles, maybe harder then."

"Yes," Nora answered. "She's angry at me for leaving town. When I got accepted here that's when our trouble began. Her name is Jill. It's so good to even say her name to someone. Aren't there any gay people in this school? I can't find them!" The worker laughed and noted she's only been there 3 weeks, and that there were! Nora said "I'm so happy I came to your office. I'll at least stay in school until our next appointment."

Students initially connect to Nora as a young adult making a difficult life transition. They are then able to listen to Nora's "hints" about "that person," then to her gayness as the educator stops and asks their thoughts. The teacher has them strategize how to bring up the subject of gayness. This, of course, is hotly debated and homophobia is inevitably examined as some students begin to judge the nature of her relationship as "symbiotic" (read "sick") with no such evidence. Someone inevitably points out that if Nora missed Jim instead of Jill, it would be seen very differently. The second paragraph is then read to show how the worker handled hearing the cues, legitimizing Nora's love, and normalizing the problem. Students enjoy seeing how this can be done comfortably and also discuss where Nora may be in the coming out process, as well as how to intervene regarding network building and individual and/or group work.

Conclusions

Human Behavior courses that have an ecological perspective are particularly hospitable to the integration of gay/lesbian and other minority group content. Teaching from a compatible theoretical perspective is a crucial basic step.

Conceptualizing which particular content is essential is the next step. The suggestion has been made that content relative to gay/lesbian identity formation and the coming out process is essential knowledge. The theoretical bases defining and explaining these processes have been offered. An outline representing this knowledge base has been presented as a device for synthesizing and integrating the material.

In reference to the teaching process, several suggestions have been made including: a discussion of the literature; use of case material to make the abstractions real; reaching for general connections in the student's own professional or personal experiences to the concepts of managing stigma; and searching for the authentic self. This helps the material to become less foreign and taboo. A process of identification can take place that helps the student open to new knowledge and develop empathy for the gay/ lesbian struggle. It is also suggested that both students and teacher share their discomfort with the material and examine their own homophobia. While the additional sharing of gayness may be a particular enriching ingredient for the gay teacher to use, (Lee, 1980a; 1986) these are all methods that both non-gay and gay teachers can use in the preparation and teaching of this crucial material.

References

Berger, R. 1983. "What is a Homosexual? A definitional Model." *Social Work*

Berzon, E. 1979. *Positively Gay*. California: Celestial Arts.

Blank, G. and R. 1979. *Ego Psychology II: Psychoanalytic Developmental Psychology*, New York: Columbia

Cass, V. 1979. "Homosexual Identity Formation: A Theoretical Model." *Journal of Homosexuality*, 4, 219.

Cummerton, J. M. 1982. "Homophobia and Social Work Practice With Lesbians." *Women Power and Change*. A Weick, S. T. Vandiver. Washington: NASW.

Erikson, E. 1963. *Childhood and Society*. New York: Norton.

Fischer, J. and Gochros, H. 1975. *Planned Behavior Change: Behavior Modification in Social Work*. New York: The Free Press.

Freud, S. 1953-66. The Standard Edition of *The Complete Psychological Works of Sigmund Freud*. 24 Vols. James Strachey, ed. London: Hogarth Press.

Germain, C. 1979. *Social Work Practice: People and Environments*. New York: Columbia.

Germain, C. and Gitterman, A. 1980. *The Life Model of Social Work Practice*. New York: Columbia.

Germain, C. 1985. "Human Behavior in the Social Environment Course Outline." Unpublished.

Gilligan, C. 1982. *In a Difference Voice: Psychological Theory and Women's Development*. Cambridge: Harvard.

Goffman, E. 1963. *Stigma: Notes on the Management of Spoiled Identity. New Jersey: Prentice Hall.*

Golan, N. 1981. *Passing Through Transitions*. New York: The Free Press.

Grace, J. 1979. "Coming Out Alive: A Positive Developmental Model of Homosexual Competence." XI NASW Symposium. San Antonio,Texas, November 14-17, 1979.

Grace, J. 1985. "Coming Out in Social Work: Worker Survival, Support and Success." *Lesbian and Gay Issues: A Resource Manual for Social Workers*. Eds. H. Hidalgo, T. L. Peterson, N. J. Woodman. Maryland: NASW.

Hidalgo, H., Peterson, T. L., Woodman, N. J. 1985. *Lesbian and Gay Issues: A Resource Manual for Social Workers*. Maryland: NASW.

Klaich, D., 1974. *Woman Plus Woman: Attitudes Toward Lesbianism*. New York: Morrow.

Kubler-Ross, E., 1969. *On Death and Dying*. New York: MacMillan.

Lee, J.A.B., 1980. *A Study of Teaching Behaviors for Perceived Relevance*. Ann Arbor, Michigan: University Microfilms.

Lee, J.A.B. 1980b. "The Helping Professional's Use of Language in Describing the Poor." *The American Journal of Orthopsychiatry*, 50, 4, 580-583.

Lee, J.A.B., 1986. "A Teaching Record" - unpublished.

Lehman, J. L. 1978. "What it Means to Love Another Woman." *Our Right To Love*. G. Vida, Ed. Englewood Cliffs, New Jersey.

Lewis, L. A. 1984. "The Coming-Out Process for Lesbians: Integrating a Stable Identity." *Social Work*, 29, 5, 464-469.

Massiah, E. L. 1985. "An Ongoing Grief Process: A Conceptual Framework for Coming Out as a Lesbian or Gay." 1985 NASW Professional Symposium, November 6-9, 1985, Chicago, Illinois.

Masterson, J. 1976. *Psychotherapy of the Borderline Adult: A Developmental Approach.* New York. Brunner-Mazel.

Morson, T. and McInnis R. 1983. "Sexual Identity Issues in Group Work: Gender, Social Sex Role, and Sexual Orientation Concerns," *The Journal of Social Work With Groups.* 6,4,3/4 Fall/Winter: 67-77.

Moses, A. E., 1978. *Identity Management in Lesbian Women.* New York: Praeger.

Moses, A. E. and Hawkins, R. 1982. *Counseling Lesbian Women and Gay Men.* St. Louis: Mosby.

Perman, J. 1963. "Role of Transference in Casework with Public Assistance Families." *Social Work.* 8, 47-54.

Sancier, B. 1984. "A Challenge to the Profession." *Practice Digest: Unions with Gay and Lesbian Clients.* Washington. NASW.

Simos, B. *A Time to Grieve.* New York: FSAA.

Toffler, A. 1971. *Future Shock.* New York: Bantam.

Woodroofe, K. 1966. *From Charity to Social Work.* London: Kegan Routledge & Paul.

2

Developing A Positive Self Image In A Homophobic Environment

Diane Bernard, Ph.D.

General Background Regarding Sexual Identity

Before getting to specific material related to sexual developmental differences between boys and girls and the prescriptive expectations for male and female behavior which are central to any discussion of how one might grow up as a homosexual female with a strong positive identity in a homophobic society, let me briefly review the major theories which attempt to account for a homosexual adjustment.

Causative explanations cover a wide range of theories which for the sake of convenience we can combine into four main categories:

1. *The Biological*— all the prenatal, predisposition notions fall into this category from chromosomal - genetic to hormonal - endocrine - chemical.
2. *The Behavioral Conditioning*— this area encompasses a wide range of potentially causative areas including fear of disease or injury, disgust reaction to opposite sex genitalia, observation, seduction (imagined as well as actual), and role modeling.

3.   *The Psychoanalytic*— unresolved Oedipal, early parent-
     child relationship problems including pervasive nar-
     cissism.
4.   *The Social Interactionist*— response to the social con-
     text - some degree of fluidity or flexibility over time -
     subject to redefinition.

Without denying the potential contribution of early
parent-child relations and the responses of impressionable
youngsters to observed and imagined sexual events, the
social interactionist position provides the basis for the further explorations and elaborations presented here. While
there are an infinite number of factors which may be important and contributory, no one factor has been established
as either necessary or sufficient to account for the development of a homosexual identity. There is neither a common
cause nor a common experience. Significance and meaning
is particular for the individual and there is a uniqueness in
both the development and the maintenance of a homosexual
identity. No one factor or combination of factors has proven
predictive, but rather it is the way that events interact with
each other and the meaning such interaction has for the
individual. Somewhere between the "more to be pitied than
scorned" concept of an intractable condition over which one
has no control, to the free choice notion of selecting arbitrary,
insolent and defiant behavior, the social interactionist position ascribes an active role to the individual with respect to
the selection and influence of experiences encountered, and
the significant meanings associated with events that contribute to the development and maintenance of homosexual
identity.

It is important to make a distinction between homosexual
acts and homosexual identity. There is a common prevalent
assumption which presumes an equation between activity
and identity which "ain't necessarily so." Sexual behavior
neither accounts for nor eventuates in a particular sexual
identity. The connection between sexual activity and sexual
identity is not a direct one and sexual activity per se is not the
only basis for identification. Similar acts may imply different
identities for different people and similar identities may

eventuate in different behaviors. There is no absolute fit or congruency between doing, thinking or feeling. Individuals may identify as homosexuals without ever having same sex experience while others who engage in flirtations with the same sex, have same sex fantasies, and may actually have same sex experience may not view themselves as homosexual. The behavior and/or feelings may be interpreted as "playing around," "camaraderie," "drunken foolery" or any other situational circumstance. The term homosexual with emphasis on same sex genital contact is inadequate and reductionist as a means of encompassing and understanding the variety of same sex relationships. The human dimension is lost by limiting the diversification to a constricted category. The reasons for sexual behaviors other than erotic interest are wide ranging (such as financial, procreative, manipulative, etc.). Sexual behaviors may be meaningless in terms of erotic attraction or significant relationship, while conversely non-sexual reasons for choosing a homosexual identity may be of equal or greater importance (such as political, reduced role demands and expectations, etc.). In short, sexual behavior is only one criterion for identifying as a homosexual to oneself or others. More important than behavior is acknowledging feelings of sexual-emotional attraction to the same sex whether or not these feelings have been, or will ever be, acted upon.

There is considerable confusion surrounding terms like gender identity, gender role, sexual object choice and sexual orientation. This confusion is coupled with an assumption that one's biological sex determines the outcome, despite the fact that neither anatomy nor physiological function are necessarily associated with each other. Most homosexuals, like most heterosexuals, have no doubt about their gender identity and are clear about being male or female. Gender role relates to learned behavior in accord with a particular culture's concepts of male and female behaviors. Homosexuals may or may not evidence opposite gender personality or behavior traits. Sexual object choice relates to choice of sexual partner. Identity as a homosexual requires accepting the implications of same sex attraction, and sexual orienta-

tion involves acknowledging the significance of one's preference for sexual activity with the same sex.

In our society, gender roles are idealized. There is a public
image of the ideal male and female. The heterosexual model
provides the pervasive cultural framework for all sexuality -
maintained by myriad cultural forces. With so much at stake
emotionally, people do not want to be distracted by facts that
do not coincide with conventional sex roles. Body image,
body awareness and body functions have profound psychological meaning and anatomy and function tend to be
socially elaborated. The heavier male skeleton and muscu-
lature and protruding sex organs create the need to dominate
and penetrate and are associated with intellectual objectivity
(read external) while the smaller framed female with hidden
genitalia is built to passively accept penetration with the
associated attribution of intellectual subjectivity (read internal). Anatomy is not necessarily destiny but all the forces
of a homophobic society pressure one to accept it as both
inevitable and permanent, despite the fact that what is meant
by masculine and feminine is constantly being redefined and
modified. They represent a constellation of interrelated and
overlapping attributes that are not polarized dichotomies but
variations by degrees along a continuum alternating and
responding to differences in our society of class, education,
ethnicity and family culture.

In addition to the ever changing conception of masculine
and feminine, sexual identity itself is not static. While the
majority of the population may experience a stable sexual
identity, redefinition can occur at any stage in the life cycle
regardless of sex or marital status. Depending on experience
and the recognition accorded to same sex erotic feelings and/
or sexual activity, one's fundamental view of self and others
will vary if one is a fifty year old married man with grandchildren, a fourteen year old boy, a thirty year old feminist-
activist, or a forty-two year old married woman who falls for
the woman next door (or any other variation in life experience
you can think of).

To summarize, resolutions of experience and personal
biography are subject to individual interpretation impacting

on social definitions. On conscious and unconscious levels, individuals select, reject, refine and change the meanings of identity and themselves.

Differing Social Pressures on Males and Females

The power differentials between the sexes and their implications for social control and sexual behavior must be considered in any attempt to understand the development of positive self esteem under adverse conditions and how this might differ for boys and girls.

The primary basis for homophobia or the homosexual taboo in Western society rests on the threat to patriarchy. Social control is maintained through the male role and it represents the basis for enforcing social conformity. The male role has greater prestige among both sexes and virtually all adult male homosexuals deny any interest in being females.

Legal opinion reflects social attitudes. The seduction of a boy by an older man is considered a crime against nature and results in heavy penalties in all states. Where females are concerned, a seduction on rare occasion may result, for example, in the discharge of a teacher, but legal action is virtually unknown. Male homosexuals are constant targets for law enforcement officials but crusades against female homosexuals are essentially nonexistent. It would seem that a sexual act lacks social significance unless a penis is involved. Sex role stereotypes view only or principally males as sexual beings. The stereotype of the unmarried male is sexual - most usually, the randy bachelor. Grown men living together are thought of in sexual terms. The stereotype of the single woman is more typically asexual. Grown women living together are usually thought of in terms of mutual economic support. Emotional relationships between women, whether or not they have involved overt physical expression, have tended to remain invisible and insignificant to researchers (be they historians, psychologists, sociologists or sexologists). The differences for men and women in the development and maintenance of homosexual identity and life style have been largely ignored and reflect the lack of cognizance given to female sexuality in general, and lesbianism in particular. Given society's preference and privileges accorded to males, the link between role preference and sexual preference is viewed differently for women. Cross gender preference among women is viewed with greater acceptance as it is perceived in terms of status and opportunity and is not necessarily equated with homosexual behaviors. When a male rejects his role, he is rejecting society's basic values. When a female strives for part of the male role, it is understandable because it is preferred. Tomboyish and masculine behaviors are not only not negatively sanctioned, they are frequently encouraged while sissy or girlish behavior is shameful. If a woman's adult identity breaks down into childish behavior she is perceived as losing her adulthood, but not her femininity. If a man's adulthood breaks down, he becomes a baby, dependent, and his masculinity collapses. The fear or threat implicit in male homosexuality is the fear of being non-male. A woman who is threatened by competitive, aggressive and other presumably male aspects of her personality may have emotional or sexual problems but is not likely to fear becoming a non-woman.

Men are brought up to be concerned with the reactions of other men to their conduct while women are raised to be cared for and to be found attractive by the significant other. Female socialization combines the establishment of intimate relationships with sexuality as a form of service. The basic difference in male and female scripts for love and sex are played out in that females are trained to be non-sexual and romantic while males are encouraged to be sexually active and non-romantic. Romance and emotional attachments usually precede sexuality for women. In general, females have fewer options and are more narrowly controlled socially. They are impelled into marriages by friends and family and submerged into the heterosexual world. The embarrassment of spinsterhood is feared rather than homosexuality. On the average, lesbian women come out later than gay men and a much higher percentage of homosexual women than men have been married. There is a prevailing heterosexual assumption in society as well as a category of asexual single women which is both believable and acceptable.

As a result, lesbians need to function in a heterosexual world without a heterosexual mate and for the most part do so by maintaining conventional social norms and a facade of social respectability. Because they must become economically independent, they usually attain a high level of education and may achieve important professional status. They are frequently viewed as ideal employees as it is to the employer's advantage that they are more dependent on incomes and need to be self supporting. In addition, without obligations to husbands and children, they are better able to adapt to unusual working conditions (travel, split shifts, etc.). Job stability, financial security and some professional acceptance make it somewhat easier for lesbians to pass and maintain a responsible mode of living, but they do so at the expense of social isolation. Even the homosexual milieu is primarily male.

Growing Up Gay and Dealing With Difference

In addition to the prevailing norms that sex without a penis does not much count and women are sexual objects rather than sexual beings, sexual development for girls is generally slower than for boys and overt sexual activity is not a typical aspect of early childhood development for females in our culture. Males become sexually active at an earlier age and, since social groups during childhood and early adolescence are largely sex segregated, they are more likely to engage in same sex behavior as part of sexual experimentation without the stigma of homosexuality. By the time girls become sexually active they may gain positive strokes for avoiding heterosexual encounters - daddies are not anxious to lose their daughters to other males and mothers fear early pregnancy. Tomboyish behavior if it doesn't last too long is considered cute while being boy crazy is not an attribute. Early signals to girls in our society neither stimulate nor

support opposite sex behaviors. (Good girls go with other girls
- girls who are fast or bad go with the boys.)

Given the heterosexual assumption and homosexual
taboo in our culture, people are initially socialized to believe
they are heterosexual. However, the socialization of females
which delays sexual activity while encouraging romance and
intimacy communicates a conflicting message. Through
childhood and adolescence girls are most usually rewarded
and given approval for behaviors which are the opposite of
those expected of young adults. A nagging sense of difference
may occur early on, although cognitive awareness of oneself
as homosexual does not typically occur until early adolescence with the onset of formal abstract thought and capacity
for self reflection. Confusion can arise not only from accepting oneself as gay, but from how to incorporate one's
gayness into one's life. Insecurities may give rise to compensatory behaviors to compete and achieve. Surviving the
turbulence of adolescence is difficult enough without the
added burden of social condemnation as sick or bad or
freakish. The resulting guilt can create either negative consequences of further isolation or positive efforts toward
acceptance. There is a positive correlation between guilt and
higher education. Being good at something (school, hobbies,
performing arts) is a frequent solution, and academic success facilitates educational and occupational attainments as
an adult. To be excellent in something is one means of
avoiding negative responses from peers, obtaining rewards
from adults, and preventing alienation. The internalization of
societal censure toward homosexuality makes for increased
responsiveness to external demands for conformity. The
desire to gain acceptance, recognition, and self esteem is
frequently interpreted as ambition. Virtues may be acquired
through adversity in pre-adulthood. The acquisition of some
special strength or ability is a useful adaptation for future
success and a protection against fear of failure and ostra-
cism. Such social conforming strategies produce model
citizens who pay for their hard earned self esteem with
certain compulsive self restriction. Persistent gender deviance takes guts and since most homosexuals are self sup-

porting and conduct their lives without the intervention of police or mental health authorities, their coping capacities and alternative solutions are amazing considering the stigmatization and, in some states, potentially criminal aspect of their sexual preferences.

Once the label of homosexual is assigned, other aspects of an individual's identity become secondary. It is paramount, outweighing the significance of social class, profession and other personal qualities. Homosexuals are a mixed group not bound by the same minority group loyalty as Blacks, Jews, and other oppressed ethnic groups; they are of many classes, backgrounds and personality types, having varying sexual habits arising out of different motives and emotions, and for the most part have no more in common than any group put together at random. There are clusters of gay subcultures which some homosexuals belong to during some part of their lives and to varying degrees. The non-sexual function of the subculture (gay bars, clubs, organizations, etc.) serves as an island of security in a non-gay world and a substitute for the majority perception which views homosexuality as pernicious. It is a place to gain recognition, affirmation and acceptance. Paradoxically it reinforces the primacy given to sexual identity by becoming the chief determinant in one's life. The choice is frequently isolation through internalizing society's negative views and living with the fear of being found out versus deep involvement in gay life which can alienate one from the mainstream of society.

All oppressed groups attempt to bolster self esteem by developing an ideology enlisting historical, psychological, scientific and legal justifications for their way of life which acknowledges difference by claiming special or superior qualities. Suffering and discrimination at the hands of the majority elicit traits of victimization. Traits considered psychological components of homosexuality are actually common characteristics of any victimized or denigrated group.

Paradoxes are inherent in all labeling and stereotyping in that they both aid and destroy identity simultaneously. They serve the forces of domination and control by restricting and limiting experience while stimulating radical innovation and creative strategies for accomplishment and eventual triumph. Derogatory labels are used by the victims as well as the victimizers and while self ridicule may reduce the pain and reinforce group identity it also serves to erode self esteem.

In short, all of the aspects contributing to homophobia and social rejection create potentials as well as limitations in human adaptation. Individual growth and development occurs not only because of but also in spite of. The need for an integrated positive sense of self outweighs individually internalized and socially reinforced views that homosexuality is unacceptable.

Difference has frequently transformed outcasts to trend setters as harbingers of style from fashions in dress to hair, jewelry, cosmetics, music, drama, film, etc. Homosexuals are recognized in some circles as economic assets since they tend to combine fewer commitments with higher disposable incomes and are therefore better consumers. Being perceived as different encourages one to perceive differently. As a result, homosexuals develop a sensibility which may include a comprehension of social structures at variance with the mainstream. Their very presence ridicules the majority social concept of masculine and feminine and makes a mockery of other social sacred cows.

Growing up gay means growing up different. Despite the multiple pejorative terms to describe the uncommon including pervert, queer and undesirable, there are at least an equal number that describe the unconventional as original, unique and exceptional. Difference does not preclude the establishment and maintenance of a positive identity as a homosexual - what we have to insure is that the price to be paid is not to the forces of tyranny which demand conformity at the expense of individual development. This is especially true for females who have diminished status and fewer options for achieving positive self esteem in our society irrespective of sexual orientation.

3

Affirming Gay and Lesbian Adulthood

John Grace, M.S.W.

This chapter will explore the ongoing, life-span challenges of evolving a self-defined and integrated lesbian/gay
adulthood and maintaining this positive sense of self within
a culture that continues to place formidable obstacles in the
path of sexual/affectional minority persons. Specific external barriers in the form of homophobia (described in a
typology of active, passive, personal and institutional dimensions) and homophobia-instigated shame integrated
with identity and shame-based defenses will be used to
explain the frequent and often puzzling phenomenon of
"developmental lag" found among many gay and lesbian
clients. Developmental lag is defined as significant and
problematic discrepancies between chronological age and
psychological maturity that impedes successful identification and mastery of essential psychosocial milestones. A
competence-based model of the stages of gay identity development will be used to examine major life tasks and
common developmental obstacles that retard or arrest
positive stage movement.

Understanding the concept of homophobia is a prerequisite for explaining the developmental dilemmas faced by

gay and lesbian clients. Weinberg introduced the term as ".
. . the dread of being in close quarters with homosexuals"
(Weinberg, 1973). We can expand this definition to include
the irrational fear, avoidance or rejection of anyone or
anything known or merely suspected of being homosexual. In
order to fully appreciate the ubiquitous nature of
homophobia and its pervasively negative effects on identity
development, the following typology is proposed:

	active	passive
personal		
institutional		

Four categories of homophobia can thus be described:
personal/active, personal/passive, institutional/active and
institutional/passive.

- The *personal* dimension includes both
  intrapersonal and interpersonal experience, i.e.
  homophobia internalized within the individual as
  well as interactions between individuals.
- The *institutional* dimension involves a relationship between an individual and a societal institution, e.g. family, school, church, business,
  government, community organization, etc.
- The *active* manifestation of homophobia is expressed through physical assault, verbal abuse,
  stigmatizing labels, punitive judgments, hostile
  stereotyping, and coercion to "be straight" directed toward those individuals and groups
  known or merely assumed to be gay.
- The *passive* manifestation of homophobia appears as ignorance about homosexuality and the
  gay/lesbian experience, neglect toward this
  population's basic rights and needs, and the
  presumption of heterosexuality.

What is the Relationship Between Homophobia and Gay/Lesbian Identity Development?

As recent research and clinical evidence continues to repudiate an illness model that indicts homosexuality per se as pathological or dysfunctional (see Gonsiorek, 1977), attention has shifted to non-stigmatizing longitudinal perspectives on the actual life experiences of lesbian women and gay men. A number of authors have generated descriptive models of the "coming out" process (whereby an individual learns to identify, understand, accept and share their lesbianism or gayness) containing specific stages of positive identity formation. Grace, for example, offers a five stage model of coming out: 1) *emergence*, where initial feelings of difference and ambiguous attraction to members of the same-sex are first noticed; 2) *acknowledgement*, when more explicit homoerotic feelings and desires manifest, and beginning attempts are made to understand and label same-sex identification; 3) *finding community*, in which the individual searches for peers; 4) first relationships, containing a sense of primary commitment and "true love" with another person; 5) *self-definition and reintegration*, an open-ended stage which entails the continuing establishment of a positive and proactive self-concept, one that is not defined in ignorance and shame or in hasty reaction against heterosexist values and lifestyles. The person in this stage increasingly displays self-awareness, identity pride and compassion, and explores the synthesis and integration of lesbian/gay identity with all other aspects of adult living. While the above model is inferred from clinical data obtained with gay men, Feigal (1983) has corroborated the model's applicability for women with the reversal of finding community and first relationship stages to reflect different socialization patterns.

In order to fully understand the harmful effects of homophobia on the pace and quality of the coming out process, a non-pejorative theory of motivation needs to be employed. The concept of competence or competence motivation has been explained as characterized by self-direction, selectivity, and persistence, with its common property being the urge for mastery. This urge is rewarded both by tangible accomplishment of desired goals and a general feeling of efficacy in one's life:

> The person or group who interacts with an environment sensitive to his competence needs enjoys a high probability of achieving competence and skill and, most important for stage development considerations, a positive sense of himself as a competent human being. "A positive sense of self-competence" is considered to be the primary condition for establishing "readiness" for movement to higher stages of social-emotional development and potential achievement of self-awareness (White, 1959).

A simple schema of *private self* and *public self* is also helpful to understand how an internal sense of competence, an intuitive sense of who you are and what you want, can be manifested in public behaviors and roles. In an ideal (and probably Utopian!) pro-competence and non-sexist environment, *emergence* of same-sex emotional attractions and openly affectionate involvements would be tolerated, even encouraged; *acknowledgement* of homoerotic feelings would be supported by respectful attitudes toward homosexuality as a viable expression of love; *finding community* would be a public exploration of visible, diverse, and easily-accessible resources; *first relationships* would occur in a context of positive sanction and community recognition of their importance and value, and *self-definition and reintegration* would be a time where individuals would simply address the same existential questions faced by the majority culture. In sum, an honest sense of private self would result in a congruent, satisfying and competence-based public identity to share and enjoy with others. Early identity confusion could be tolerated, examined and eventually resolved from an inner locus of decision making that valued honesty over conformity.

Unfortunately, the great majority of lesbian women and gay men share childhood and adolescent histories where confusion about sexual identity or affectional needs was quickly equated with danger; or, in those cases where people observed homophobic behavior directed elsewhere, a lingering sense of dread was the result. Clients recall the sense of threat that emerged early in their lives, often well before a clear sense of sexual identity had crystallized—fears of physical injury, verbal humiliation, abandonment by loved ones, or rejection by specific individuals or society at large.

The family environment is where the different types of homophobia are manifested earliest. Active and passive expressions may range from parents' invectives against homosexuality as a "mortal sin" resulting in "eternal damnation," through well-intentioned criticisms of atypical gender role behaviors, to a deafening silence in the family about sexuality in general. Other passive institutional dimensions of homophobia may be expressed through family expectations or assumptions of heterosexuality in all its members.

Throughout childhood and adolescence, personal attacks and proscriptions against homosexuality as well as institutional "norms" and presumptions of heterosexuality are repeatedly encountered in school and church, community groups and peer interactions. Very serious consequences result from experiencing this chronic sense of danger. First, increasing amounts of time and energy must be devoted to survival and defense rather than intimacy and growth. Second, people may develop a generalized view of the world as threatening and develop a sophisticated "negativity radar" that can generate self-fulfilling prophecies of danger everywhere. Third, public self may become a form of disguise and armor, with private self consequently becoming increasingly alienated from the rest of the world. Finally, this growing isolation may foster a sense of shame about one's core identity and basic needs.

What is the Role of Shame in Creating and Maintaining Developmental Lag?

In his book, *Shame: The Power of Caring,* Kaufman describes shame as feeling exposed and painfully diminished, leaving the ashamed person with a fundamental sense of defectiveness or deficiency. This may be accompanied by an urgent need to flee, hide or mask shame in whatever way possible (Kaufman, 1980).

Gay and lesbian clients often talk about guilt when they really mean shame. The following sentence dyads proved helpful in one of my workshops as a means of distinguishing the two words:

Guilt says, I made a mistake.
Shame says, I am a mistake.

Guilt asks, what is to be done?
Shame says, nothing can be done.

With guilt, reparation may be made.
With shame, the damage seems beyond repair.

Guilt can be sobering.
Shame is intoxicating (with the emphasis on toxic!).

Guilt energizes.
Shame paralyzes.

Guilt motivates us to improve or accept ourselves and
    the world.
Shame intimidates us to destroy and reject ourselves
    and the world.

Guilt awakens us to here and now responsibilities.
Shame stupefies us into past remorse and future
    dread.

Guilt can reveal the truth.
Shame always lies.

Kaufman's central thesis is that shame originates
through early interactions between people, but at some point
becomes internalized and self-generating, leaving the
ashamed individual set up to become their own worst enemy.
Over time, shame can bind increasingly to any and all of a
person's interactional and internal experiences. Eventually,
basic affects, needs and drives can become distorted by
shame (Kaufman, 1980).

Examples of this destructive binding include:

-   *Shame and feelings (affect).* Anger contaminated
    with shame can boil over into rage and violence or
    freeze into resentment, cynicism and contempt.
    Sadness may become damned up by shame to
    create a sea of despair or chronic melancholy and
    self-pity. Fear may escalate into acute panics,
    chronic suspiciousness, and lingering dread. Joy
    may be squashed by shame entirely, disqualified
    by a concurrent sense of unworthiness, or am-
    plified into over-idealization of self or others,
    grandiosity and an irrational sense of entitle-
    ment. And guilt may be corrupted by shame into
    unfair and unrelenting self-criticism, acts of self-
    punishment, depression and suicide.
-   *Shame and sex.* Sex (activity and fantasy) be-
    comes "dirty". Sex, intimacy and power become
    confused. Violence is mistaken for passion.
-   *Shame and basic needs.* With shame, basic needs
    for relationships, identification with role models,
    differentiation and individuation, nurturing, and
    affirmation are denied, belittled or become ad-
    dictive cravings.

Shame can become a catalyst for internalizing
homophobia and subverting competence motivation. Repeated experiences of homophobia-inspired shame may add

to a person's sense that private self is defective, worthless, bad, unlovable, that it is to be hidden at all costs rather than exposed. Competence drive remains, but now the process gets reversed. If truth is impermissible, then the person will become a competent liar. If authentic self-disclosure is forbidden or fraught with danger, then the person will become a competent fraud. If the primary task is survival rather than growth, the person will competently build walls rather than bridges.

These shame-based defenses serve a two-fold purpose: to protect against additional shame from the world outside, and to contain internalized shame and prevent it from being reactivated by exposure to others.

Sadly, the individual who unconsciously denies the private self or consciously deceives the outer world as a way of warding off shame faces a terrible paradox. They lie or deny to contain their growing sense of self-loathing, yet through denial or deceit they actually increase its internal spread and intensity. What results is an increasingly impenetrable mire of shame between private self aspirations and public self presentations. This can be represented in the following diagram:

Private AND Public	PLUS	Shame	=	Denial,
Self Self				Deceit
				and Self
				Alienation

Returning to the stages of gay and lesbian identity formation, we can begin to examine in more detail how shame has the potential to contaminate that coming out process and stall growth and maturation.

Early social and performance anxiety is a typical response to shame during the emergence stage. The individual may face strong approach/avoidance conflicts about engaging with an environment that demands clear and consistent adherence to heterosexual norms and typical gender role behaviors. Individuals experience a double-binding fear of being noticed if they don't behave "correctly" and being noticed if they don't try at all. What often results is either anxiety-impaired performance or, in situations where people can "pass" effectively, conditional self-acceptance only for "appropriate" heterosexist roles and denigration of the rest of private self.

Shame and fear may escalate during the acknowledgment stage, when ambiguous feelings of same-sex desire start to include more explicit homoerotic attractions and homosexual fantasy. While wide individual variations for the onset of acknowledgement exist, research indicates most lesbian women and gay men acknowledge their homosexuality to themselves by ages thirteen to nineteen (Jay & Young, 1979). This usually occurs in an adolescent environment that is vehemently homophobic and shaming.

Some people respond with denial and freeze off their sexuality from conscious awareness. Many others try to cope with their private sexual identity by disqualifying it through rationalizations that demonstrate heterosexual assumptions. They strike bargains that take the form of "if, then" statements to themselves and others. "If I'm a good student, then I'm not gay. If I'm captain of the football team, then I'm not gay. If I'm a good Christian, then I'm not lesbian. If I fool around with men (women) only when I'm high, then I'm not gay (lesbian). If I work or study twelve hours a day, then I don't have time to be _____. If I marry and have children, then I'm certainly not _____." Some people identify with their aggressors and join in the attack. Their bargain becomes, "If I harass or beat up faggots and dykes, then I'm obviously straight." Homophobic bargaining often takes on perfectionist proportions. Perfectionism is shame in disguise. If someone continues to believe they are innately bad and defective, then the only way to survive and escape detection is with "perfect" cover ups. A client describes this as learning to look good while feeling bad.

Some people in the acknowledgment stage will make it to "in groups", escape overt hostility, and achieve heterosexual peer group inclusion. Others will wind up openly ridiculed and ostracized. Shame continues to operate in both cases. In the latter, there are clear environmental sources of hostility and rejection, while in the former the shame emerges internally from knowing at some level you are lying to the world.

Most gay and lesbian persons during their chronological adolescence have little or no conceptual understanding of the concept of shame, yet certainly know the visceral sense of fear, hurt, rage, and self-loathing that can accompany it. If a person does not have the ability to understand and resolve shame, they will seek out any means available to relieve the excruciating psychic pain that accompanies the subjective experience of self-hatred. Even when connoted as bad and unacceptable, private self needs and drives remain. If unsatisfied through healthy, interdependent love relationships, they will become displaced onto repetitive patterns of activity that provide relief, however fleeting, from the pain of chronic isolation and self-disgust. A colleague calls these displacements of need "love shifts" (Smalley, 1984). In her workshops, she helps people make lists of love shifts they have observed in themselves and witnessed in others. A sampling would include: parental approval (the forerunner of perfectionism), school grades, athletic achievement, drugs, smoking, food, sex, money, credit, power, work, limerence, caretaking, martyrdom, worry, intellectualism, rage, sleep, self-starvation, dogma, violence, therapy, and so on. In making a love shift, a person sacrifices variety for intensity. Intense involvement with a love shift (which may include any of the homophobic bargains described earlier) can produce hypnotic effects that include euphoria and pain reduction. But just as denial and deceit are ineffective strategies for reducing underlying shame, love shifts may compound the problem by relieving pain at the expense of growth.

Stanton Peele articulates the harmful consequences of repeated love shifts on a person's self-esteem and identity development by describing a continuum of human activity ranging from healthy habits through destructive addictions. According to Peele, a healthy habit expands awareness, leads to other involvements, increases self-esteem, brings pleasure, and increases variety (Peele, 1981). An addictive experience, on the other hand, eradicates awareness, hurts other involvements, lowers self-esteem and, most important, is not pleasurable. Peele emphasizes what is "pleasurable" about an addictive experience is its ability to predictably (and reliably) provide a way to eradicate thoughts and feelings that are painful. His definition of addiction is very simple— losing the ability to make choices (Peele, 1981). Parenthetically, we could apply this same definition to homophobic oppression (both external and internalized) in terms of its power to deprive gay/lesbian persons of healthy choices. Peele also notes that any habit can become an addiction.

The cumulative effects of homophobia, shame, love shifts and addictive detours can result in what Cass calls *identity foreclosure* (Cass, 1979) where the individual is unwilling or unable to proceed any farther in the coming out process. This may occur in the emergence stage with ongoing denial of same-sex feelings, or in the acknowledgement stage with the admission of homosexuality accompanied by resolute attempts to repress or change sexual/affectional orientation.

When identity is not completely foreclosed, developmental lag may still slow the process of gay and lesbian psychological maturation. This is particularly evident in the finding community stage, where lesbian women or gay men who have honestly acknowledged their sexual identity now attempt to establish a sense of community or find a peer group where private self can be shared more publicly. Finding community can be understood as a "gay and lesbian adolescence." It is an opportunity to make up for time lost during a person's actual teenage years that were partially or completely spent hiding or acting out "pseudo-heterosexual" roles and facades. The continuing issue of identity, shame and developmental lag may now present as a two-fold dilemma: (1) if a lesbian woman or gay man's chronological adolescence was a time of hiding or "passing", developmental adolescence may not begin until early or even middle adulthood; and (2) the shame they have previously internalized may cause them to react to the "younger" parts of themselves and others with contempt and self abuse, creating yet an additional source of delay, identity confusion, and continuing self-alienation.

The finding community stage can provide powerful op-

portunities for realizing and asserting a wide range of intimacy needs honestly, appropriately and effectively with other
lesbians and gays or, if the momentum of shame continues
unabated, simply become a repetition of the original pain
filled chronological adolescence with the new focus on
finding the "right" way to be gay or lesbian.

People may still feel inadequate about how to initiate and
maintain relationships, behave in social groups, or handle
disappointment, loss and conflict. Love shifts and addictive
patterns may again be employed to cover the pain of adolescent ignorance and awkwardness, and unsure, self-con-
scious individuals may succumb to the pressures of the peer
group to act in ways that are still incongruent with private self
needs. What may start out as a sense of infatuation and over-
idealization with the gay or lesbian community can become
soured and turned into cynicism and social withdrawal.

If people do not have compassionate explanations for
developmental lag, they will subscribe to homophobic stereotypes that reinforce the old propaganda that gay and
lesbian individuals and their community are sick, superfi-
cial, hostile, obsessed with sex, etc. Adult clients often report
a great sense of relief and understanding when I suggest that
they may have significant differences between their chronological and developmental ages. They quickly identify
situations where they and others felt or acted like "young
teenagers." Contemptuous and shaming responses to unidentified developmental lag can then be replaced with a more
respectful, benevolent and responsible "re-parenting" of the
younger parts of oneself. A colleague who works extensively
with adult children of alcoholics notes that one of their typical
problems is that they have lacked responsible adult role
models. As a result, they are often left alone to guess about
what it means to be "grown up", and they frequently guess
wrong. Without an adequate understanding of homophobia-
instilled shame and its stultifying effects on maturation,
adult lesbian women and gay men face the same risk. Both
groups are vulnerable to what I describe as "internal child
abuse and neglect" where their sense of shame and isolation
creates perfectionistic and unrealistic expectations for in-

dividual and community behavior, with consequent punishment and rejection when a person or peer group doesn't measure up. Honest admission of immaturity and ignorance is, paradoxically, an adult response to "adolescent" puzzles and frees people to competently identify and master unresolved life tasks.

The next stage of the coming out process, first relationships, contains a sense of deepening involvement with another gay or lesbian individual. A primary commitment will usually involve a number of sub-stages: 1) the *dream world stage*, where both the partner or lover as well as the relationship itself are idealized and only positive qualities are emphasized; 2) the *disillusionment stage*, where the couple starts noticing dislikes and areas of difference; 3) *misery*, which can precipitate a relationship ending or, if worked through successfully, lead to 4) *enlightenment* where a couple decides to seek help and each partner begins to take individual responsibility for their relationship role; and 5) *mutual respect*, where both people can honestly acknowledge their potentials and limits, areas of commonality and difference, and make a loving decision about whether to remain together or move apart (Schroeder, 1980).

First relationships can result in great healing or serious damage to the psyches of the involved men or women. The dream world or honeymoon phase can provide a wealth of nourishment for basic needs like affirmation, physical and sexual contact, and emotional nurturing that may never have been gratified in such a balanced, ongoing and intense manner. The psychic armor built up over the years to protect one's private self may be suddenly discarded so that people can enjoy the unadulterated pleasure of saying and hearing words and expressions of love.

If a couple has acquired competence in the developmental tasks required in previous stages and so approach a first relationship with a solid base of self-esteem and as a natural evolution of their growing intimacies with others, they have a good chance of establishing a viable relationship contract. This may range from spoken expressions of shared love and commitment to specific written agreements about the roles, rights and responsibilities of each partner. Successful first relationships are characterized by flexibility and mutuality. They form a "good bargain" basis to support individual and collective happiness and progress. Healthy adult relationships also recognize the truth that everyone we love will eventually disappoint us, so they include respectful strategies and processes to cope with disillusionments, losses and, if necessary, loving good-byes. Partners learn to accept each other as human and fallible, and can express and resolve conflicts without chronic abuse or interminable power struggles. The two people retain their individuality while choosing to work on an interdependent partnership that provides shared benefits and rewards. They are honest about the potentials, faults and limitations in themselves and their partners. They can openly express and satisfy their respective needs for both intimacy and privacy within the relationship and with other lesbian/gay and non-gay friends and acquaintances. Their social networks in the gay community and the larger society contain people who affirm and enrich the relationship. Most importantly, healthy first relationships reduce shame and increase pride.

What happens, on the other hand, if lesbian women and gay men enter the first relationship stage with a coming out experience contaminated with shame? After the initial dream world experience, disillusionment and misery may be experienced as catastrophic. People may feel a sense of panic that this was their only chance and desperately attempt to "shape up" themselves or their partner to restore their relationship ideal. In healthy relationships, the misery stage is expressed intimately through the emotions of grief, but in a shame-laden partnership misery may turn into rage and violence or despair and depression. Shame has the power to explode two people apart at the misery stage or foreclose further growth by encouraging love shifts and addictive distractions within the relationship that leave it enmeshed and stagnant.

Self-definition and reintegration constitutes the final stage of coming out, and is an ongoing process that will last the rest of a person's life. Lesbian and gay adulthood can continue to be affirmed and consolidated in this stage by pursuing healthy lifestyles characterized by variety, choice, and responsibility.

Social workers can help their gay and lesbian clients through the coming out process by: 1) providing education about homophobia and shame; 2) helping clients identify and resolve love shifts and addictive patterns that impede or arrest growth; 3) addressing remaining areas of ignorance and stress that contribute to developmental lag; and 4) facilitating access to lesbian and gay-affirmative experiences that foster self-awareness, identity pride and respect for difference. In sum, uncover shame, recover competence, discover adulthood.

References

Cass, V. C. Homosexual Identity Formation: A Theoretical Model. *Journal of Homosexuality*, 1979, p. 220.

Feigal, A. The Other Side. In M. Borhek (ed.), *Coming Out to Parents*. New York: Pilgrim Press, 1983, pp. 84-113.

Gonsiorek, J. Psychological Adjustment and Homosexuality. JSAS Catalog of Selected Documents in Psychology, 1977, 7, 45. (MS. No. 1478).

Jay, K. and Young, A. (Eds.) *The Gay Report: Lesbian and Gay Men Speak Out About Sexual Experiences and Lifestyles*. New York: Simon and Shuster, 1979.

Kaufman, G. *Shame: The Power of Caring*. Cambridge: Schenckman, 1980, vii, pp. 37-79.

Peele, S. *How Much is too Much?* New Jersey: Prentice-Hall, 1981, p. 5-6, pp. 52-56.

Schroeder, M. *Hope for Relationships*. Hazelden Foundation, 1980, pp. 5-11.

Smalley, S. Personal communication.

Weinberg, G. *Society and the Healthy Homosexual*. New York: Anchor Books, 1973, p. 4.

White, R. W. Motivation Reconsidered: The Concept of Competence. *Psychological Review*, 1959, 66, pp. 297-333.

PART II

DIRECT PRACTICE WITH LESBIAN AND GAY POPULATIONS

Introduction

Examples of areas of practice with lesbian and gay clients follow the introductory chapter which describes how to integrate content in direct practice curricula. Additionally, the attention to children and young adults provided in the chapters by Bernard and Grace in Part I is supplemented by consideration of other age groups and populations within lesbian and gay communities.

Forrister begins Part II by delineating content and methods for including knowledge related to client intervention. The author explores the reasons for requiring specific content (professional mandates, uniqueness of this population, and values issues). He then identifies ways in which such knowledge can best be integrated within practice courses. Forrister gives examples of "moving from familiar to less familiar content" and increasing student interaction around new learning. Educators' roles in facilitating this process are described and illustrated. Forrister recommends combining didactic teaching with discussion, role modeling, and initial faculty participation in role-playing so as to encourage student involvement. Examples of specific lesbian and gay issues are included throughout the chapter.

Lenna describes a group often ignored when considering lesbians and gays. In his attention to adolescents, he reenforces earlier chapters which explored how stigmatization and homophobia among peers can be particularly devastating to this age cohort which has few role models and even fewer resources. Use of group intervention is then presented as a logical modality for lesbian and gay teenagers. Lenna describes two levels of group activity. Level I stresses cognitive and educational growth in a structured series of meetings. The author identifies topic areas and questions for consideration in each group session. Level II of the interventive process focusses on personal growth within a supportive social situation. Again, the author specifies group goals and strategies. The article concludes with caveats relative to confidentiality and the relevance of involvement of significant others.

In approaching social work with non-traditional families from a dual perspective, Gunter describes how practice theory can or may not be appropriate with various family configurations of which lesbian and gay members are a part. Distinctions between family of origin and family of choice are highlighted with particular emphasis on the need for social workers to attend to the latter structure. Gunter also addresses the special multiple issues of rural, elderly, and ethnic minority lesbian and gay persons. The author identifies a breadth of problems frequently encountered within and between diverse family structures and suggests interventive strategies with these various systems.

As Terry explains in Chapter 7, relationship termination and loss are not experiences encountered only by lesbian women and gay men. However, the author elaborates on the unique stressors encountered by this population. Using the traditional modes of coping identified by Kubler-Ross, Terry then identifies particular strategies for coping frequently observed by clinicians in working with lesbians and gays facing this problem. Interventive strategies are suggested which can support reestablishment of a positive identity in a homophobic society.

4

The Integration of Lesbian and Gay Content in Direct Practice Courses

Daniel K. Forrister, M.S.W., Ph.D.

Introduction

Why Introduce gay and lesbian content to social work practice courses? Although this may appear to be a valid question to some educators, the reality is that lesbians and gays comprise a significant segment of the population. Also, CSWE has determined that content related to sexual orientation should be included in the preparation of students for practice with diverse client populations. Additionally it is ethically imperative to expect the beginning practitioner to have a variety of courses to support expectations and values of the profession. The knowledge gained from the Human Behavior in the Social Environment component and experiences working with diverse client populations during field practicum require theoretical practice education for work with lesbian and gay clients.

Expectations are placed on social workers to perform in a variety of settings, to assist clients who may differ from themselves, and to apply interventive skills for problems they may never, personally, experience. Preparing students to meet these expectations requires professional education including learning experiences in as many different areas as possible. As indicated, the profession calls for the inclusion of lesbian and gay content in social work education. The question to be considered, therefore, should not be "why include lesbian and gay content?" but instead "how can we integrate this content into the educational process?"

The intent of this paper is to point to the integrative potential in direct practice courses for lesbian and gay content. Potentials for integration appear readily and are described relative to the professional value system, the application of practice skills, and the modalities of teaching commonly used in teaching direct practice. These three areas of potentiality are discussed independently. Social work values and the utilization of them as resource for establishing practitioners' responsibility for the provision of services for lesbians and gay clients are considered. In the subsequent section, the applications of some general practice skills for lesbians and gays are discussed. Mention is made in this brief consideration of practice skills of some of the differences which may be unique to lesbians and gays, as well as similarities they share with other client populations. In conclusion, two of the modalities, discussion and role-play, which are considered effective in preparing students for work with diverse client populations are discussed.

Social Work Values and Practice With Lesbian and Gay Clients

Opportunity to introduce students in direct practice courses to lesbian and gay content presents itself in the professional value system. There are three major reasons for the utilization of social work values as an introductory device. First, most students come to direct practice courses with some existing knowledge of social work values. Second, discussion of values can be carried out in the abstract, reducing the emotional involvement necessary for the initial consideration of controversial content. Finally, the legitimacy and validity of social work values can provide the impetus for students to understand their responsibility to lesbian and gay clients.

Social workers' professional values charge them with responsibility of serving all clients equitably (Fox, 1983). Programs of social work education are designed to provide an introduction to the professional value system and to reinforce these values. When sexual orientation is a factor, however, it is evident that some practitioners have difficulty in fulfilling their professional responsibilities (Dulaney & Kelly, 1982; Gambrill, Stein & Brown, 1984). There are several possible explanations for this. Practitioners may not have completely internalized professional values. Personal values may conflict with professional values, preventing the generalization of professional responsibility to lesbian and gay clients. Or, a lack of information and experience may preclude the application of professional values to social work with lesbian women and gay men. These three problematic conditions can exist independently or in some combination. However, their existence can be alleviated by a thorough review of professional values early in direct practice courses.

There is pedagogical significance in re-examining social work values at the beginning of a direct practice course. A review of professional values can be used to: assess students' understanding of them; identify which of the three explanations mentioned above may be applied to their failure to apply social work values to lesbian and gay clients; and make an initial introduction of lesbian and gay content to the course. The timely review of professional values enables instructors to introduce content pertaining to sexual orientation at the point where students are ready to consider it.

As mentioned above, students will likely have been made aware of social work values elsewhere in their professional education. Yet, a direct practice course may be the first opportunity they have to consider the application of them to intervention with lesbian and gay clients. Adhering to pedagogical precept that instruction should progress from content with which students are most familiar to that with which they are less familiar, discussion of professional values can facilitate the introduction of lesbian and gay content. The comfort included in this educational process serves to reduce the resistance students may have to the newer materials. For example, a discussion of the value of the "client's right to self determination" might first be discussed in general abstract terms. Secondly, students might be asked to reflect on those practice situations where this value is obviously significant. Then, they may be encouraged to consider practice situations where they may find it difficult to employ this value. Finally, if students do not pose the problematic situation of the gay or lesbian clients' right to choose an alternative life style, the instructor may want to initiate a discussion pertaining to this. A similar process may be used to review such values as a "non-judgmental attitude" or "acceptance."

Preparation for practice with lesbian and gay clients entails a combination of cognitive and affective learning. Olson and Moss (1980) suggest that these learning styles be carefully mixed. Consistent with the educational precept of moving from the familiar to the less familiar is the suggestion that affective learning moves from situations requiring less self-disclosure to situations requiring more self-disclosure (Englund, 1980). Student comfort inherent in the cognitive transition mentioned above is further protected when values are discussed in abstract terms. Once students are comfortable with abstract applications of social work values to lesbian and gay clients, they can proceed to discussion requiring more personal and emotional involvement, and the example provided by Lee in Chapter 1 demonstrates this principal graphically. Social work values are an instructional resource providing opportunities for both the structuring of the presentation and mixing of cognitive and affective learning exercises.

Changes in attitude and behavior expected of students at the inclusion of lesbian and gay content in direct practice courses may prove difficult or even painful for some students. Two ways instructors can utilize professional values to minimize this discomfort have been discussed and reflect a learning process. Each step of this process requires students to requires students to increase their personal involvement with the content. For example, "equal access" might first be discussed in terms of democratic principles. Second it might be discussed in terms of the economically disadvantaged. Then, it could be discussed in terms of the socially disadvantaged. Finally, students might be asked to generalize to lesbian women and gay men. At this point, the class might explore the degree to which they accept the concept of equity for their lesbian/gay clients. Do gays and lesbians have the right to equal housing, to parent, to teach in public schools?

A third use of social work value lies in the student's motivation to identify with the profession. Values of the profession and particularly their representation in the NASW Code of Ethics can be used to substantiate, validate, and legitimize the responsibility of social workers to diverse client populations, including lesbians and gays.

Application of Practice Skills to Work With Lesbian and Gay Clients

In the transition from considering the application of professional values to the application of practice skills with lesbian and gay clients, instructors and students can continue the process of moving toward less familiar content and more personal involvement with the content. The least threatening practice material should be presented first. In their work, Dulaney and Kelly (1982) consider the guiding principals of social work as they apply to lesbian and gay clients. They are essentially the same for all clients, regardless of sexual orientation. They include: accept the client as a total human being; accept the client's sexual orientation; do not pretend to have all of the answers; and do not have a hidden agenda. Discussion of these or any similar set of principals, such as Biestek's (1957) Principles of the Casework Relationship, helps prepare students for work with any client population and facilitates a progression from the discussion of practice values to a readiness for the acquisition of practice skills.

Lesbian women and gay men have the same basic needs

as other clients. Sexual orientation cannot be considered the "determinant" of problems. Instead, the worker must consider such factors as: the client's perception of self; the way she/he perceives her/himself treated by the rest of society; the ways in which she/he has encountered oppressive homophobic systems; and availability of support systems (Berger, 1983; Woodman & Lenna, 1980). The processes of problem identification and assessment, therefore, are carried out using an ecological approach. This means that teaching for practice with lesbian and gay clients necessitates the motivation of students to employ their knowledge from the other components of their social work education to facilitate the application of practice skills. It is crucial that students develop an awareness of special needs of lesbians and gays and an understanding of the social forces which impinge on this vulnerable population. These special needs and social forces affect both the manifestation of problems and the development of solutions to problematic situations.

Consistent with the educational process of beginning with familiar material, students should begin considering the similarities lesbians and gays share with other client populations. Gay men who lose their lovers to AIDS have the need to grieve and are at risk for depression. Similarly, the lesbian seeking custody of her children is less likely to care about sexual behavior than the processes involved in petitioning for custody. The educational objective, here, is to assist students in developing an understanding that sexual orientation in itself is not a concern unless the client identifies it as such. Above all, it is necessary to ascertain that students are aware of institutionalized prejudices, discrimination, and stereotypes and to teach ways of countering homophobic systems.

The integration of lesbian and gay content in direct practice courses requires students to refer to their knowledge of human behavior in the social environment if they are to thoroughly understand the commonalities and differences lesbians and gays have with other client populations. However, the developmental processes that confront every individual with new challenges may include stresses unique to the lesbian or gay client. As described in Part I, all adolescents deal with sexual identity. Lesbians and gays must deal with sexual identity with few or no role models, and there are special problems that surround coming out as a lesbian or gay person. The older gay man may have many of the physical problems faced by other senior citizens, but he may be more likely to be alone. Nursing homes and senior citizens' centers may ignore affectional and social needs (Berger, 1982), and social security and other pension plans favor more traditional husband-wife couples. An educational objective for the inclusion of lesbian and gay content is the development of an awareness that problematic situations surrounding sexual orientation are most likely a result of institutionalized prejudices and discrimination. There is a need for students to understand the social conditions which give rise to the special needs of their lesbian and gay clients.

Just as it is necessary for practitioners to appreciate the needs which may be specific to their lesbian and gay clients, there is a need for them to understand environmental forces which are important factors in making assessments of and assisting clients in developing and utilizing support systems. As with any client, the lesbian or gay person comes to the social work situation with strengths and weaknesses unique to her or him. Similarly, her or his environment consists of particular resources which may be utilized to facilitate change and deficits which exacerbate a difficult situation.

As a result of their work in other components of social work education, students should be aware of societal values which result in policies excluding lesbians and gays from services that heterosexuals take for granted. Because of discriminations based on both gender and orientation, lesbians are at double jeopardy. In general, relationships between members of the same sex are discounted in our society. Consequently, social policies favoring the traditional marriage and household may place lesbians and gays and their lovers at greater risk. Society is not as generous in its provisions for lesbians and gays as it is for heterosexuals, and present day social policies contribute to the problems of lesbians and gays. If society is not willing to move toward equity for all its members, social workers need to be prepared to assist their lesbian and gay clients by acting as advocates in a social change process.

In preparing for practice with lesbian and gay clients, students must become knowledgeable of those services in the community which meet the needs of this clientele, and they should be aware of services which are designed specifically for this population. Lesbian and gay clients have the right to expect social workers to assist them in finding a variety of services, and students in direct practice courses should take the responsibility of locating these services in their geographical area.

Within their immediate environments there are conditions unique to lesbians and gays which must be considered if effective services are to be provided. Students in direct practice courses need to be aware of these unique conditions and be prepared to consider them in their assessment with lesbian and gay clients. Such conditions include but are not limited to:

1. Friendships are important to lesbian women and gay men (Bell & Weinberg, 1978). A circle of friends may be substituted for the family. The reality is that this population does not share its minority status with family members (Potter & Dorty, 1981). In a crisis, lesbians and gays may be more likely to call upon friends than family members for support. This is particularly true for lesbians, who often feel alienated from their families (Sanford & Forrister, 1983).

2. Lesbian women and gay men tend to have more positive relationships with former lovers than heterosexuals do with former spouses. The "ex" in a lesbian or gay person's life may have the special status of best friend and may often be called on in times of stress. This individual may know the client better than anyone else (Sanford & Forrister, 1983).

3. Contrary to popular stereotypes, lesbian women and gay men do form and maintain relationships which have qualities similar to those of marriage for heterosexuals (Bell & Weinberg, 1978; Berger, 1982).

4. Lover relationships for lesbians and gays are more egalitarian than they are for heterosexuals. In the lesbian or gay household the division of labor is likely to be done by skills or abilities rather than role expectations.

Cognitive learning that occurs in direct practice courses is necessary in preparing the prospective social worker for work with lesbian and gay clients. Of more importance is the potential for affective learning. Experiential learning exercises in direct practice classes have the potential for fostering the acceptance of lesbian and gay clients and helping the student feel comfortable with those of a different sexual orientation. Such attitudinal changes are most necessary if the profession is to equitably provide services for lesbians and gays.

Modalities for Integrating Lesbian and Gay Content in Direct Practice Courses

The most common approach to education is the transmission approach (Crompton, 1974), where information to be acquired by the student is presented by the instructor. This method, effective in the transmission of knowledge, does not encourage tolerance and acceptance, foster the development of skills to communicate acceptance, nor prepare one for the possible behaviors of the client (Crompton, 1974). The achievement and teaching modalities which encourage students to interact affectively, as well as cognitively with minority content are necessary (Brownstein & McGill, 1984; Crompton, 1974; Englund, 1980).

Of most importance in the establishment of an environment conducive for experiential learning is the instructor's involvement with both the class and content

(Crompton, 1974; Jurich & Hastings, 1983; Webb, 1984). Indeed, Jurich and Hastings (1983, p. 368) refer to the instructor as the "primary ingredient." The instructor's role is evident in the suggestions that the teaching of practice be approached as the practice of group work (Crompton, 1974; Webb, 1984). The instructor utilizes her/his practice expertise to assist students in their interaction with lesbian and gay content and preparation to serve this clientele. This is accomplished by modeling practice behaviors and demonstrating the skills of practice.

Preparation for teaching lesbian and gay content for practice is similar to preparation for work with a small group. Thorough knowledge of the content to be taught is necessary (Jurich & Hastings, 1983); however, knowledge of the content is not sufficient. Experiential learning requires that instructors be aware of their own biases (Crompton, 1974; Jurich & Hastings, 1983); comfortable with the educational techniques to be used and willing to participate with students (Gabriel, 1982); tolerant of others' viewpoints (Webb, 1984) and aware of their own image (Jurich & Hastings, 1983).

Approaching teaching as practice, the instructor ascertains for students that there are no hidden agendas. Educational objectives are openly expressed and the pedagogical rationale for classroom activities is always provided. The major objective here, is for the instructor to create a supportive and nonthreatening environment for learning.

Two common modalities for developing situations of experiential learning are discussion and role-playing. Discussion can be used independently; however, effective role playing includes the use of both modalities.

Discussion

As a primary modality for dealing with lesbian and gay content, discussion can be utilized to foster personal interactions among students. It becomes an opportunity for students to explore their own feelings and value biases. The instructors' contributions to this process are to ascertain that factual information pertaining to lesbians and gays is presented and to provide structure. Jurich and Hastings (1983) note four guidelines proposed by Irvine and Helms for fostering such learning. Briefly stated, the guidelines suggest that everyone has the right to be heard; the positive is to be accentuated; the individual is always reaffirmed as a person; and everyone's right to privacy is respected.

The educational precepts of moving from the more to the less familiar content and from less to more self-disclosure while mixing cognitive and affective learning expectations may be applied to the structuring of discussions to maximize their potential as experiential learning situations. Using a group approach, with students as with clients, discussing a situation which includes a great deal of anxiety can be part of a problem solving process resulting in changes in attitude and behavior (Englund, 1980; Jurich & Hastings, 1983). As Gambrill notes (1983, p. 139), "Only when issues are addressed openly and honestly can people confront and overcome their irrational fears." Open and objective discussion may have the positive effect of helping class members unsure of their sexuality deal with it and identify resources in the community which may be beneficial should they desire further assistance in dealing with this issue. The fortunate class will have a lesbian or gay member who is knowledgeable about lifestyles, special needs, and values of her or his community and can comfortably share this knowledge with classmates. If there is no such class member with the appropriate knowledge or experience, responsibility falls totally on the instructor to make appropriate references to reading materials and community resources for lesbians and gays. Nonetheless, discussion allows this to be done matter-of-factly without jeopardizing anyone's privacy or drawing attention to a particular individual.

Role-Playing

The primary modality for teaching lesbian and gay content presented in this paper has been discussion. However, it is often used in conjunction with and as an integral part of role-playing, which is commonly cited as an activity of choice for teaching skills which may be used in practice (Crompton, 1974; Gabriel, 1982; Shaw, Corsini, Blake & Mouton, 1980; Swell, 1968). This modality provides the opportunity to consider life-like situations within the classroom (Glenn, Gregg & Tipple, 1982; Meinert, 1972; Swell, 1968). It is an experiential learning modality which encourages students to express themselves and try new behavior in a nonthreatening environment (Shaw, Corsini, Blake & Mouton, 1980; Swell, 1968). The apparent ignorance of the special needs, or even existence of lesbian and gay clients (Dulaney & Kelly, 1982; Gambrill, Stein & Brown, 1984) indicates that practitioners need the understanding and empathy that may be developed in role-playing. Further, once students are comfortable with this modality, they tend to see it as a valid vehicle for learning and as a practice technique which may be effectively used in practice settings.

Anxiety which may surround participation in role-playing may be reduced if the instructor appeals to students' motivation to become a professional (Swell, 1968), and explains the qualities of role-play as a rehearsal for practice. Certainly, the educational precepts of moving from the more to less familiar and from less to more self-disclosure should be followed. Accordingly, role-playing involving lesbian and gay content is best preceded by class discussion related to professional values and lesbian and gay issues and other role-plays of less controversial content. General preparations for role-playing require instructors to invest their energies in development of rapport, acceptance, and trust with and among students.

As a teaching modality, role-playing is adaptable. It can be structured to meet various needs of students in covering specific aspects of lesbian and gay issues. Structure can include a brief definition of roles and setting (Gabriel, 1982; Shaw, Corsini, Blake & Mouton, 1980) and an explanation of the practice skill objectives of a particular role-play situation (Shaw, Corsini, Blake & Mouton, 1980). These structural specifics can be typed on index cards and given to participants for the particular role-play, allowing for both necessary structure and creative interpretation. Specific skill objectives need to be consistent with course objectives, and instructors should be comfortable with role-playing techniques and be prepared to play any role they expect students to take (Gabriel, 1982).

In introducing role-play, volunteers should be used as much as possible (Gabriel, 1982). Thus, those students most comfortable with role-playing and lesbian and gay content provide early models for the attitudinal approach expected of the class in this experiential learning. Volunteers, then, should be positively reinforced for their willingness to participate. Once the class is comfortable with role-play and discussion of sexual issues, it may be feasible to randomly make assignments for role-playing.

A major attribute of role playing is that it offers an opportunity for students to interact with lesbian and gay content both as social worker and as a lesbian or gay client. By using such techniques as role reversal (Shaw, Corsini, Blake & Mouton, 1980), students may experience alternately what it is like to attempt to provide services for the lesbian or gay client and what it is like to be the lesbian or gay client seeking services. The latter is more likely to bring about attitudinal change. At this point, students are often surprised to discover that sexual orientation does not necessarily determine one's communication patterns and how one feels, or that there are differences in one's needs that are not readily met by institutionalized means in our society. Indeed, they are likely to come aware of institutionalized discrimination and prejudice.

Role-playing is most effective when it includes discussion, which should immediately follow the role-play (Gabriel, 1982). Ideally, the role-plays are video taped. Then, they may be replayed for discussion. Using this technique it is possible for students to stop the tape at any point for discussion. Video taping permits students to deal with various aspects of the role play, such as practice skills, verbal and nonverbal communication, content of the session, or policy issues.

The discussion following role-playing offers students an opportunity to discuss their personal reactions to the role-play situation. Interpersonal interaction between students at this time can result in a verbal formalization of attitudinal change. Changes in a direction consistent with the profession's value stance can be positively reinforced by the instructor and classmates. Consequently, the use of role-playing and discussion can bring about and confirm attitudinal changes which may be necessary to work with lesbian and gay clients.

Admission of attitudinal change can serve to open discussion for other areas where change may be necessary if social workers are to serve diverse client populations. Thus, the discussion becomes a tool for assessment. Instructors and students can explore together other client groups or problematic conditions with which they feel comfortable. The inclusion of lesbian and gay content in direct practice courses can then be generalized to other social work practice situations.

References

Bell, A. & Weinberg, M. (1978). Homosexualities: A Study of Diversity Among Men and Women. New York: Simon & Schuster.

Berger, R. (1982). The Unseen Minority: Older Gays and Lesbians. *Social Work, 27*, 236-241.

Berger, R. (1983). What is a Homosexual? A Definitional Model. *Social Work, 28*, 132-135.

Biestek, F. (1957). *The Casework Relationship.* Chicago: Loyola University Press.

Brownstein, C. & McGill, S. (1984). Practice Workshop: A Model for Teaching Base Social Work Practice. *Arete, 9*, 48-59.

Crompton, D. (1974). Minority Content in Social Work Education— Promise or Pitfall? *Journal of Education for Social Work, 10*, 9-18.

Dulaney, D. & Kelly, J. (1982). Improving Services to Gay and Lesbian Clients, *Social Work, 27*, 178-183.

Englund, C. (1980). Using Kohlberg's Moral Development Framework in Family Life Education. *Family Relations, 29*, 7-13.

Fox, J. (1983). Affective Learning in Racism Courses. *Journal for Social Work, 19,* 69-76.

Gabriel, J. (1982). Using Role-Play as a Training and Supervisory Tool. *Child Welfare, 61,* 383-387.

Gambrill, E., Stein, T. & Brown, C. (1984). Social Service Use and Need Among Gay/Lesbian Residents in the San Francisco Bay Area, *Journal of Social Work and Human Sexuality, 3,* 51-69.

Glenn, A., Gregg, D., & Tipple. B. (1982). Using Role-Play Activities to Teach Problem-Solving. *Simulation and Games, 13,* 199-209.

Gramick, J. (1983). Homophobia: A New Challenge. *Social Work, 28,* 137-141.

Jurich, A. & Hastings, C. (1983). Teaching About Alternative Life Styles: Handbook, in E. Macklin & R. Rubin (Eds.), *Contemporary Families and Alternative Lifestyles,* (pp. 362-378). Beverly Hills, CA: Sage Publications.

Meinert, R. (1972). Simulation Technology: A Potential Tool for Social Work Education. *Journal of Education for Social Work, 8,* 50-59.

Olson, T. & Moss, J. (1980). Creating Supportive Atmospheres in Family Life Education. *Family Relations, 29,* 391-395.

Potter, S. & Dorty, T. Social Work and the Invisible Minority: An Exploration of Lesbianism. *Social Work, 26,* 187-192.

Sanford, L. & Forrister, D. (1983). Relationships of Gays and Lesbians. Unpublished Paper. Presented at the Mid-South Sociological Association, Birmingham, Alabama.

Shaw, M., Corsini, R., Blake, R., & Mouton, J. (1980). *Role Playing: A Practical Manual for Group Facilitators.* San Diego: University Associates, Inc.

Swell, L. (1968). Role-Playing in the Context of Learning Theory in Casework Teaching. *Journal of Education for Social Work, 4.*

Webb, N. (1984). From Social Work Practice to Teaching the Practice of Social Work. *Journal of Education for Social Work, 20,* 51-57

5

The Outsiders: Group Work
With Young Homosexuals

Harry R. Lenna, Ph.D.

Introduction

In an interview regarding one of his very popular novels for adolescents, Robert Cormier stated, "There's just so much intimidation— and of course, when you're a teenager, you're easily intimidated. Kids that age want to be independent and free, and think they are, but they're one of the most conformist groups in the world because they want to fit in with the peer group and run with the pack."

The statement quite aptly summarizes the young person's social ecology as he or she seeks to interact and find acceptance among peers. It is no less true for the gay or lesbian youth. The issue, of course, is that such young people either know or suspect that in one vital dimension of self they are decidedly different from most of their peers. They are also most likely very sensitive to the fact that their personal reality is one that can bring stigmatization, and homophobic rejection from the very same peers with whom they so desire to fit in. If their homosexual orientation has already been discovered they have very likely experienced the agony of rejection and social isolation. Even if not yet generally known, the specter of such discovery can be a constant source of fear and anxiety. Clark (1975) characterized this double barreled emotional trauma as a condition of oppression in which:

> Fear, then, is created by an experience that either brings about the deprivation of needs or the expectation that needs will be deprived. Anxiety is related specifically to the relationship of oneself to another; hence it is grounded in the need of people to be confirmed and affirmed by other people. (p. 34)

The model for group work with adolescent and early post-adolescent lesbians and gays offered here seeks to provide a context where these twin dynamics of homophobic oppression can be challenged and find some resolution.

Most social work with gay and lesbian young people has been minimal and has tended to focus primarily on intra-psychological stress related to homosexual orientation per se. Some social workers have moved away from the cure and change goals of treatment to a more enlightened approach of resolving emotional stress and anxiety related to homoerotic feelings. However, this focus on the individual's self-acceptance as lesbian or gay is only a beginning. Broader needs expressed by clients also require work with the person-in-situation realities associated with identity issues. Ignoring social and interpersonal relationships results in inadequate or even injurious behavior by the professional. Citing real or imagined obstacles to involvement in the social spheres and needs of the young lesbian and gay client often replaces creative intervention. Furthermore, professional aloofness can heighten feelings of oppression and alienation for the youth, causing a variety of negative ramifications. These may include denial, repression or suppression of a homosexual orientation; depression with its secondary results of withdrawal, anti-social acting out, and even suicide; and, unfortunately for significant others, involvement in socially demanded intimate heterosexual relationships (Woodman & Lenna, 1980).

Social workers are particularly geared toward recognizing the influence of social systems on the developmental process. As professionals, we accept the need for self-actualization predicated on gaining self-esteem and giving self-esteem to others as a part of interaction. Therefore, the author recommends intervention which will promote validation for lesbian and gay adolescents in their efforts to develop responsive and responsible life styles and interactions.

Assumptions Related to Working with Lesbian and Gay Adolescent Groups

An ecological approach to lesbian/gay adolescence is particularly relevant because it accounts for the person as a unique configuration of components. The young persons are in the process of growing and developing uniquely within a breadth of other systems such as the family, peer, school, legal, and spiritual networks. To ignore any aspect of the intra-personal or external is a disservice. For example, both gay and non-gay adolescents who are sexually active are exposed to sexually transmitted diseases. Overlooking this reality denies understanding of various physical and social repercussions. Conversely, the social worker must recognize that integrating a lesbian/gay identity does not necessarily include overt sexual behavior. Of even more importance is that the professional not fall into the heterosexist trap of questioning the youth's ability to know his or her homosexual orientation without having heterosexual experiences. Some adolescents encounter particular conflict because of religious oppression, yet do not have the freedom to make changes in affiliations. At the same time they may not want to eliminate the spiritual foundations which provide meaning and value for their development of internalized ethics. Social workers must be sensitive to such issues. Also, they can help their young clients accept differences and be empathetic to struggles of peers in identity development. In the group process which the author describes, such knowledge provides a base for establishing individual and group norms and, coincidentally, group cohesion.

Knowledge about lesbian and gay issues should include an understanding that many individuals self-identify in childhood, early or late adolescence (see, for example, Bell & Weinberg, 1978). Therefore, social workers cannot assume that early acknowledging of self as gay or lesbian is just youthful experimentation or a development phase. Neither can the counselor depreciate adolescents by considering them incompetent to know what they are "going to be" in later years. This dimension of competency judgement applies both in an emotional sense (the youth is not sick or mentally ill) and in cognitive ability (cognitive stupidity is not a factor in homosexual identification.)

In exploring resources with the adolescent youths, social workers should not use such homophobic myths as recruitment of children by adults or child molesting to avoid lesbian and gay community contacts. Nor should these myths be a rationalization for negating group intervention. The reality for adult gays and lesbians is that they often want to be available as role models and helping persons for young people but definitely prefer age-peers for social, intellectual, and intimate relationships.

Finally, the social worker and lesbian and gay young people must interact within the parameters of the legal realities of their communities. It is important that these be recognized and that creative adaptation within such legal strictures be employed. More crucially, legality should not be used as a rationalization for avoiding work with homosexual adolescents. We do not avoid problem solving with hetero-sexually active adolescents and adults who engage in pre-marital sexual behaviors or consider them felons or criminals, regardless of prevailing but unenforced statutes. So too, we must be flexible with lesbian and gay youth, while helping them to be cognizant of the legal ramifications and the dangers of some behaviors such as cruising in public places.

In summary, the social worker will begin with a knowl-edgeable and empathetic framework to work with gay and lesbian young people to facilitate self-esteem and responsibility to self and others. This interventive process involves responsibility for self including the biological, emotional and social dimensions; accepting the need for defining identity for self and with others in social situations; and implementing change in social institutions so that they can provide for continued self-actualization.

Principles Underlying a Model for Lesbian and Gay Adolescent Groups

A clear sense of identity and a strong commitment to act on that identity are considered by various authors (Weinberg & Bell, 1978; Woodman & Lenna, 1980) to be core aspects of a creative and self-actualized gay or lesbian life style. However, for many self-acknowledged homosexual young persons, there may be considerable emotional and psychological distance between identity acknowledgement ("I am a homosexual") and identity commitment ("My homosexuality is a positive aspect of me as a total person.") Coming out is the term used to describe this process of moving from an essentially covert, passive and reactive social stance to behavior that reflects commitment which is assertive and proactive.

The therapeutic process involves two psychodynamic points of reference that should underlie the social worker's interactions within the group process. The first of these is opportunity for sentiment clarification by the participants. The second is that of providing an appropriate cognitive-affective structure that can assist group members in developing a positive proactive sense of self.

Participants of the target group are quite likely to begin the group process in a state of considerable confusion, emotional stress and negative self-imaging. Sorting out their personal sentiments as related to sexual orientation must be given careful attention. Sentiment, as used in this instance refers to the concept as presented by Becker (1964).

1. thoughts/feelings regarding what has been, is, and can be— the reality aspect.
2. thoughts/feelings regarding what ought to be— the value aspect.
3. thoughts/feelings regarding what is wanted— the desire aspect. (p. 154)

The principle of pro-activity calls, first of all, for participants' development or reinforcement of a positive sense of self in regards to both the personal and social dimensions of their homosexual orientation. Second, a positive sense of one's sexual affectional self must find context and opportunity for concrete self-expression. As Jourard (1971) pointed out, some level of self-disclosure is a necessary element of mental health and growth.

> I say that self-disclosure is a means by which one achieves personality health. I mean it is not until I am my real self and I act my real self that my real self is in a position to grow. (p. 34)

Intervention through the group process being discussed seeks to accomplish three basic therapeutic goals. The first goal is to provide clients with accurate information about homosexuality and homosexual life styles. A second purpose is to help the clients translate knowledge into personal, reality based, proactive choices about behaviors. The principle to be stressed is that each participant has the power and responsibility to establish his or her identity so that it can enhance self and others. Finally, the development of a sexual identity includes a demand for opportunities to test and find validation for what is genuine for self and appropriate to social contexts. Unfortunately, gay and lesbian youths do not have access to the institutions of the gay sub-culture that are usually available to adults who are in the process of coming out. Therefore, it is of even greater importance that help be made available so that these young people may comfortably self-disclose and consider the varied potentialities and problems of living as a lesbian or gay youth.

The author has found the group process especially efficacious. Several considerations underlie a preference for this interventive modality. First, homosexual teenagers are likely to be moving from a social position of protective isolation into more expanded contacts with social institutions. This is particularly the case in regard to their sexual-affectional self. Just being able to interact with a group of other gays and lesbians is socially satisfying. The group context can provoke discussion of diverse viewpoints regarding homosexual identities and life styles, and, in turn, enhance opportunities for positive development based on thoughtful consideration. Additionally, the homogeneity of a group where members share sexual-affectional orientation can reduce feelings of risk in verbalizing personal emotions and ideas frankly and openly. Finally, peer groups are a typical source of support in testing adolescent identity issues. Involvement in a lesbian/ gay peer group fills the void which might exist as a result of exclusion from heterosexually oriented friendship networks.

It is not suggested that the group context is the most appropriate therapeutic context for all issues or problems facing the young homosexual client. In many instances he or she may find greater comfort in individual counseling for self-revelation or exploration of possible homosexual identity. Where symptoms of excessive stress, anxiety, or a sense of panic about one's recently acknowledged or suspected homosexual orientation are evidenced, they would seem best resolved in individual sessions. Woodman and Lenna (1980) placed dynamics such as denial, identity confusion, attempt to "bargain" away reality, depression related to sexual identification, wishful thinking or self-destructive behavior as possible initial crisis or incipient crisis dynamics that, when manifest, need priority of attention. Initial identity resolution, on the whole, seems better resolved where focus can be directly and intensively related to the individual troubled client's most immediate needs.

The use of groups as proposed here is seen as most apt for those adolescents who have achieved at least some basic resolution and acceptance of their sexual-affectional orientation. They, therefore, are apt to be more focused toward exploring and developing self-actualizing understanding, social contexts for asserting and validating themselves, and methods of coping with and resolving real or potential conflicts that may be a part of negotiating their social environments.

Where possible, groups should be composed so as to minimize wide variation in developmental stages as well as psycho-social development. The stresses and issues of a thirteen year old may seem childish and inconsequential to a sixteen year old who has dealt more fully with such issues of separation and autonomy. Such disparities can, in adolescent groups, evoke at best lack of empathy or, at worse, hostility and disparagement by older participants.

The Intervention Process

The approach to intervention within this model is divided into two major levels. Level I is primarily addressed to education and information sharing. Level II focuses on affective and social commitment to self-actualization as a lesbian or gay person. Depending upon the context and its resources, implementation of the two levels is recommended to be successive for any given cohort of participants. Once the cycle of planned educationally oriented meetings has been finished as a way of introducing the various aspects of a lesbian or gay life style it can be repeated in whole or part according to the expressed need of participants to explore in more depth issues that have emerged. Level II focuses more intensively upon individual affective and social issues within a social growth perspective, with emphasis upon self as lesbian or gay.

Level I

The first level of intervention stresses a cognitive focus. From the facilitator's point of view, the goals of the cycle of topical meetings are intended to:

1. Provide accurate information about homosexuality and gay and lesbian life styles.
2. Provide a context where participants can relate this information to their own lives and social situations.
3. Provide a comfortable group setting for increased social contact and interaction with other gays and lesbians of generally similar ages.
4. Help participants discover the positive meanings their sexual-affectional orientation can have for them.
5. Develop awareness of the variety that is a part of what has been called a gay or lesbian life style.
6. Instill the principle of self-empowerment for making realistic and proactive choice in defining and enacting one's own lesbian or gay identity and life style.

Seven general topic areas [1] are suggested as a format for the cycle of meetings.

1. Images of Ourselves: New and Old
2. The World Out There
3. Lifestyle Variations
4. Exploring Our Sexual Selves
5. Exploring Our Feelings
6. Intimacy: Boyfriends/Girlfriends
7. Intimacy: Developing A Caring Network

The first session, Images of Ourselves: New and Old, has as its primary focus the relationship of sexual-affectional orientation to self-identity. The goal is to help group members conceptualize and further clarify what being gay or lesbian means to them. A sample of possible questions that might be used by the facilitator to evoke discussion includes:

-   How do the participants view the personal attribute of a gay/lesbian sexual orientation?
-   How does it influence their behaviors?

- If their homosexuality is known to others, how do people react to them and how do they respond to these reactions?
- How do they or might they "explain" their sexual-affectional feelings to others?
- If they had a "straight pill" that would make them different, would they want to use it? Why? Why not?

In the second meeting, related to "The World Out There," the focus is on the general attitudes of others toward homosexuality and how group members have been made aware of these reactions. The goal is to eliminate internalized negative stereotypes and find new ways of responding effectively to homophobia. Discussion areas can be:

- What are some attitudes toward homosexuality?
- Where do they come from?
- Are they true or false representations of gays and lesbians? Why? Why not?
- Do group members have ideas and attitudes about themselves which are similar to those they have identified?
- How do the participants feel about the attitudes of others?
- What experiences have made them aware of these attitudes?
- What are some effective responses to homophobic attitudes?

The third area to be explored is "Lifestyle Variations." The goal is to identify the diverse patterns in lesbian and gay relationships and to demonstrate ways in which integration of the sexual dimensions of self and general life experiences is possible. More specifically, questions for discussion are:

- How would the participants relate the concepts of life style and life style diversity to their adolescent years?

- What roles will or can people they care about play in their lives?
- How are lesbian/gay life styles different from other life styles?
- Does being lesbian/gay affect vocational, educational, career goals?

The fourth meeting focuses on "Exploring My Sexual Self." The intent is to deal with myths and misinformation, to provide an opportunity for evaluating responsible sexual behavior, and to provide adult validation for the fact that homosexual behaviors are not evil or causative factors in mental illness. Areas of exploration can include frank discussion of sexual behavior and may include such questions as:

- Do we know why some people are homosexual and some are not? Does it really make a difference?
- Regarding sexual behaviors themselves, are some of them OK and others not so?
- Is there a difference between responsible and irresponsible sexual interaction?
- What needs to be known about sexually transmitted diseases, particularly for lesbians and gays?
- Are my sexual-affectional preferences the end-all and be-all of who I am?

Having explored sexuality, the next session moves to "Exploring My Emotional Feelings." The purpose is to gain greater understanding about possible conflicting emotions associated with being a lesbian or gay adolescent. The responses to the following queries should include ideas about both positive and negative affective reactions.

- How do I feel about myself as a lesbian or gay teenager?
- How do these feelings affect how I choose to behave?

- How do the attitudes of non-gays who are important in my life affect my personal feelings?
- What can I do to maintain good feelings about
  myself if others are being negative?

The final two sessions are related to issues about intimacy. The goal now is to help members evaluate the need for
responsible and responsive support systems which will
promote self-actualization. In the first of these two sessions,
same-sex relationships with boyfriends or girlfriends should
be explored. Depending on the life situations of the participants, this topic can be approached from life experiences or
hypothetical ideas, or a merger of the two can occur. Topical
areas would include:

- Do I want a steady relationship? Why? Why not?
- What would this involve for me and the other
  person?
- What would this mean to my parents, relatives
  and friends?
- How would my friends and I deal with the reac-
  tions of others?
- Can we have close friendships with other people?

In the last session, questions addressing the importance
of developing caring supports can be raised. As group
members explore the processes of networking, the facilitator
can provide information and referral services related to
resources that are available to young gays and lesbians.
Additional discussion can focus on how informal networks
are formed. Questions can be:

- Why do I need social supports and affirmation
  from significant and empathetic others, including
  religious groups?
- Where do I/we find these supportive others?
- Are there adult gays and lesbians who can be
  supportive?

During this first level of group sessions which focus on information and education, the group structure can be an open one with members free to attend or skip sessions. In addition to providing participants with the topical calendar, handouts of materials pertinent to the next week's discussion are helpful. Also, giving examples of the possible questions to be discussed at the next meeting helps the members focus their ideas prior to the session and enhances group interaction.

The primary role for the facilitator during Level I interactions is that of educator. Information sharing and discussion are the major interactional dynamics. Dangers for facilitators when working within an educational focus can be that of becoming too didactic and too much the center of the participants' activity in the role of expert. Despite the need and desire for information, young people are likely to tune out if the worker relates to the group participants as passive recipients of data. A preferred approach, particularly with this age group, is to generate the participants' ideas about the particular focus of a given session. Correction of mis-perceptions, clarification of ideas and the transmission of additional knowledge can best be facilitated by offering or eliciting the same through discussion among the group participants. Feedback from the group leader is best directed toward the thinking generated by the group with a minimum of focus on correction of false information or misunderstanding directed at individual members.

At this initial level, the facilitator can expect that shared information and insights will, in the earlier stages, have a more generalized, intellectual flavor and relatively less of what is personal. Although application of ideas to self should be encouraged, pressing for intensely personal feelings probably will prove counter-productive. The adolescents first need to develop comfort in openly discussing the whole area of homosexuality and homosexual life styles. They also must have a high level of trust in other participants before they venture into acknowledging more personal feelings and problems. Support should be given to those who wish to limit their involvement to general fact sharing. Where this first level of groups has been offered as an ongoing cycle for open groups, many participants repeat the series before deciding to become involved in the more intensive closed groups that make up the second level of the process.

Level II

The second level of group process has both an affective and social focus dealing more specifically with personal sentiments, problems, and needs. These groups should be closed and set for a specific number of weeks. Those who take part should agree to attend all of the sessions. Membership usually is made up of those from the information and education groups who have expressed the desire to have this more intense level of interaction. In some instances, the social worker may initiate referrals based on client-worker agreement that such a group experience would be beneficial for the young persons. The basic approach for Level II can be characterized (generally) as a social growth approach. Toseland and Rivas (1984) have offered a useful summary for the points of goal reference for activities among participants:

> (1) their assessment of their own needs, (2) their previous experience in trying to accomplish these goals, (3) the environmental, social and familial demands placed upon them, (4) their assessment of their own capacities and capabilities, and (5) their impressions or experiences of what the social service agency sponsoring the group has to offer. (p. 155)

Overall, the group process should be much more non-structured and focus on the personal issues brought by the participants. The primary points that distinguish this group effort from the primary level of education and information are:

1. Placing emphasis on clarification of each individual's thoughts, feelings and behaviors.

2. Attempting to achieve better integration of thoughts and feelings about one's homosexuality into a positive gestalt which can enhance self-image.
3. Reinforcing the principle of the right and need for each person to be responsible for self-definition, rather than being defined by others.
4. Making conscious and focused decisions about what should be done to make one's gay/lesbian identity and life style more proactive and self-actualizing.

Participants should be encouraged to expand both their ideas and actions for positive social interaction beyond the boundaries of their group. Decisions and efforts related to asserting a homosexual identity outside the group should be discussed in relationship to purpose and probable outcomes. Consideration within the group session can assist the young members to develop principles to guide future decision making. Lesbian and gay youths need to be sensitive to the possibilities of homophobic reactions to disclosure of their gay/lesbian identities. Adolescents, given their dependent status, need to develop the capacity as well as the opportunities for making decisions about when self-disclosure may or may not be appropriate. "Appropriate" in this instance means that self-disclosure will create the potential for self-actualization within a specific situation.

The author has found fantasy exercises that permit the young people to develop and expand a sense of the ideal self as lesbian or gay to be a useful technique. It presents the opportunity for group members to free themselves from the normal constraints and inhibitions that may still be a part of relating to their sexual orientation. The development of a sense of the ideal self will, of course, then need to be modified to the reality constraints of their individual personal and social situations. The use of role play also has been found helpful in this regard.

Not all participants in Level I activities may feel a present need to move on to Level II, and some participants may not be judged appropriate for a particular Level II group being formed at a given time. Principles enunciated by Klein (1972) for group composition have been found useful.

(1) Compose the group so there is homogeneity with regard to the developmental task.

(2) Compose the group so that there is heterogeneity of coping patterns and defenses.

(3) Compose the group so there is balance and at the same time so that it is weighted toward the positive.

(4) Compose the group so that there will be both stimulus for interaction and movement toward change in behavior.

(5) Compose the group so that levels of remission are not very different.

(6) Assess and predict the probable role behaviors one can expect each potential member to enact.

(7) Avoid bringing people into the group when their behavior will be palpably ego-alien to any other member.

(8) For group work to be a treatment of choice, the members must have some degree of social hunger.

(9) For group work to be indicated, potential members must be able to communicate with others in the group in a meaningful way. (pp. 60-63).

In summary, this level of group process provides for greater development of self-actualization in an adolescent lesbian or gay life style. It permits for acknowledging and sharing fantasies and working through negative stereotypes, social prohibitions, and negative experiences from prior social interactions. The social worker and the group can help in ameliorating internalized guilt feelings, self alienating behaviors, alienation from others, and self-destructive acting out which impedes building a positive lesbian or gay self-image. Moving into meaningful social contexts such as vocational/career, recreation, spiritual, and cross-gender groups also is a goal of the Level II groups. Accepting adolescent love relationships which are guilt free, involve mutual sharing and are growth producing is yet another potential outcome. In essence, through use of the group experience, the adolescents can incorporate the various dimensions of self which have particular meaning including their lesbian/gay identities.

Involvement of Significant Others

School, church related, youth organizations and other avenues need to be explored as a means of reaching out to teenage lesbians and gays. The fear of negative reactions from adults and non-gay peers to self-disclosure requires that the professional community be assertive in wide distribution of materials about available services while respecting the feelings of the potential users of such resources. Clear indication of professional sponsorship should be provided in order to allay suspicion from parents and concerned others about the intent or competence of those involved. Also, it should be explicit that anonymity for those seeking information will be accepted and respected. Circulating information is crucial. When presentations are given to school, church or community organizations, handouts should be provided to all listeners. If posters are used in various teen settings, there should be tear-off sheets providing only the address and telephone contact number for the series of group meetings. In this way, there need be no explanation for the teenager's having the unidentified data. The setting chosen for the group meetings should be such that regular gatherings of teenagers will not arouse comment or speculation as to intent or purpose.

When possible, it is strongly urged that groups for parents/ guardians be established and run concurrently with the adolescent groups. Similarly to the youth groups, the first level of meetings for related adults can be dedicated to information and education. The topics can mirror those being discussed in the teen groups. However, the emphasis might be on parental understanding and responses to the issues, problems, and concerns of the lesbian or gay teenagers. If and when young persons enter the second level of group involvement described by the author, parents also may focus more on personal feelings, problems and issues. At these sessions, alleviation of guilt and anger related to their children's homosexual sexual-affectional orientation may very well be a primary focus of discussion. The therapist should be prepared to cope with the projection and other defensive reactions to such feelings.

It then may prove therapeutic to combine the adult and adolescent self-actualizing groups for special sessions toward the end of the second level of intervention. The purpose would be to facilitate an exchange of ideas, concerns and suggestions for future growth on the part of all involved. Parents and guardians also should be informed of and encouraged to form or become part of existing groups such as Parents and Friends of Lesbians and Gays. Interaction with such resources can offer valuable ongoing support to concerned adults.

Supporting or providing contexts for age-appropriate social and recreational activities for gay and lesbian youth and accepting non-gay peers is another area that can be worked on jointly by the teenagers, their parents/guardians/relatives and social workers.

Footnotes
1.   The seven subject areas suggested for the initial level of group discussions have been adapted from those used by the Men's Coming Out Group, Gay and Lesbian Community Center of Colorado; Denver, Colorado.

References

Becker, E. (1964). *Revolution in psychiatry.* New York. Free Press.

Bell, A. P., & Weinberg, M. S. (1978). *Homosexualities: A study of diversity among men and women.* New York: Simon and Schuster.

Clark, D. (1977). *Loving someone gay.* Mibrea, CA: Celestial Arts.

Jourard, S. M. (1971). *The transparent self.* New York: D. Van Nostrand.

Klein, A. F. (1972). *Effective groupwork: An introduction to principle and method.* New York: Association Press.

Toseland, R. W., & Rivas, R. F. (1984). *An introduction to group work practice.* New York: Macmillan.

Woodman, N. J., & Lenna, H. F. (1980). *Counseling with gay men and women.* San Francisco, CA: Jossey-Bass.

6

Social Work With Non-Traditional Families

Patricia L. Gunter, Ph.D.

Introduction

Social work as a profession is in a unique position to address the many and varied problems encountered by gay men and lesbian women within the conceptual framework of family. The dual perspective of social work, focusing on both the individual and the social environment, provides a foundation for effective interventions with gay and lesbian people. The choice of a particular method of intervention must be based on the client system's willingness to work toward problem resolution and the practitioner's understanding the nature of the problem within the context of the environment.

Problems encountered by gays and lesbians are often found within the framework of family dynamics. Social work methods and theories relative to family intervention and change may or may not be effective when applied to family interactions and relationships with gays and lesbians. Moreover, the social worker who recognizes societal stigmatization and its effect on family values and attitudes has a better understanding of the potential benefits family interventions will have for an individual gay or lesbian person, parent, or couple.

It is difficult to discuss work with non-traditional families without first examining the many and varied problems that a gay or lesbian person encounters with the family of origin. The relationship with the family of origin or lack of relationship may be in fact important to the work with the gay or lesbian person engaged in an alternative family setting. Given that many problems encountered by non-traditional families are a result of a combination of factors based within society and the complexity of systems interaction, the non-traditional family operates within a dual family concept.

Principles of Practice

Whether the focus of intervention is on the individual within the family system or on the family as a separate entity, neither the individual nor the family can be treated without consideration of the impact of the social environment. There are two factors of which the practitioner must be aware if effective services are to be provided gays and lesbians from a family focus.

The first factor important to practice with gays and lesbians is to recognize the diversity of family configurations. New forms of family, variant from the traditionally recognized concept of family, are becoming more recognized as viable lifestyle alternatives. The increasing numbers of childless couples, single parents, and gay and lesbian couples holds many implications for practice. Traditional theories of intervention may not be appropriate in light of these new family forms. The interactions of new family forms within the social environment has the potential of not only changing the nature of relationships between family members, but also changing how each individual perceives family functions and identities.

Gay and lesbian individuals face a particularly difficult situation given their relationships and interactions with two or more family systems. The family of origin, a highly complex system, may be the contributing factor in producing an individual's or a couple's problem or provide a framework for solution of the problem. Conversely, relationships, positive or negative, between the individual and the family cannot be assumed to be the locus for all problems. The locus of a problem can be within the individual or have its origin within larger social systems. Generally, however, many of the problems of gays and lesbians are reflective of family attitudes and values as well as a reaction to society's attitudes toward homosexuals and homosexuality.

The family of choice as identified by the members themselves has received little recognition in terms of family systems theory. Little attention has been paid to the qualitative differences between family of origin and family of choice. Important elements for consideration are: formation of membership; boundary system maintenance; establishment of goals; and types of structure. Gays and lesbians often have a primary identity with a family of choice for a variety of reasons: 1. rejection by or rejection of the family of origin; 2. the need to identify with or establish a primary family unit; and 3. expectations of society that of individuals have a family identity.

Practitioners must recognize the family of choice as a viable mechanism for change as well as a possible potential problem area for gays and lesbians. Where the client is gay or lesbian and the family unit is one of choice the worker must be cognizant that structural operations within the system may act to distort or inhibit the individual's ability to function and develop, just as the family of origin may. The family of choice may also serve as the informal resource and support system utilized by the individual and one upon which he/she becomes dependent.

The second factor to consider when examining issues pertinent to effective family practice with gays and lesbians is the concept of social environment. Historically, social work has recognized the importance of the family and the social environment as elements affecting individual behaviors. Individuals and families traditionally have been the focus of all levels of social work practice. However, during the 1920s a shift in social work's theoretical base produced interventions that by and large ignored the importance of the social environment until the reemergence of this emphasis in the 1950's.

When social work incorporated psychoanalytic theory into practice it rendered social factors peripheral. This focus stressed interventions whose primary concerns were with individual personality, ability to adjust, developmental patterns as reflection of inner-self, past events, experiences in the family of origin and, finally, pathology. The adoption of the psychoanalytic perspective over the psychosocial perspective as a foundation for diagnosis and treatment placed the gay or lesbian person in a vulnerable position. The emphasis of treatment based on a pathological focus versus the recognition of the interaction between social environment and the individual reinforced the concept of homosexuality as a disease and treatment as leading to "cure".

The acceptance of such treatment patterns was to ignore the reality of the situation. The exacerbation of problems for non-traditional families by the social environment was and often continues to be overlooked in practice. Yet in many cases, this is the first step toward effective practice rather than assuming dysfunction is centered within the individual. The ever expanding core of knowledge and practice methods that give a primary emphasis to the family as a system of patterned activities which shapes attitudes and behaviors of its members refers infrequently to the same sex oriented individual. There is little evidence that serious attempt has been made to develop interventions focusing on the gay or lesbian person from a family perspective given the reality of the social environment.

Implications for Practice

In developing effective practice that will meet the needs of gays and lesbians, the practitioner must continue to place an emphasis on both the individual and the family. The importance of the family as a contributing factor to dysfunctional behaviors or in situational responses cannot be overlooked. It must be realized that society is experiencing a change within families and with new forms of family patterns. The need to broaden and expand the concept of family is evident - particularly beyond the limited definition of family as "a group of individuals united by bonds of blood, marriage or adoption." Further, addressing both the legitimacy of the family of origin as well as the family of choice is necessary to the development of effective services for gay and lesbian populations. Both the family of origin and family of choice provide ample opportunities for intervention and positive change based on family theory.

The practitioner needs to evaluate the theoretical basis of family treatment as well as constructs of small group practice. This should help to determine if the person-in-the environment is in actuality the framework for services. In this process, the worker can identify those elements of interventions not consistent with the realities of gays and lesbians functioning within a dual family concept.

Any examination of practice theories and methods should indicate limitations of following preset and predetermined treatment modalities. By reversing the process of focusing on the individual as the center of attention to focusing on family and social climate, the importance of the dual perspective is quite evident. Attention is directed toward societal factors and conditions. The responding behaviors are based on a complex set of relationships and structures. Thus, the individual is no longer assumed to be the locus of the problem, exhibiting maladaptive behaviors.

This approach allows the worker to utilize interventions that incorporate a dual-family concept into practice so that the worker, client, significant others, and families can work together to engage in mutual helpful and supportive activities. This multi-dimensional focus recognizes that problems are similar whether occurring in the family of origin or family of choice. The problems may be similar in terms of family dynamics, but differ in how individuals view potential options, solutions and alternatives. Attention should be given to the specific patterns of relationships between the individual, family members, and various aspects of the social environment.

There are, however, potential areas for concern that most frequently are encountered by gay and lesbian populations. Depending on whether the issues are generated from the family of origin or the family of choice, the practitioner may need to address the problem areas from different perspectives. Identification of common concerns related to each type of family constellation and how this affects positive interventions for the gay or lesbian person can help to broaden the direct practice framework for practitioners.

Family of origin, as a concept, has been shown to have a major influence on the way its individual members function, develop and interact with the social environment. However, attempts at empirical documentation of the influence of the family on determining an individual's sex orientation have been of little or no value. Although a number of studies have been undertaken to correlate family dynamics with same sex orientation, it cannot be assumed that either individual or family pathology can be associated with a client's sexual preference.

It is much more appropriate to focus on the gay or lesbian person's current situation with family rather than on an assumed problem in the family's background. Problems typically encountered by the gay and lesbian person within the family of origin are related to the individual's same sex orientation. If there are perceived or actual patterns of disruption that either interfere with an individual's or family's ability to function, interventions need to address the immediacy of the situation.

Parental, spousal, partners', friends', and children's expectations are all potential sources of difficulties. Family members have, over a period of time, established rules of behavior based not only on family needs and expectations, but expectations held by groups, community, and society within which individuals are expected to function. For many gay and lesbian people, these expectations produce the most stress, emotional reaction, and generalized anxiety. The majority of family members have been conditioned to internalize society's homophobia, along with placing emphasis on the importance of continuing the family unit. When the family as a unit is threatened by an internal behavior not within the set of expectations, the unit reacts defensively.

The expectations and demands on gay or lesbian persons place them in situations that often dictate not only the way they feel about self, but also how they will choose to continue interaction with the family system. In some cases, the individual and family are successfully able to adjust to include an alternative lifestyle; for others the resolution may be to follow socially prescribed behaviors. Some choose to separate psychologically and physically from the source of stress and pressure.

Feelings of loss and failure may accompany the individual who recognizes the inability to share a family identity and to function within a family system. The attempt to maintain family identity while functioning as a different person with others produces not only anxiety, but fear. Fear is not only related to the possibility of discovery and possible confrontation, but the fear of punishment. A reaction to this for many gay or lesbian persons may be to actively deny a same sex orientation within the family unit. The type of emotional and physical strain that this produces will interfere with an individual's ability to engage in positive relationships, not only with family members but with potential same sex partners.

Many gays and lesbians feel that the most stress-producing and threatening component related to their sexual orientation is the process of coming out. This can be voluntary or as a response to a particular situation. In either case, the process is complicated and can give rise to many types of reactions. The nature of the complex relationships between family members and whether the family is either an open or closed system will affect the manner in which these reactions are formulated.

To compound the issue, individual family members may react differently, while the family as a unit reacts as a single respondent. No matter what the reaction is to the initial information, the responses are likely to reflect the feeling that the family is in jeopardy. It is difficult to project possible outcomes even when family dynamics are well understood.

After the initial confrontation, the family begins to question its structure, assignment of roles, patterns of communication, acceptance of relationships outside its boundaries, and the way feelings are handled.

All of these impact on the family and the individual and have importance as to how well the family can or is willing to work toward resolution. This in turn may provide the family with a perception that there are only three options acceptable in maintaining the integrity of the unit. The most positive and hoped for would be the acceptance and integration of the gay or lesbian person back into the family, although a role change will usually occur. Option two provides a neutral acceptance of the situation with the establishment of certain conditions that the family and the individual are expected to honor. The final option is for the family to fully disengage from the individual and to restructure its boundaries to accommodate for the loss.

The structure of relations and how the family accommodates diversity within individual members is probably the key to the unit's ability to accept the individual and maintain a productive functional family system. The effect upon the gay or lesbian person is of major consequence, even when the transition to acceptance is smooth. If an event or situation is seen and/or experienced as negative, the consequences for both the individual and family can be devastating.

Families of choice are also sources of problems, issues and concerns that gays and lesbians must confront. Associated with such issues and problems is the realization that the legal system has failed to provide recognition for this family type. This has created an additional set of problems especially since statutes and court decisions have usually provided legal justification for discrimination and non-recognition. Society has been given a legal affirmative vote to continue oppression. Neither the individual's identity nor the family of choice is recognized within the scope of the legal system and failure to do so produces additional intra-family and interpersonal strains.

Gay and lesbian parents with children are mostly ignored as recognizable family units. Yet gay or lesbian parenthood is certainly not unusual, and it cannot be ignored when addressing family problems and relationships. A major issue is the well-being of children as affected by parental and family relationships. Elements of this issue center around questions relative to the role of gay and lesbian parenting. Gay and lesbian parents must confront a set of attitudes and circumstances rarely encountered by any other group or parents.

Myths and stereotypes abound about the negative consequences of gays and lesbians raising children despite the fact that research does not provide any evidence that the gay or lesbian person is any less effective as a parent than the heterosexual. However, the parent has often incorporated these misconceptions into a personal perception of how fit he or she is as a parent and additional strain and anxiety arise when attempting to cope with the normal tasks associated with parenthood. Although there appears to be a higher percentage of families with lesbian mothers than of gay fathers (probably more a reflection of societal roles and expectations than differences between gays and lesbians), the problems and issues for both are much the same surrounding parenting.

Foremost in the mind of any gay or lesbian parent is the well-being of the child(ren). Associated with this is the issue of child custody. Child custody may involve the other natural parent, other family members, social service agencies, and the legal system. Homophobic attitudes provide the basis by which determination is made as to what is or is not beneficial for a child. Even if custody is not an issue, the parent reacts as if his/her lifestyle and relationships are being monitored. The basic motivation is to protect the child(ren). However, this occurs within a framework of anxiety and fear of discovery. A parent may decide to willingly grant custody to the other parent or another family member, and consequently will experience negative feelings about him/herself. Relative to these are negative reactions from others who are aware of his/her decision to give up the child. No matter what the specific circumstances, the parent must come to grips with the reality of the possibility of loss or deal with actual loss.

Parenting roles and skills should be handled within the concept of family. A decision has to be made as to whether or not to come out to the child(ren) or to wait until the question becomes an issue from the child(ren)'s perspective. In either case, all involved will be affected by the knowledge and how well the process is handled, along with expected and unexpected reactions. The parent may determine that it is important to help the child(ren) to develop skills necessary to cope with differences between types of families. Because of societal homophobia, children may need preparation in how to confront and handle negative reactions from peers, teachers, and parents of friends. They also will need guidance in developing relationships within a variety of family systems.

A gay father or lesbian mother must make a decision as to choice of lifestyle— openly with same sex partners, or more traditionally. The final consideration is how the parent perceives his/her sexual preference which may or may not affect the well-being of the child. Gay and lesbian parents who become engaged in the process of being identified as a couple with a same sex person may encounter difficulties they did not expect in terms of integrating family systems. Many of these problems are similar to those of non-gay couples, but without the traditional societal or family approvals and supports. The role of an adult lover introduced into what has been a family identified as parents and children changes or alters the relationship between parent and child. The participation of a new partner in parenting and the reactions of each member of the couple dyad and the child(ren) to the new situation can be expected to produce, if not at times a crisis, at the minimum an upheaval within the system. This places a strain on relationships between partners, along with strain from external pressures of non-approving relatives and individuals who view the situation as being "unnatural" and "unhealthy".

Couples of the same sex actively involved in parenting roles are confronted with a formidable task of establishing and maintaining a family of choice. The primary focus of the relationship is often centered upon structuring the family unit for benefit of the child(ren), rather than integration of the various members into the system. Other relationships of the family may be strained between families of origin and families of choice. Pressures may become so anxiety and stress producing that individual members may not be capable of integrating into the family unit, thus producing a non-beneficial situation for all involved.

Same sex couples are often ignored by professional social service practitioners. Work with heterosexual couples has been recognized as a valid focus for social work intervention, yet application of interventions with same sex couples has received little attention. The lack of legal, social and familial recognition of the same sex couple as an independent family unit leaves these individuals with little or very few social and professional supports.

The lack of role models has affected the way in which same sex individuals have attempted to establish a bonded relationship. The model available has been the socially approved traditional heterosexual marriage. Either through modeling on the traditional concept of couple formation or having to alter the traditional pattern of coupling, a same sex couple develops a set of behaviors and roles unique to their particular circumstances. Because of the lack of skills to develop such relationships, individuals may have difficulty in defining roles, both as a couple and individually.

Relationships are influenced by two quite different sets of external expectations affecting the members as part of a dyad and relating to each one as an individual. These effects can impact on how the individuals function as a couple and also can be perceived as a threat to the relationship. Society, by not recognizing same sex individuals as a couple, continues to view each person as being single. Social expectations demand certain behaviors of a single person and how he/she is to react in various situations. This involves factors around the work environment, relations with non-homosexuals, and how leisure or social time is spent. The extent to which one or the other of the partners is comfortable in being identified as a member of the relationship is important. This is very evident when one of the individuals feels that he/she may need to remain closeted because of employment or difficulties with the family of origin. The other partner may be completely open and have difficulty in maintaining a low profile in the relationship.

The second set of expectations is frequently generated from gay or lesbian communities. Roles and behaviors for couples may be established by community members to provide a frame of reference for the partners' interactions between each other and other gay or lesbian individuals. In most cases, the gay or lesbian couple may have limited interaction with other couples of the same sex and handling of the relationship may be based on external guidance rather than directing energies toward problem resolution between themselves. The gay or lesbian couple often lacks family or primary friendship supports enjoyed by traditional heterosexual couples.

Other problems encountered by such couples include: financial concerns; differences in attitudes and values; expression of sexuality; and religious/spiritual consideration. Issues that may further strain a relationship, such as dealing with families of origin, heterosexual and homosexual friends, and past lovers generally complicate the situation where two people are attempting to develop and maintain a healthy, satisfying relationship as a couple.

The multiplicity of barriers is many. The couple in an attempt to protect a newly-formed relationship may find themselves having difficulty maintaining personal identity. The fusion of identities is a common problem within same sex relationships. The lack of mechanisms for support affects the process of a couple reaching stability. The term "instability" when applied to such relationships is not based on a realistic perspective of the nature of the social climate. Same sex couples must carve out roles and identities that have never been clearly defined or fully accepted. In an attempt to create a family for themselves, they encounter formidable barriers, including those presented by non-responsive practitioners, families, and friends.

There are other groups within gay and lesbian populations that need special mention. The gay and lesbian population is as diverse as the general population and is a representative cross-section of society at any given time. Practitioners have been educated to respond to special categories of individuals that are considered to be vulnerable and at risk. Rural, elderly, and minority gays and lesbians constitute such categories.

Rural gays and lesbians deal with many barriers that are inherent within the rural environment. They have limited exposure to resources and support systems both formal and informal. Access to accurate information and services is frequently not available and they are more likely to encounter an actively hostile environment. There is a lack of opportunity for socialization or the formation of gay and lesbian friendship systems. Service providers and agency administrators either ignore the possibility of same sex orientation or openly practice discrimination. The closed rural systems and the intimacy and overlap between these systems provide gays and lesbians with few options or alternatives.

Aging individuals face multiple problems relative to their lack of status in society. Not only do gay and lesbian elderly have to deal with conditions associated with the normal or pathological aging processes, but are affected by both homosexual and heterosexual attitudes. This is reflected in society's orientation to youthfulness as it relates to productivity. The older gay or lesbian person, because of age and circumstances, may be virtually isolated as support systems diminish and formal services do not recognize sexual preference.

Older persons who have lost a companion or mate after a long period of time may not have a support system in either the family of origin or the family of choice. Conversely, the companion's family may after many years resurface to claim traditional family roles in dealing with a deceased member. Even when there has been acceptance of the relative's same sex relationship, the family of origin often has a tendency to be insensitive to the remaining partner— the individual who is experiencing one of the most emotional, painful, and personal events he/she may have encountered. If arrangements have not been made in advance, the remaining

member of the couple may find him/herself without resources to meet basic survival needs. Not only is this individual left to cope with the grieving process but is expected
to fend for him/ herself. The gay or lesbian community may
not be available or aware of the problems because many aged
couples have remained invisible as a reaction to a
homophobic culture.

A final grouping of gays and lesbians with special needs
is those that are identified as minorities of color. Racial
minorities within society are visible in their difference and
this is also true within gay and lesbian populations. The
family of origin, because of cultural expectations and a need
to protect its boundaries and identity from the majority
culture, often places greater demands on its members. Gay
and lesbian minority individuals therefore suffer biases and
pressures from multiple groups. It may be extremely difficult
for these individuals to function effectively in gay or lesbian
relationships without some form of alienation from the family
of origin. It is much more difficult for minority individuals to
integrate alternative lifestyles within the boundaries established by the majority culture, either heterosexual or homosexual.

Practitioners need to be aware of the specific difficulties
encountered by minority gays and lesbians and how these
impact on their ability to reach their potential as adults and
the effect on developing positive identity as a family. Gays
and lesbians of color encounter much more rejection and
frequently are forced as a couple to become more protective
of their relationships. A worker must be aware that the
perception of threats is real and not a reaction to guilt or
internalized fears.

Practitioners' Roles

There are many opportunities to serve gay and lesbian
individuals through family systems theory and interventions. Gays and lesbians did not arrive from a vacuum, nor
do they function within a vacuum. A primary system affecting
the well-being of any individual is the family. In the case of

gay and lesbian persons, family systems may be perceived as the locus of a presenting problem. An individual may seek help as a result of an inability to deal with dual identities, feelings of guilt, failure, and anxiety and/or depression in relation to family of origin or of choice. Frequently, an individual seeks guidance and support after the family has reacted to knowledge of the person's sexual orientation or behavior contrary to expectations.

It is imperative that worker and client collaborate in making a series of decisions. A determination must be made as to whether the client or the family will become the primary focus of intervention. Is the purpose of intervention to be to develop coping skills and changes within the individual or to engage the family in the process?

Relationships between individuals and family of origin should be explored in depth with the individual coming to an understanding of his/her perception of the family's expectations and feelings. Dependent upon past and current family dynamics all family members may not perceive a need to reach a resolution of issues. The function of the practitioner is to help the client by providing guidance and direction as well as support.

Depending on the expected outcomes, the worker may need to work with the person in accepting alienation from the family. Another alternative is to help the individual through the process of terminating family relationships. This is important so that the person does not view him/herself as a failure, but understands that a complex combination of multiple factors within the family and within society have created a situational response.

The worker can be a guide through this process so that problems and issues can be reassessed and/or readdressed, providing an opportunity for the individual to restructure and establish an identity outside the family unit. Encouragement should be provided to examine the strengths and weaknesses of the family system to prevent internalization of rejection. Nor should the grieving process be discouraged. Allowing the individual to grieve provides a framework for understanding and coping with feelings related to losses and insecurities.

There are basically three reasons why the family as a unit will seek help or agree to become engaged in the treatment process: one, to find out where mistakes have been made; whose fault is it? The second is to search for a cure for the family member; and third, to seek help in resolving a situation for which they do not have the skills or knowledge necessary to cope successfully. Families and family members have the same difficulties as the rest of society in dealing with a relative's same sex orientation. Their knowledge is based on the same homophobic myths, stereotypes and fear of same sex lifestyles as incorporated in the general populations' attitudes.

Families experience feelings of failure, guilt and uncertainty. They are not prepared to cope with an issue that encompasses such biological, religious, and social implications. The inability to cope may bring about unusually strong emotional reactions that place the family unit in crisis. When family identity has been threatened the system responds to such threats. Exploring this often leads to expressions of grief and failure of individual members to live up to prescribed expectations.

The worker engaged with family systems must be prepared to provide counseling, support, guidance, and direction on specific issues. Helping the family to deal with such emotions as fear, anxiety, and anger is as important as helping them to express themselves to one another. From this point of validating feelings, concerns and expectations, the worker should be prepared to provide correct and adequate information to help alleviate unrealistic perceptions or correct actual mis-perceptions.

Given societal views of same sex orientation, attention should be directed toward passive or homophobic behaviors expressed by family members. The worker, the gay or lesbian person, and family members should work openly and honestly in addressing this issue. It is the one area that, because of underlying dynamics, may be the most difficult to resolve. The family will also need education and direction in how to handle attitudes and inquiries from outside the family unit. It is appropriate for referrals to be made to resources that can

provide informal community based supports. These resources can be valuable in helping the unit to accept the
realities of the situation.

Practice with the client and the client's identified family
system is focused on bringing about resolution to a particular
set of problems. Work with individuals and the family system
can help define issues, facilitate problem solving, open
communication between members, and encourage development of a process for utilizing internal and external resources
and support. The resolution phase begins when participants
can agree upon terms for acceptable behaviors and realistic
expectations given the importance of maintaining family
integrity.

It is important that the practitioner be aware that similar
problems and difficulties arise in a family of choice. The
similarity of problems indicates use of similar methods for
intervention. The major differences are that specific
boundaries and guidelines for expectations and behaviors
have not been clearly defined. The worker should keep in
mind that without these boundaries or expectations the
family unit may need first to clarify the role of a family unit.
Confusion and disorganization have the potential of diverting
energies and problem-solving capabilities away from the
growth potential for productive, positive relationships.

Problems arising in the family of choice may need much
more directive action on the part of the practitioner. In
situations where children are involved, the worker must work
with both adults and the children. This can be approached by
working with each individual and then, through the use of
family and small group processes, involve the family unit.
Important to this aspect of intervention is that the worker
recognize the external pressures experienced by each
member and what skills individual members and the family
unit will need to cope with the social environment. The goal
is to improve the functioning of the family as a unit and to
help them develop behaviors that are responsive to individual
needs as well as family needs.

A final family configuration that is important is the gay or
lesbian couple. Again, many of the problems stem from

external sources and perceived negative behaviors are reactions to stress produced by uncertainty. Problems within couple relationships are typical of the difficulties of individuals attempting to bond without recognized boundaries or roles and a specific identification as a couple.

In working with gay or lesbian couples, it is necessary to help them to identify a framework within which to operate. This includes the development of skills necessary for each individual to retain his/her identity, as well as function in response to tasks and activities as a partner. The focus on communication and openness should produce an atmosphere where clients and worker can move toward concrete resolutions of conflicts in a positive, productive manner. The worker, in enabling individuals toward this goal, will want to provide each partner with opportunities for self-awareness and self-actualization, thus providing the individuals an opportunity to better express and understand their needs personally and in terms of a couple relationship. Exploring why a couple is together and how they perceive the relationship and long-term goals is an effective way to introduce the use of problem solving as a skill.

The worker should always be cognizant of external threats from families of origin, friends, or the gay and lesbian community. Many couples have not had opportunities, other than heterosexual, to interact with others in couple relations, leaving their expectations of a new form of family ill-conceived and ill-defined. They may be devoid of support systems to encourage working toward resolution.

In some cases, the worker will need to become actively involved in providing guidance and direction to aid in helping the individuals to terminate a relationship. The termination process is important if individuals are to understand and accept the fact that neither individual may be to blame, but that priorities, long-term goals, and needs are not compatible. Where the relationship can be identified as stagnant or destructive, the focus in termination should be placed on awareness and understanding. Neither individual should be left with a sense of failure and become fearful about establishing positive adult relationships in the future.

Other populations of gays and lesbians need special attention by the worker. Individuals, because of being geographically isolated, elderly or belonging to a minority of color, will need the worker's energies to focus on developing special strategies and resources on their behalf. The unique position of these individuals places both the worker and client system in a situation where traditional interventions may not be effective. These individuals are confronted not only by homophobia but also racism and ageism and need more than just adaptation of traditional strategies. There is a need for a worker's active role in systems change and development of resources both formal and informal.

Summary

To provide effective and positive services to gays and lesbians, the social worker must have a knowledge base and skills that not only engage a client, but must understand the gay or lesbian person's position within the social environment. Social workers have been educated to give practice attention to the multiple factors that influence an individual's well-being and achievement of life's needs and goals.

Practitioners cannot be fully educated or effective with gay and lesbian populations unless they are willing to apply, test and evaluate the many theories and strategies utilized in practice with families. This means that not only does the worker have a responsibility to serve the family of origin, but have full realization that practice with the family of choice is just as important in terms of positive change for the gay or lesbian family.

Conceptually, practitioners often limit their scope of practice to traditionally accepted professional and societal guidelines. However, to fully meet the needs of individuals and families, effective practice is not only starting with the individual but, in the case of gay and lesbian populations, recognizing that alternative family groupings are primary factors. Only from this position can workers hope to fully educate themselves as to the many possibilities for positive interventions.

It is necessary from an ecological perspective to return to the basics of the casework approach rather than the psychotherapeutic approach. Recognizing the dual family concept as a reality and a potential for broadening the base of intervention, the worker is forced to review those societal elements that oppress and prohibit full realization of an individual's and family's potential for growth and self-fulfillment. Work with gays and lesbians cannot be successful if taken out of the context of the social environment. Nor can it be effective if diverse family groupings and lifestyles are not addressed as being valid systems that may need and seek professional help.

The challenge in education for effective practice is not only to become knowledgeable about issues and potential problem areas, but to recognize the need to establish a practice framework based on traditional social work roles. Additionally, it goes further by demanding that the practitioner assume responsibility for services based on the realities of the situation and actively become engaged in changing systems that fail to recognize variance and diversity among gay and lesbian populations. Until professionals act upon this basic premise, the commitment to underserved, powerless and vulnerable populations will not be met, particularly for those families where social and the legal systems are actively rejecting and/or denying rights to an identity.

Suggestions for Further Reading

About our children. (1982). Los Angeles, California: Federation of Parents and Friends of Gays, Inc.

Alyson, S. (1981). *Young, gay and proud*. Boston: Alyson.

Berzon, B. (1978). Sharing your lesbian identity with your children. In Vida, G. (Ed.) *Our right to love: A lesbian resource book*. Engelwood Cliffs, New Jersey: Prentice-Hall.

Borhek, M. V. (1983). *Coming out to parents: A two way survival guide for lesbians and gay men and their parents*. New York: Pilgrim Press.

Brooks, V. (1981). *Minority stress and lesbian women.* Lexington, Mass.: D. C. Heath & Co.

Brown, D. G. (1963). Homosexuality and family dynamics. *Bulletin of the Menninger Clinic, 27*(5), 227-232.

Cass, V. C. (1979). Homosexual identity formation: A theoretical model. *Journal of Homosexuality, 4,* 219-235.

Decker, B. (1984). Counseling gay and lesbian couples. *Journal of Social work and Human Sexuality, 2.*

Di Bella, G. (1979). Family psychotherapy with the homosexual family: A community psychiatry approach to homosexuality. *Community Mental Health Journal, 4.*

Dulaney, D. and Kelly, J. (1982). Improving services to gay and lesbian clients. *Social Work, 27*(2), 178-183.

Gochros, H. (1978). Counseling gay husbands. *Journal of Sex Education and Therapy, 4,* 6-10.

Gonsiorek, J. (1982). The use of diagnostic concepts in working with gay and lesbian populations. In Gonsiorek, J. (Ed.) *Homosexuality and psychotherapy: A Practitioner's handbook of affirmative models.* New York: Haworth Press.

Hall, M. (1978). Lesbian families: Cultural and clinical issues. *Social Work, 23,* 380-385.

Hammersmith, S. K., and Weinberg, M. S. (1978). Homosexual identity: Commitment, adjustment, and significant others. *Sociometry, 36,* 56-70.

Harry, J. (1983). Gay male and lesbian family relationships. In Macklin, E. (Ed.) *Contemporary families and alternative lifestyles: Handbook on research and theory.* Beverly Hills, CA: Sage.

Harry, J. and Lovely, R. (1979). Gay marriages and communities of sexual orientation. *Alternative Lifestyles, 2*(2), 177-200.

Jones, C. R. (1978). *Understanding gay relatives and friends.* Sommers, CO: Seabury Press.

Krestan, J. and Bepko, C. (1980). The problem of fusion in the lesbian relationship. *Family Process, 19,* 277-289.

Lewis, K. G. (1980). Children of lesbians: Their point of view. *Social Work, 25,* 198-203.

Malyon, A. K. (1981). The homosexual adolescent: Development issues and social bias. *Child Welfare, 60,* 321-330.

Martensen-Larsen, O. (1975). The family constellation and homosexualism. *Acta Genetica et Statistica Medica, 7,* 445-446.

McWhirter, D. and Mattison, A. (1983). *Stages: A developmental study of homosexual male couples.* New York: St. Marten's.

McWhirter, D. P. and Mattison, A. M. (1978). The treatment of sexual dysfunction in gay male couples. *Journal of Sex and Marital Therapy, 4,* 213-218.

Miller, B. (1978). Adult sexual resocialization: Adjustments toward a stigmatized identity. *Alternative Lifestyles, 1*(2), 207-223.

Morin, S. F. and Charles, K. A. (1983). Heterosexual bias in psychotherapy. In Murray, L. and Abramson, P. R. (Eds.) *Bias in psychotherapy.* New York: Praeger.

Morin, S. G. and Schultz, S. J. (1978). The gay movement and the rights of children. *Journal of Social Issues, 34,* 137-148.

Moses, A. E. and Hawkins, R. O. (1982). *Counseling lesbian women and gay men: A life-issues approach.* St. Louis, MO: C. V. Mosby Co.

Needham, R. (1977). Casework intervention with a homosexual adolescent. *Social Casework, 58*(7), 387-394.

O'Leary, B. (1978). A mother's support. In Vida, G. (Ed.) *Our right to love: A lesbian resource book.* Englewood Cliffs, New Jersey: Prentice-Hall.

Pagelow, M. D. (1980). Heterosexual and lesbian single mothers: A comparison of problems, coping, and solutions. *Journal of Homosexuality, 5*(3), 180-204.

Peplau, L., Cochran, S., Rook, K. and Padesky, C. (1978). Loving women: Attachment and autonomy in lesbian relationships. *Journal of Social Issues, 34*(3), 7-27.

Potter, S., and Darty, T. (1981). Social work and the invisible minority: An exploration of lesbianism. *Social Work, 26*(3), 187-192.

Riddle, D. I. (1978). Relating to children: Gays as role models. *Journal of Social Issues, 34*(3), 38-58.

Steinhorn, A. I. (1985). Lesbian mothers. In Hildalgo, H., Peterson, T. and Woodman, N. (Eds.) *Lesbian and gay issues: A resource manual for social workers*. Silver Spring, MD: National Association of Social Workers.

Toder, N. (1978). Couples: The hidden segment of the gay world. *Journal of Homosexuality, 3*, 331-343.

Weinberg, M. S. and Williams, C. J. (1974). *Male homosexuals: Their problems and adaptations*. New York: Oxford University Press.

Woodman, N. J. and Lenna, H. R. (1980). Counseling with gay men and women: A guide for facilitating positive lifestyles. San Francisco: Jossey-Bass.

Woodman, N. (1985). Parents of lesbians and gays. Concerns and interventions. In Hildalgo, H., Peterson, T. and Woodman, N. (Eds.) *Lesbian and gay issues: A resource manual for social workers*. Silver Spring, MD: National Association of Social Workers.

7

Relationship Termination for Lesbians and Gays

Pat Terry, ACSW

The strains which promote tenuousness of lesbian and gay relationships are reality based. The reasons are numerous and many are related to societal attitudes, lack of traditional support systems and in general, minimal relationship "binders." The stress of oppression and the struggle to integrate other areas of one's life into the relationship lifestyle can be overwhelming.

The termination of a relationship either by separation or death can seem to be a crisis that will never end. The pain of loss is not unique to the lesbian and gay lifestyle. However, the lack of available resources and support is the predominant aspect that must be seen as requiring specific attention. Recently, there has been an increase of literature and networks for divorced individuals. Lesbian and gay individuals also need the validation and support of others as they face the crisis of loss. This chapter will specify the aspects of grieving most known to clinicians but will include the particular dimensions applicable to counseling with lesbians and gays.

The Grief Process

Disbelief

The initial awareness that the relationship is ending is accompanied by shock. The loss of control over one's life and the situation is confusing, bewildering and frightening. Preoccupation with the situation and the internal emptiness seems to block out all other aspects of life. One tends to become forgetful and is often unable to carry on with routine activities. There is a general sense of "this can not be happening to us or to me." It is a stage of the process where activity and time seem to stop. Behavioral responses may differ depending on the individual and the situation. Withdrawal, for some may be the coping mechanism. This behavior is frequently displayed by individuals who are not comfortable with sharing their pain or are embarrassed by their own feelings of vulnerability. Others may immediately seek support. This is a time of extreme vulnerability no matter what behavioral indicators are in place.

Lesbians and gays may face more serious problems during this stage. Many may not have support systems to which they can turn. This is particularly true of individuals who have chosen to isolate from others or have not identified as lesbian or gay outside of their couple relationship. Traditional institutional supports such as the family or church often are not available to this population. Answers to questions as to what is wrong or what happened to your "roommate" require preparation if one is to carry on with the facade that all is well.

Perhaps fabrication is a way to cope and deal with the loss because simultaneously dealing with the loss and coming out is too stressful. Individuals who have identified to others face a similar problem in that many lesbian and gay social relationships and socialization patterns were developed as a couple. This is a time for the social worker to take advantage of support systems that do exist and allow concerned others to provide support. There, in fact, may be others who have experienced similar situations and can provide an empathetic ear. There is a tendency, however, to assure the individual that all will be well. What really is needed is to be able to help the individual deal with the pain, anger and feelings of isolation accompanying the loss.

The realization that this stage of disbelief, shock, pain, confusion, preoccupation, and bewilderment is temporary is crucial. Dysfunctional behavior needs to be viewed as "normal" and not perceived as neurotic, psychotic, or maladaptive. Caution does need to be used regarding the making of major life choice decisions. Impulsive decisions may only prolong this stage or complicate the situation. An example of impulsive decision making would be the destruction of all former ties that bound the couple.

Denial and Bargaining

Denial, perhaps, is only an extension of disbelief. One begins to have thoughts that the relationship really is not over and that it is a temporary disruption that will be resolved in the near future. This may be accurate in some situations, but more likely than not this is an indicator that one or both partners are having difficulty letting go of the support they have found in each other and the relationship. Statements such as "someday" or "let's just take a time out" can just be an indicator of the denial process. This stage is characterized by feelings of confusion, fear, and diffused anxiety. There is acute pain related to the void in one's life and in one's self. The intense concern of loss of control and isolation can provoke fears of going crazy. The lesbian and or gay individual may be suffering from the loss of the only support system for her or his lifestyle.

Disengagement at the emotional level is often another form of denial. This type of disengagement is essentially a denial that the person ever meant anything. During this particular stage many lesbians and gays enter into a world wind tour of the local bar scene with the intent of proving to oneself that the terminated relationship was insignificant or that the person can be replaced. The individual has already experienced perceived rejection and further rejections will only exacerbate those feelings. Bars are full of sad people who have rejected or been rejected. Should one encounter someone and begin another relationship during this stage the carry over effects of not completing the grief process will only surface in the newly formed alliance. Denial, can be helpful. It does allow the individual to do some emotional regrouping and relief from the intensity of shock and disbelief.

Bargaining with each other may emerge from the denial. Promising changes or relationship restructuring may be efforts to maintain a status quo. An inability to perceive any limitations or weakness in the relationship may dominate the thinking and enter into the entire fantasy. The relationship is viewed as having been perfect, when in fact, problems did exist. The clinician's sensitivity to the significance of loss is essential. Seeking therapeutic help to "make it all better again" is not uncommon. The clinician must be alert to this and not fall into the trap but also can not be brutally confronting in breaking down this defense when the client is still vulnerable. Validity must be given to the person and the relationship. The lack of such sensitivity and validation not only discounts the client but can exacerbate feelings of worthlessness as well as reinforcing negative social and institutional mythologies relative to homosexuality. Along with validation, the therapist may have to assume a temporary role of an intensive support system seeing the client as often as the situation mandates. In addition, the client may need to be encouraged to enter pro-active social or therapeutic group situations with other lesbians and gays to avoid severe isolation. Assurances by the therapists that the feelings of loss of control or "being crazy" are time bound become important components of the supportive process. Validation of the loss, support, and social networking are key factors for the clinician to provide during the denial stage. This will decrease the devastating effects of severe isolation and the fear of loss of control.

Anger/Blame/Guilt

Anger may seem like an illogical, purposeless emotion but it is there in a loss. Appropriate releases for anger need to be established. One has a right to be angry at loss and the lost person. There is anger at one's self for allowing vulnerability.

One may blame one's self, the partner or others for intruding and invading the relationship's space. The guilt of terminating a relationship can be as difficult as the feelings of not being cared for. Doubt about relationship capacity and self worth promote the anger and guilt. There may be a tendency to overestimate the power of a third party, should that be a factor. In a sense, it is a "you love what you suffer for" belief. This is a feeling that a new relationship must be made to work no matter what, since one may have disrupted their entire lifestyle for another person. The danger of course is that one can spend many years living this out and being unhappy.

It is during this stage that the former partner is deglorified as well as the relationship. Unlike denial, one begins to identify relationship patterns that were unpleasant but tolerated. Perhaps, one even begins to feel and/or realize that the relationship was not as productive as it appeared. This can be a healthy sign of objectivity as well as a signal that the acuteness of the crisis may be ending. As objectivity develops, there is a return to a new post-crisis functional level. Regular activities are resumed and old priorities begin to return. Periodic "panics" may still be there as well as moments when the person may wonder if they will ever "care" about someone. There are also times when one can begin to evaluate what they really want in a partner. This stage should minimize the contact one has with a former partner. Although the anger is there and that anger is natural, one must take care that the anger does not become a consuming emotion with eruptive possibilities towards the former partner or others.

There are generalized feelings of anger and rage during this stage which can either be person-specific or diffused. Focused anger may be directed at the partner and other involved parties. Contact with the former partner can be with the intent of saying and doing hurtful things. Individuals who previously supported the relationship are painful reminders of the loss. Diffused anger at the intrusions of "unwanted" others is not unusual in that the individual feels vulnerable and can resent the strength evidenced by others. In addition, the individual may experience angry feelings towards others who seemingly are content with their relationships. Lesbian or gay lifestyles may also be a target for anger. The individual's behavior may take the pattern of blaming self, others and one's orientation or lifestyle. Retaliatory acting out, frantic bar hopping, rebound relationships and spiteful behaviors can be dominant during this stage.

Unique within this lifestyle is the potential, once again, for the reinforcement of negative stereotypes. Constant sexual affairs and increased substance abuse only serve to convince the individual that the stability and permanence of lesbian and or gay relationships is non-existent. The lack of legal resources and support during the beginning or termination of a relationship forces individuals to deal directly with one another, increasing emotional tensions and anger at powerlessness. The clinician must be sensitive to the displaced anger. It is too easy for an individual to attribute all difficulties to the lifestyle. Directing the anger at the former partner is difficult since it acknowledges rejection. Also, there is fear that, if anger is expressed, it will result in loss of the partner forever. The issues of rejection and abandonment need to be explored by the clinician with the client. Alternatives to anger and new patterns of stress reduction can be encouraged. It is imperative that the clinician not reinforce negative stereotypes about lesbian/gay lifestyles but instead assist the client in revitalizing empowerment as a lesbian or gay person. Support for the reality reasons for the anger toward loss must be provided and the clinician can not be afraid of allowing angry feelings to be expressed.

Self blame, self abnegation and shame may be paramount in this stage. Religious and social sanctions against homosexuality may be internalized and a general malaise that God is punishing one for engaging in a same gender relationship can exist. The client may exaggerate and perseverate on perceived faults within self leading to a belief she or he is not good enough for anyone. Internalized negative sanctions and limited reality testing can progress to a reaction formation regarding one's lesbian or gay identity. There may be frantic heterosexual dating or compensatory behavior with self attempts to be perfect.

This may be a crucial point for the client and clinician. It is important that the client not internalize negative social and institutional stereotypes. Sensitivity and awareness of the client's feelings and knowledge regarding how oppression increases self doubt is important. The clinician needs to be a facilitator for the client in changing those characteristics the client wants to change for him/herself rather than change for change's sake or for the sake of others. It is at this time the client may need to work or rework identity issues. Judgmental attitudes or statements by the clinician may result in the client fixating at this stage with guilt dominating almost all of the emotional aspects of life. Reality testing with the clinician about the client's own strengths, abilities and goals can be a focus of treatment. Areas in relationships and relationship style can be worked on by the clinician and client.

Sadness

In general a chronic pain accompanied by sadness can be prevalent during this next stage. As one starts to remove the emotional layers of anger, blame and guilt the feelings of hurt, sadness, and loneliness begin to surface. The mind and body, working together, have prepared the individual for this stage of intense emotions. Those feelings need to be attended to and if done, one soon realizes that life goes on and survival is possible.

The unique sharing that develops between same gender partners is a major factor that is dealt with during this stage. There may be a sense of a part of self being gone. Integrity must be regained and those sad times are an indication of awareness that the individual is taking that part of their personal power back. This may be a time for the two individuals to put closure on what was and look toward what is left or should be. It is time to deal with the fact that what was good about the relationship as it was now is no longer there. During this stage, the client may continue to withdraw from all close relationships as well as from places and objects associated with the terminated relationship. There may be a disruption in eating and sleeping patterns as one walks through this painful stage. Ambivalence may increase with seemingly a decrease in decision making ability.

There are unique dimensions of self-actualizing for the lesbian and gay individual. One may continue to work on or reaffirm their identity. For some, the identity issue still may not have been resolved. Withdrawal from usual contacts can result in further isolation. The generally closed system of the community makes isolation more probable due to some fears of encountering one's previous partner. When one seeks out different social contacts through the "bar scene" the depression can increase as one is exposed to others encountering similar situations. The behavior at this time can increase the potential for the individual to have to come out in terms of explaining the interruption in usual behaviors. The most dangerous factor during some of this stage is self destructive behavior as the individual struggles with identity issues, isolation, and chronic pain.

The therapeutic milieu may be the one place for grieving for the client since friends often exhaust their ability to listen before the individual has completed their debriefing and verbalizing. Subsequently, the clinician's validation of the client's pain, rejections, and depression needs to continue. The therapeutic support is necessary to help the client move through the grief process. The clinician's awareness that this is a crucial time in terms of self destructive behaviors and isolation is important. Disruption of isolating behavior and development of feelings of empowerment for the client are treatment goals during this time.

Recovery and Acceptance

It seems incomprehensible to the client that she or he will move from the devastating stage of chronic pain and sadness to recovery and acceptance. Obviously this is a gradual process and expectations that it "just happens one morning" are unrealistic. Time is essential to this process. This stage will differ with each person and one must be aware that recovery and acceptance are gradual. One can anticipate clues that recovery is progressing. The client will begin to demonstrate increased feelings of self worth. Objectivity about the former partner as well as other life areas begins to return. There is a decrease in feeling intensity towards the former partner as investment in other life areas begins to return. Preoccupation with resentment and bitterness decreases. The client is less concerned with the former partner's new life and begins taking care of his/her own needs. The feeling of foolish vulnerability diminishes. There is a realization that this has been a painful experience but perhaps a necessary one. Realistic anxiety about finding someone new or living by one's self will surface. The future becomes important and the client looks forward to encounters with new people or a new person.

Behaviorally, the client will return to restructuring reality. Old friendships and enjoyments may be renewed. There is a thinking and verbalization in terms of self rather than "us". Social activity will become more selective as compared to frantic sexual or social involvements. The client may demonstrate increased energy and commitments to other areas such as work, school, or gay activities. The behavior towards the former partner can show dramatic changes. Where vindictive behavior once prevailed, there is now a more balanced perspective where the former partner is seen as separate from the client and decisions regarding contact are based on individual choice rather than need. Acceptance by both partners of each other's emotional and physical space is important in maintaining the separateness.

The client's self worth as a lesbian or gay individual is renewed or solidified. The closed community system can still present some barriers and difficulties as it is highly probable that seeing one's former partner in social situations is present. Establishing sexual or non-sexual relationships with individuals who do not know the former partner is difficult. The "coupling phenomenon" where most social activities are for or with couples is difficult for the client who is not in a new relationship. This can present a social barrier for the individual as well as friends who are in dyadic relationships. For the client, feeling comfortable at a social activity where the participants are in couples is a difficult task with feelings of isolation once again surfacing. In addition, those friends in a relationship are often threatened by the presence of a "single."

The client can begin to work through this discomfort as part of the treatment program. Again, the sensitivity of the clinician is essential. During this stage, therapeutic time needs to be spent in helping the client explore alternatives to a one-to-one live-in relationship so that the individual will have time and avoid rebound situations. Dealing with feelings of panic or depression over the fear of never finding anyone may be necessary. A treatment priority is assisting the client to understand and accept slippage or setbacks. Each time the client faces situations previously encountered with the former partner the potential for a setback exists. Time and increased coping skills, hopefully gained through the grief process, will allow for a decrease in duration and intensity of those setbacks.

The client and clinician have come through an intense experience together. Ideally at the termination of therapy the client has returned at least to the original functional and coping levels. In many cases, the painful experience of loss and of coping with grief and grieving will result in the client increasing functional and coping levels. Fears of loss, although still present, are recognized as natural consequences of this painful experience rather than being immobilizing. Relationship alternatives and relationship styles may change thereby promoting new and rewarding experiences. During this process, the therapist has undoubtedly become a major support system for the client and termination should involve re-examination of immediate and long term goals. The client can be helped to examine areas for continued change within self and in relationships to maximize the gains and strengths realized through resolving this crisis. Above all the client must have assurances that the clinician will be available if needed in the future.

The lesbian and gay culture needs a sensitivity to this phenomenon. The traditional supports are not there and consequently lesbian and gay individuals need to develop support networks for each other. Loss is painful for all humanity; for the lesbian and gay person it is often a time of increased painfulness due to isolation from traditional supports.

Summary

Oppression is a social disease. Stress, alienation, powerlessness, and isolation from the societal mainstream as well as an inequality with the customary entitlements of life can exacerbate any crisis for the lesbian or gay individual. There are unique aspects of loss and crisis with lesbian and gay clients. When there is a lack of social and institutional support a crisis can escalate into long-term dysfunctional patterns. The institutional oppression experienced by individuals in an alternative lifestyle increases stress in a society already burdened with enormous stress. Due to the limited socialization environments, the lesbian and gay person tends to utilize bars thus increasing the potential for substance abuse. Absence of the support system of a life-mate may perpetuate an identity crisis or the reemergence of a crisis unresolved. Those lesbian and gay persons who have remained hidden from the gay culture as well as the majority culture face a higher risk of isolation during a crisis. This becomes a prime time for reinforcement of negative lifestyle stereotypes. Helping professionals have not generalized knowledge about loss and grief to the lesbian and gay lifestyle and therefore may not be available as a support system. Lesbian and gay therapists comfortable in their lifestyles are also limited in number. The absence of legal supports such as reconciliation counseling, custody agreements, and financial agreements perpetuate the practical and emotional complications of relationship terminations. These factors all contribute to the increased risk of suicide, isolation, identity questioning, internalization of homophobic attitudes and general dysfunctioning of the lesbian and gay individual experiencing a loss and crisis.

The clinician's sensitivity and awareness to the unique aspects of loss and crisis is stressed throughout this chapter. Validations of the significance of the loss and a lesbian and gay lifestyle as part of the client's identity is necessary in order to minimize internalization of negative social and institutional stereotypes. Therapeutic intervention with the lesbian or gay client requires an acceptance that there are unique aspect of loss and crisis. The grieving process can be applied to the general population; however, effective interventions with the lesbian and gay client must also take into account specific social and institutional variables.

References

Bell, A. and Weinberg, M. (1978). *Homosexualities*. New York: Simon and Shuster.

Brooks, V. (1981). *Minority Stress and Lesbian Women*. Lexington, Mass.: D. C. Heath & Co.

Clark, D. (1977). *Loving Someone Gay*. Millbrae, Calif.: Celestial Arts.

Kubler-Ross, E. (1969). *On Death and Dying*. New York: MacMillan.

Moses, A. E. and Hawkins, R. O. (1982). *Counseling Lesbian Women and Gay Men*. St. Louis: C. V. Mosby Co.

Siegal, R. L. and Hoefer, D. D. (1981). "Bereavement Counseling for Gay Individuals," *American Journal of Psychotherapy* XXXV(4), October 4.

Tanner, D. (1978). *The Lesbian Couple*. Lexington, Mass.: D. C. Heath and Co.

Woodman, N. J. and Lenna, H. R. (1980). *Counseling with Gay Men and Women*. San Francisco: Jossey-Bass.

PART III

ADMINISTRATION AND COMMUNITY SERVICE

Introduction

Section III begins with Hidalgo's chapter identifying knowledge, value and skill components of this curriculum area. Again, the reader is reminded of the social work mandates for such learning. Of greatest significance is the specification of content which can and should be included in administration and community development courses. Also noteworthy is the emphasis on practical social change experiences for students which move them beyond the theoretical and intellectual spheres.

In Chapter 9, Terry provides the reader with an excellent overview of the civil rights acts of the nineteenth and twentieth centuries. She proceeds from this to the implications for civil liberties for lesbian women and gay men, demonstrating how administrative policies (as well as future legislation) can be expanded and implemented to prevent continued homophobia and oppression. Concern for client services as well as safeguarding the rights of professional workers is well documented. Terry further demonstrates the need for viewing civil rights as "human rights," validating her basic premise of "Entitlement Not Privilege." Thus, the spheres of knowledge and values addressed by Hidalgo are given further clarification for professional practice.

Burnham provides social work educators, students, and practioners with basic steps for implementing community organization experiences in a wide variety of arenas. Included are: social worker as broker; social networking; consultation to gay and lesbian groups and organizations; establishing a "phone help line;" organizing for community education and advocacy; and organizational roles for "closeted" individuals. This very practical article helps to diminish the misperception of limited avenues for social work intervention with lesbian and gay communities. In essence, Burnham demonstrates that, when professionals are not blinded by homophobia, knowledge and skills can be expanded to include this population and facilitate self-actualization.

•

8

Integrating Lesbian and Gay Content in Program Planning, Administration, and Community Practice

Hilda Hidalgo, Ph.D.

Introduction

Traditionally, social work curricula have been compartmentalized into courses which offer students little opportunity for integrating practice related knowledge, skills, and values. Students in the administrative track, for example, seldom experience learning situations in which they are asked to assume primary responsibility as a change agent by demonstrating conscious synthesis of specific knowledge, skill, and value components of an administrator's practice protocol.

Providing learning experiences which emphasize such synthesis requires careful identification, analysis, and organization of both educational content and educational processes. What knowledge, for example, is "basic" to understanding in a specific area of focus? What skills are required to provide a specific service? What value issues or perspectives are important? And, finally, how are these components best ordered and approached for maximum learning and practice use?

This chapter offers some information and guidelines for structuring education so as to focus on learning activities which will meet the needs of gay and lesbian clients and staff. Particular emphasis is given here to key knowledge, skill, and value components for such activities. Additionally, the chapter identifies administrative perspectives which will be aimed at addressing gay and lesbian issues and services.

Rationale for the Selection of Educational Experiences Centered on Lesbian and Gay Concerns and Issues

At least ten percent (10%) of the total population in the United States is lesbian or gay oriented. It is almost certain that *all* social service agencies have lesbian and gay clients. If the homosexual population is invisible in the agency, it could mean that the agency is sending an explicit or implicit message: "lesbian and gay men need not to apply" and/or "make sure lesbian or gay identity remains in the closet to avoid penalties and discrimination!"

The frequency distribution of homosexuals among the population makes it possible to target the needs of this minority population as a focus for educational experiences regardless of the practice setting of the social work student—whether they be administration or social work community organizer students.

The NASW Code of Ethics (1976), the NASW Public Social Policy Statement on Gay Issues (1977), and CSWE Baccalaureate and Master's level Evaluative Standards (1983) all provide the ethical and professional rationale for an educational experience centered on lesbian and gay concerns and issues.

Educational Objectives of Experiences Centered on Gay and Lesbian Concerns and Issues

Learning activities should be designed to provide social work-administrator students and social work-community organizer students with the opportunity to:

1. Test, reinforce, internalize social work values related to social justice and respect for difference under circumstances that will probably require facing personal values;
2. Synthesize knowledge and theories in all the core curricular areas: human behavior and the social perspective of their specialization;
3. Practice a variety of skills such as those needed in tasks such as: staff education, conflict resolution, power field analysis, community needs assessments, program development, and program planning.

Change Focus of Educational Experiences

The focus of an educational experience should be directed toward achievement of clearly identified goals that involve change. Possible goals for the experience could be:

1. Changes in negative attitudes (e.g., of agency staff and/or community members) in relation to lesbians and gays;
2. Changes and/or modifications in existing agency programs/policies that will result in making existing agency services and practices sensitive and responsive to lesbian women and gay men (clients/staff);
3. Planning new programs designed to meet specific needs of lesbians and gays in the community.

A single goal or a combination of goals should be identified by the students and the instructor. The selection of a goal or goals should be based on a realistic assessment of what can possibly be achieved, given time constraints and level of knowledge and skill achievement of students. If none of the goals identified can be achieved in a real exercise, analysis of why such goals are *not* possible can be in itself a good educational experience. Another action possibility is to engage in a role-play situation constructed for the purpose of achieving one of the goals listed above.

In order to maximize the educational value of learning activities for students of administration and/or community organization, we have identified specific knowledge, skills, and values to be considered in planning such activities. Knowledge and theoretical components should include:

Social work as a profession
- Historical overview of the profession as advocate for change agent with oppressed populations, including the contributions of our lesbian founders
- Professional ethics and practice values

Social Policy
- Role of policy as guidelines for practice
- Social and legal sanctions in the oppression of gay men and lesbian women

Human Behavior and the Social Environment
- The function of homophobia in society
- Concept and function of social worker's role in "labeling" processes and in defining "deviance" in society
- Concepts of how people change within systems and of how systems change
- "Coming out" as a developmental process for gays and lesbians
- Lesbian and gay life-styles and issues
- Information on AIDS
- Lesbian and gay community resource systems and networks

Research
- Attitude development/attitude changes
- Instruments and procedures useful in measuring attitude change
- Data collection and presentation

Practice-Administration and Community Organization
- The problem solving model as a practice model for administrators and community organizers
- Value concepts and dilemmas in social work practice
- Bureaucratic factors inhibiting and facilitating change
- Formal and informal operations within a bureaucracy, or agency, or community
- Authority as a concept; using the authority of office and the authority of expertise
- Power field analysis
- Concept of power in individuals, institutions, and groups
- Power alliances in relation to source, uses, and formation
- Organizational innovation and change, definitions, and processes for:
  a) innovation through a new program or service
  b) change as alterations in resources in the internal structure of agencies
  c) symbolic or real change
  d) steps and stages of organizational change

Practice Skills
- Clarifying worker's own attitudes, beliefs, feelings, expectations, responsibilities
- Self-assessment in reference to personal values
- Recognizing "professional" and "non-professional" behavior in self and others
- Identifying areas needing change
- Gathering and presenting data useful to implementing programs to address needs of lesbians and gays
- Applying research studies to practice problems and situations

- Clarifying and acting on accountability as an individual professional in a bureaucratic structure or community
- Using personal and professional power
- Identifying, clarifying agency organization objectives, ideologies and missions
- Using the supervisory structure in practice
- Using organizational procedures (formal and informal) appropriately to achieve objectives and change
- Identifying and using organizational ambiguities or groups in the organizational structure to facilitate change
- Using conflict and confrontation appropriately
- Assessing relative power and strength of conflict and confrontation participants
- Developing and planning an educational activity
- Framing issues in political terminology
- Forming intra- and interagency coalitions
- Working for change within organizational structure
- Analyzing organizational structure and procedures to identify entry points for change efforts

Professional Values
- Respect for individual dignity, individuality, self-determination
- Competence and accountability as a professional
- Importance of sound knowledge and skill base for effective professional practice
- Responsibility to advocate
- "Taking a stand" on issues of importance for social justice

Implementation of Learning Relative to Agency-Related Administrative Issues: The Meaning of Field Placement for the Student:

In order to provide a real educational experience for students of social work administration and community practice in relation to gay and lesbian issues, it is important that the student be placed in a real administrative field practice position. In other words, it is crucial that the student's role in the agency allows him/her to make some administrative judgments and have some supervisory responsibility. Without these components, the field experience is nothing more than an exercise in administration. For this reason, a field assignment that involves dealing *in the role of administrator* with a gay and lesbian programmatic issue is important. Such an assignment can provide opportunity to test and develop the array of needed administrative skills, and apply a broad range of knowledge. If the agencies that serve as field placement for the student are unwilling or unable to provide such opportunities, it is possible to look at alternative settings or programs— such as gay and lesbian activist organizations in the community. Because these organizations usually have limited funds, they are likely to welcome a student who can test his/her knowledge base and practice skills while, at the same time, providing a real service. It could well be that these non-traditional field placements offer a *richer* educational opportunity to the student than the traditional settings. As with any field instruction setting, the educator will have to do a careful assessment, as is indicated in the chapters relative to Field Instruction. However, of even greater significance, is the continuing assessment of learning opportunities related to non-homophobic learning experiences within any field agency.

This chapter has described content to be covered for the students engaged in program-administrative or community development social work education. Faculty bear a keen responsibility to assure continued monitoring of their own attention to such dimensions of learning, never assuming that such curricular issues only belong in direct practice courses. Regardless of role or setting, social work educators and students have a mandate to serve lesbian and gay populations.

9

Entitlement Not Privilege: The Right of Employment and Advancement

Pat Terry, ACSW

The right of all individuals to work and advance has its philosophical roots in our heritage and our constitution. This philosophy, as many oppressed groups know, is often restricted in implementation by discrimination. Fair employment laws and presidential orders in the 1940's and 1950's were severely limited in eliminating and preventing discriminating practices. The Civil Rights Act enacted by Congress in 1964 provided legal enforcement for equal employment. It provides that no person in the United States shall, on the grounds of race, color or national origin, be excluded from participation in, be denied the benefits of, or be subjected to discrimination under any program or activity receiving federal funds. Additional executive orders and amendments have been an attempt to strengthen anti-discriminating practices for protected groups. The term "protected groups" takes on significance in the discussion of initiating equal opportunity policies for lesbian women and gay men.

Historical perspectives are necessary for determining

intervention strategies. A brief review of the Civil Rights Acts provides this foundation.

The Civil Rights Act of 1866 was enacted subsequent to the adoption of the 14th, 15th, and 16th Amendments to the Constitution. Legislation was enacted to protect the rights of racial minorities. This act extended the right of citizens of racial minority status to contract, to sue and to participate in legal proceedings. Since employer/employee relationships have been viewed by the courts as contractual, interpretation of the Civil Rights Act of 1866 includes that the right to employment was covered. In addition, further interpretation of this law which granted racial minorities the same property rights as "white" citizens has been viewed to mean expectation of continued employment is legally recognized as "property right."

The effort to extend rights was further reinforced by the Civil Rights Act of 1871 which provided federal protection when discrimination existed under state law or custom. This Act also prohibited discrimination in employment as a result of conspiracy between two or more persons. The next major effort towards establishing anti-bias employment was in the form of Presidential Directives in 1941 which required defense contractors doing business with the federal government to have equal opportunities.

Recent federal statutes regarding discrimination in employment began with the Equal Pay Act of 1963. This statute prohibited paying different wage rates for jobs involving equal skill, effort and responsibility under the same conditions. This, clearly, is directed at discrimination based on sex. Although this Act applied to any business involved in interstate commerce and the courts have upheld that this applies not only to individuals handling such interstate goods but to all employees of the business.

The Civil Rights Act of 1964, Title VII has the strongest statute for anti-bias rules for employment. The Civil Rights Act of 1964 provides that no person in the United States shall, on the grounds of race, color or national origin, be excluded from participation in, be denied the benefits of, or be subjected to discrimination under any program or activity receiving federal financial assistance. Implementing regulations for programs receiving aid through the U.S. Department of Health and Human Services (HHS) are in Title 45, Code of Federal Regulations Part 80.

The Act also prohibits discrimination in employment if a primary purpose of Federal assistance is provision of employment (such as apprenticeship, training, work study, or similar programs). Revised Guidelines adopted in 1973 by 25 Federal agencies, prohibit discriminatory employment practices including unequal treatment of beneficiaries, hiring or assignment of counselors, trainers, faculty, hospital staff, social workers, and others in organizations receiving Federal funds. Although Title VI does not explicitly bar sex discrimination, various Federal agencies have prohibited such discrimination in their own regulations.

Title VII of the Civil Rights Act of 1964 prohibits discrimination because of race, color, religion, sex or national origin in all employment practice including hiring, firing, promotion, compensation and other terms, privileges and conditions of employment. The Equal Employment Opportunity Act of 1972 greatly strengthened the powers and expanded the jurisdiction of the Equal Employment Opportunity Commission (EEOC) in enforcement of this law. Title XII now covers all private employers of 15 or more persons, all educational institutions (public and private), state and local governments, public and private employment agencies, labor unions with 15 or more members and joint labor-management committees for apprenticeship and training. Executive Order 11246 issued in 1967 requires Affirmative Action Programs by all Federal contractors and subcontractors which includes that firms with contracts over $50,000 and 50 or more employees develop and implement written programs, which are monitored by an assigned Federal compliance agency. In addition each contract awarded by the federal government amounting to $10,000 or more contains an equal opportunity clause which is binding for the team of the contrast. Contractors are required to:

1. Not discriminate against any employee or job applicant because of race, color, religion, sex or national origin.
2. State in all solicitations and advertisements for employees that all applicants will be considered on basis of these qualifications.
3. Advise all unions with which the contractor does business of the commitments under Executive Order 11246.
4. Include the same type of EEOC agreement in every subcontract or purchase order, unless exempt, so that provisions will be binding upon subcontractor or vendor.
5. Ignore policies of foreign governments that would require discrimination on the basis of race, color, sex, religion or national origin in hiring persons in the United States for work to be performed for, or in, such foreign country." (*Labor Law Reports*, 1981 Guidebook to Fair Employment Practices," Commerce Clearing House, Inc., Chicago, Issue 1033, 21-22).

Employment bias regarding age was addressed in the Age Discrimination Act of 1967 and extended to public employees in 1974. This Act provides protection against discrimination to employees or applicants if they are between the ages of 40 and 70 and if occupational qualifications do not require physical factors. Any employer of 20 or more workers for 20 or more weeks a year is subject to this Act.

During the 1970's anti-bias employment rules were again extended. Not only was the 1964 Act strengthened by the establishment of the Equal Opportunity Commission in 1972 to enforce the Act but the Rehabilitation Act of 1973 (section 503 and 504) extended coverage to the handicapped for those programs receiving federal assistance. This protection was extended to disabled veterans and veterans of the Vietnam conflict in the Vietnam Era Veterans Readjustment Act of 1974.

There are numerous interpretations regarding Fair Employment Laws and I would encourage the reader to pursue this subject in the Labor Law Reports published by Commerce Clearing House, Inc., 4025 W. Peterson, Chicago, Illinois 60646. What, unfortunately, is quite clear from this brief overview is that with the exception of rare state laws and city ordinances there is no mention of sexual orientation. Even more alarming, is the realization that Civil Rights Acts began in 1866 and, one hundred years later, racial and ethnic minorities are still waiting for full implementation. The 1963 Equal Pay Act still is far from implementation. Studies continue to show comparable worth discrepancies. Harassment on the basis of sex is a violation of Section 703 of Title VII of the Civil Rights Act of 1964. However, women still are subjected to unwelcome sex advances with implicit and explicit messages that their "right to property" will be jeopardized if they are unresponsive.

Conclusive then is that, even with laws, discrimination exists. What about lesbian and gays where there is no federal protection and minimal legal backup at state and city for discriminating employment practices?

Service programs at all levels generally have some federal financial assistance. It would seem that a major strategy would be to impact at the national level with legislative or presidential actions. This is a must in order for lesbians and gays to be afforded basic constitutional rights. Such political activity can not be minimized and all persons have a responsibility to promote and support this effort. However, this approach must be concurrent with activity at the local level so that we may begin to immediately negate the impact of discriminatory practices based on sexual orientation. As resources are devoted to legislative inclusion, there must be action within agencies in terms of advocacy for equal opportunity policies. It is at the policy level that changes can happen more quickly and impact upon service delivery.

There are two major areas where homophobic policies and procedures affect lesbians and gays. First in employment and advancement and secondly in actual service provision.

Let us examine the employment aspect. The components

we are dealing with are recruitment, selection and promotion. The general scenario for a lesbian or gay individual is to "hide" their sexual orientation at least during the recruitment and selection phase. Very few lesbian or gays will believe that their sexual orientation can be anything but a barrier to employment. The fact is the qualifications of the individual should be the deciding factor. Reality tells us that very often qualifications would not be the deciding factor if sexual orientation were known. There are of course exceptions to this in businesses that have lesbian women and gay men as their clientele. Generally, speaking majority culture businesses want "majority culture" employees. Usually this is applied equally to public service.

From the very beginning, we have the lesbian and gay individual not only dealing with the anxieties of employment but also feeling that somehow their employee "worth" will be affected by sexual orientation. Visible minorities have been facing this all along. In some sense the "invisible minority" has an advantage in that minority status can not be overtly discriminated against if it is not known. This certainly can work for the Caucasian and non-handicapped male. Once employment has been established and recruitment and selection completed, the individual faces the process of competing for advancement opportunities. Again, such opportunities should be based on performance and qualifications. Again, in many cases, if sexual orientation is known performance and qualifications can become secondary considerations. The lesbian and gay individual's organizational success may be dependent on remaining an invisible minority. If organizational advancement is obtained, the lesbian and gay individual wants to maintain that position. Performance may be at an exceptional level, yet sexual orientation somehow can become the issue rather than job skills. What has developed from this "get on, stay on, go on" organizational scenario for lesbians and gays is the reinforcement of homophobic administrative policies. The lesbian and gay individual not only remains fearful and hidden but falls into the over-achiever syndrome in order to compensate for an alternative lifestyle.

Nevertheless, it is true that being an identified lesbian woman or gay man involves organizational risk of being terminated. Basic constitutional rights and security needs are threatened every day.

There need to be efforts made to change this scenario without endangering the individual's livelihood. Those lesbian and gay individuals within organizations need to examine how they best can begin to change homophobic policies. For some, it may mean coming out and being a role model for other lesbians and gays as well as promoting the concept of qualifications and performance as opposed to sexual orientation. For others, simply practicing the equal opportunity/affirmative action concepts as an administrator can lead to organizational direction toward the right of all persons to work and advance on the basis of merit, ability and potential. Programs, policies, and practices which are directed towards employment and advancement and treat qualified individuals without bias should be developed, supported, and promoted. Opportunities for all minorities, visible and invisible, should be provided. Discipline should be administered equitably and carefully documented. One's own biases and fears need to be overcome when administrative or management decisions are made. Employee job performance should be judged on capability, not for any other criteria. Administrative policies should prohibit racial, religious, ethnic, handicapped, gender and sexual orientation epithets or slurs even in jest. Personal life and job life must be kept separate and far apart. As an administrator, manager or service provider, lesbians and gays can ill afford to fall into the homophobic perceptions of promiscuity or "converters." Ideally, all administrators and managers should be seen as proactive individuals in equal opportunity practices including non-homophobic role modeling for staff and personnel.

With legal sanction and enforcement, equal opportunity practices are difficult. Without legal sanction, as in the case of lesbian and gays, equal opportunity practices are dependent upon agency policies, administrative directions, and administrative attitudes. Lesbian and gay administrators at the minimum must mirror in attitude and action a proactive approach to equal opportunity practices. Hopefully, they will be risk takers, maintaining and reflecting a pride in their own identity. The organization will benefit from this approach as production is closely linked to job satisfaction and a positive work environment. Fear stagnates production and inhibits creativity. It certainly is equitable to deal with employment based on capability and performance rather than majority culture judgments.

Another aspect of homophobic administrative policies is the reflection upon the consumer. Obviously, the policies of community and service agencies have impact on quality of delivery. For purposes of this discussion, service delivery systems are the identified focus. Helping professional and human service workers continually face the question of whether intervention is the same regardless of ethnicity, age, gender and sexual orientation. Effective intervention must keep cultural, age, gender and sexual orientation in significant perspective. Human service workers have a professional and ethical responsibility to understand the culture and lifestyle of their clients.

Lesbian and gay individuals and members of the larger community share some commonalities as well as differences. Awareness of these commonalities and differences is essential for the non-gay as well as the lesbian or gay human service worker. We know that lesbian or gay clients will be seen be non-gay workers as a result of the numerical majority of non-gay professionals or for a variety of reasons of preference. We know that differences in philosophy and approach exist even within the professional lesbian and gay helping community. There are similar questions that need to be asked if we are to serve our lesbian and gay clients in a professional and ethical manner.

First we must determine the treatment modality or approach. If the client is the factor in determining a particular approach, then a sensitivity to lifestyle, resources, and frame of reference must be present. Lesbian and gay clients have unique lifestyle issues. Self validation, coming out, economic security, relationship, and religious concerns are only a few of those issues. Non-gay human service workers must be aware and responsive to these.

If it is the problem that determines the approach, then systems factors must be the priority consideration. For example, a lesbian or gay client with a substance abuse problem faces some unique dilemmas. One of those problems is the environment that often is available for socialization within the lesbian and gay community. Although socialization alternatives have increased over the last few years, the bars are still a primary environment for social activity and meeting others. The alcohol abuser often must decide which to give up—the substance or socialization. Therefore, individuals have their sobriety programs challenged on a continual basis due to the limited social alternatives in the lesbian and gay community.

Residential treatment is often an approach utilized in alcohol and drug treatment. Entering a residential program with same gender participants can be complicated if the client's lesbian/gay orientation is known. Programs often refuse clients on this basis. Should a lesbian or gay client access a residential program it often is the beginning of a complicated and painful time. Assaultive statements regarding one's lifestyle and self are frequently directed at the individual. Identity issues arise for the lesbian and gay as well as other participants in the program. Treatment of substance abuse focuses on the need for honesty by the client with self and others. Dealing with one's life style and same gender sexual orientation in a non-supportive substance abuse treatment environment with homophobic staff and program participants poses personal and systemic problems.

When the human service professional is the determining factor in the treatment approach her or his lifestyle, resources, skill level and attitudes become prospective issues. Consider, if you will, a client who is referred to a therapist whose particular expertise is in reality therapy. The reality of being lesbian and gay is that it is not an easy lifestyle. Positive and easy should not be confused as synonymous. A reality therapist might confront the client about mannerisms which could provoke others to demean or verbally assault her or him. The zealous therapist makes a statement to the effect "that if you walk like that, you must be prepared for the consequences." The "therapeutic" message is clear. It is one of disqualification. It is a message to change one's self as there is something wrong with you. Perhaps the true reality is that being comfortable with how one walks, talks, behaves and feels can not be defined by homophobic institutional norms. In this example, the therapist chose to negate the individual rather than archaic social expectations.

Self definition for lesbians and gays is a survival issue and generally is accomplished after many years of personal struggle and final negation of the majority culture perspective. Make no mistake in that lesbian and gay human service workers can be as or in many cases more homophobic than non-gay human service workers.

The problem, concerns and issues for lesbian and gay clients are unique. Human service workers need to have an awareness, understanding and sensitivity to this unique lifestyle. We need to be asking questions as to the relationship between the client's sexual orientation the responsiveness to treatment and the therapeutic relationship. Lesbians and gays have been programmed to handle their own problems as disclosure often has an end result in rejection from significant others, loss of economic security, difficulty with the legal system, lack of needed treatment from the medical community, abandonment from religious leaders and social isolation. Oppression increases stress making simple life activities such as a company Christmas party an issue. Disqualification by others, including one's therapist, leads to internal degradation which at best results in a negative self esteem and at worse— self destruction.

Non-lesbian and non-gay human service workers at a minimum need to have an understanding of alternative lifestyles and an awareness of their own values and attitudes. It is the non-gay human service worker that will provide most of the services to the lesbian and gay client. Sensitivity and responsiveness become an imperative. Lesbian and gay human service workers face additional challenges. We, too, must deal with the gay perspective as a professional and personal mandate. In addition, we must be guardians and monitors of services to the lesbian and gay population providing leadership in policies, practice, theory, and system design. We must challenge traditional systems that are oppressive and dysfunctional. There must be risk taking in terms of providing ideas for programming, policies, and procedures. Strategies must be developed which provide services which are relevant and non-homophobic. Administrators and decision makers are key to implementing the guidelines and setting the atmosphere for responsive services for lesbians and gays.

The writer has attempted to set forth two administrative responsibilities in providing a non-homophobic agency environment. The review of Fair Employment legislation and directives is essential to understanding the system intervention that must be made if lesbian and gays are to have protection from biased employment practices. In addition to homophobic employment practices, there must be close scrutiny of service delivery and the policies and procedures guiding human service delivery. As lesbians and gays continue the struggle to access equal opportunities at the national, state and local levels, the struggle at the agency or enterprise level must also move forward. Equal opportunity is not just a "gay rights" issue—equal opportunity and entitlement, accessibility, availability, and acceptability are human rights issues.

References

Labor Law Reports, Commerce Clearing House, Inc., 4025 West Peterson Avenue, Chicago, Illinois 60646.

10

Social Work Roles in Local Community Organization ExperiencesWith Lesbian Women and Gay Men

Doug Burnham, Ph.D.

It is the intent of this chapter to explore ways social workers, regardless of sexual orientation, can be involved in developing and maintaining local community organization experiences for lesbian women and gay men. It should be kept in mind that social workers who are trained as generalist practitioners have been exposed to a broad body of information and skills in working with individuals, families, groups and organizations that are basic to work with any population group. Applying information and skills differentially depends on the worker's understanding, in this instance, of lesbian women and gay men and their experiences, individually and collectively, in this nation's particular social/ cultural context.

The social worker who delivers services directly may be in the most strategic position to offer members of oppressed populations (including lesbian women and gay men) encouragement, support, advocacy, consultation, and direction in organizing to impact environmental systems. This work may or may not be done within agency or program context.

It is ideal to have lesbian women and gay men use agencies and programs that exist to serve the whole community. Social workers have a responsibility to work toward this ideal. The reality is, however, that many resources either do not have the necessary knowledge or skills or do not operate from a value perspective that is helpful in serving lesbian women and gay men. As social workers are striving to modify agencies and programs in order to better serve lesbian and gay people, they must also become involved in activity that creates opportunities for this group to meet their needs as members of a community and the larger national society. The social worker will not only be working in an agency or program but also as a professional and a citizen working on community based efforts to build supports and services. The material in this chapter is for all social workers, whatever their setting.

Social workers can use principles and theories which are traditional to the profession to guide their involvement in enhancing local community and organizational experiences for lesbian women and gay men. Much of that which has served to divide and segment social work practice can be brought together by working with lesbian and gay people in a community or organizational context.

Kramer & Specht's (1983, p. 14) working definition of community organization may serve well as a basis for local community practice with lesbian women and gay men:

> Community organization refers to various methods of intervention whereby a professional change agent helps a community action system composed of individuals, groups or organizations engage in planned collective action in order to deal with social problems within a democratic system of values. It is concerned with programs aimed at social change with primary reference to environmental conditions and social institutions. It involves two major interrelated con-

cerns (a) the interactional processes of working with an action system, which include identifying, recruiting and working with the members and developing organizational and interpersonal relationships among them which facilitate their efforts; (b) the technical tasks involved in identifying problem areas, analyzing causes, formulating plans, developing strategies, mobilizing the resources necessary to effect action, and assessing the outcomes of program.

The definition indicates that a practitioner must work with large numbers of various size systems to be effective. It also suggests that the worker must be prepared to fill the roles of broker, enabler, mediator, advocate, and activist. Much of this thinking is a synthesis of writers and theorists such as Murray Ross (1955), Roland Warren (1978), Floyd Hunter (1952), Jack Rothman (1971) and a host of other time honored professionals as well as Kramer and Specht's own work.

These are fundamental concepts for engaging in local community based work with lesbian women and gay men. One does not have to consider him/herself a "community organizer" to be effective with this population. In reality, very few social workers have positions that are primarily organizational by description. The worker must, however, have a clear understanding of social work foundation knowledge and skills. This includes an understanding of social oppression and its effects on the daily lives of lesbian women and gay men.

The worker's sexual orientation will, of course, affect his/her perspective on community work with lesbian women and gay men. The worker's effectiveness, however, is more dependent on ability and willingness to view a whole situation, skills in community assessment, and self awareness.

Similar to Shirley Cooper's (1974) contentions concerning the race of the worker with Black clients, the gay and nongay worker will have different interpersonal struggles in relationship building with lesbian and gay clients. Cooper (1974, p. 128) says that the white worker with the Black client "influenced by a culture rampant with racism and unfamiliar with the intricacies and nuances of the lives of ethnic people may, even with the best of intentions, fail to recognize when social and cultural factors predominate" in affecting attitudes. On the other hand she notes that ethnic workers are "vulnerable to the opposite form of . . . error. Because they are so centrally involved, they may exaggerate the importance or impact of ethnic factors."

In our national culture, it is impossible for any person to completely let go of their homophobia and heterosexism. As with sexism, racism, ageism, and classism, everyone has absorbed a certain degree of homophobia and heterosexism. One's sexual orientation does not determine the extent of that absorption. Even though it may manifest itself in different ways, every worker has to examine and/or struggle with this phenomenon.

Local organizational opportunities with lesbian women and gay men are plentiful and the efforts may range from the development of informal support networks, to formal clubs, to political organizations, to extensive service programs. The size of the organizational effort is not as important as the recognition of what is needed at a particular time by a particular group of people in a particular environmental context. The development of a lesbian literary collective in Paint Lick, Kentucky is as valuable as the development of a multi-service center in New York, New York. It is the quality of the organizational experience that determines its value.

The remainder of this chapter will cover a few ideas concerning various opportunities for the social worker to assist in local community organizational experiences with lesbian women and gay men. These ideas are not meant to be exhaustive but should give the reader a perspective of the variety of opportunities for creativity.

Social Worker as Broker

It is important for lesbian women and gay men to have access to other gay and lesbian people. Such contact on an informal level can serve as basic support, helping to meet what Charlotte Towle (1965) calls "common human needs." Much of what social workers do is focused toward helping people find, build, and maintain meaningful informal resources. Some lesbian and gay people have a great deal of difficulty making that first move to reach out and make contact with other gays and/or lesbians. Workers may well expect to spend a portion of their energy exploring this issue and its ramifications with a prospective client. Gay and lesbian workers may use their own involvement in community activity as a spring board for introducing a new person to available opportunities. Non-gay and non-lesbian workers, if they have successfully established relationships with gay and lesbian resources, can call on people in these resources to serve as facilitators for the new person. Such use of indigenous persons is a respected social work method.

Connective experiences for gay or lesbian people may begin on a formal level e.g., membership in clubs or organizations. These resources may hold regular meetings and have a focus or purpose such as political, religious, or recreational groups, but they also provide an initial sense of belonging. Since social isolation and alienation are major issues for some gay men and lesbian women this feeling of fitting in can be a rewarding outcome. It also allows an opportunity for a gay or lesbian person to meet others with whom they may be able to build more spontaneous relationships and thus leads toward the development of an enriching informal resource system.

To link gay and lesbian and people with existing resources is certainly a role well suited for the social worker. Knowledge of all societal, formal, and informal resources is, of course, necessary for any social worker. Because of a dearth of social contexts for lesbian women and gay men, information about formal and informal resources takes on even greater significance. Some communities have a well organized system of gay and/or lesbian cultural/social institutions, programs, and opportunities. These locations will usually have a gay and/or lesbian phone line which may be a starting place for the social worker to learn more about the availability of resources. Written directories of services may be available but they are almost always a little out of date. The phone lines are usually informational in nature and are operated by volunteers. The phone numbers can generally be found in the phone book, local newspaper, or by calling community based referral services. It is the social worker's responsibility to explore existing services and learn the extent of their usefulness, limits, competency and referral procedures.

In many communities and for many individuals, secrecy and anonymity are paramount concerns when seeking connection with other gay or lesbian people and particularly if the group is large and recognized. While this concern should not be minimized by the worker, it should be kept within realistic boundaries. Being forced to come out may be a situation that has very real potential for damaging a person. All individuals are responsible for their own choices concerning coming out or being open about their sexual orientation. Workers need to be ready to realistically and sensitively discuss the possible consequence of these decisions.

In trying to link individual gay or lesbian people with resources, the worker needs to obtain from the referral source any policy that can impact the public nature of people involved. The resource, for example, may be an informal group that meets once a month at someone's home to set a calendar of leisure activities and there may be no formal policies. Make sure the person referred understands that. Ultimately neither social workers nor other professionals have absolute control over the ethics or behaviors of others. The best we can do is know the programs to which we refer and prepare the client for the initial encounter.

Even if a gay or lesbian client, for whatever reason, is not ready to make direct contact with other gay and lesbian people there are a variety of communication tools available that can be helpful in gaining a sense that one is not alone. Organizational newsletters, calendars of events, newspaper announcements, pamphlets, magazines, books (fiction and non-fiction), etc., all provide opportunities to be involved and contribute to the development of community and activity which builds self-esteem and pride.

Because most areas in this country do not have an organized set of resources specifically for lesbian women and gay men, brokering becomes somewhat non-traditional and largely dependent on social networking.

Social Networking

In order to connect members of gay and/or lesbian populations, it is imperative that social workers be able to tap into existing social networks or help build new ones.

Even in areas where there are no formal resources, lesbian women have frequently been able to establish strong local social networks. Reasons for lesbians' talent and ability to do this have been discussed by authors such as Wolf (1979) and Martin and Lyon (1972). These networks may exist around recreational activity, bars, professional or business interest, or feminist issues, and they serve as valuable resources. There are no formal organization guidelines, designated meeting places, or phone numbers. For workers to be able to use this resource, they must explore a variety of ways to find access. This means being sensitive to signs of networking (Wolf, 1979) and willing to place themselves in the most likely environments to obtain needed information. This may include going to recreational activities, bars, gay related or owned businesses, women's music and arts events, feminist organizations and events. The worker may purposefully establish relationships with lesbian women in order to enlist them as avenues for introducing other lesbian women to networks. The worker can then help the lesbian client learn interactional skills and approaches that facilitate entrance.

Gay men may find informal networking more difficult. As men, they are taught to avoid intimate interaction with other men. This certainly contributes to isolation of men from each other (Pleck & Sawyer, 1974). Gay men may see each other at bars and other gathering locations but may find it difficult to overcome the social learning which places a stigma on reaching out to each other (Harry & DeVall, 1978). Men are praised if they are sexually exploitive so sexual interaction does not necessarily lead to intimacy, sharing or support building (Levine, 1979). This is not to say social networks do not exist for gay men. They certainly do. It may, however, be more difficult to find them. This may mean that, particularly for the non-gay worker, establishing relationships with a few gay men may serve them well in efforts to connect gay men to informal social networks.

Helping to build new social networks may be a challenge for the social worker. Since most groups need a more clearly defined purpose than "let's get together and be supportive," the worker will want to tap into interests of the people he/she wants to bring together. If, for instance, workers in an agency find they are working with five or six lesbian clients and all of them feel a need or desire to have contact with others, the workers can introduce the idea of a group meeting. This meeting can focus on personal growth and support building or, perhaps on a more social basis— a dinner, a picnic, a trip to a Holly Near concert, a bowling party, or a trip to a cinema with coffee after. This will give the participants an opportunity to search for a common ground, check each other out, and determine if there is enough interest to merit further planning. This kind of meeting may be easily arranged but the worker can not assume it will happen spontaneously. Among lesbian women who have had very limited contacts, such a meeting may take a great deal of preparation. They may be frightened, distrustful, and lack social skills. The worker can help to lessen anxiety and transform it into positive anticipation by openly expressing enthusiasm. Techniques such as role playing and rehearsing can also be helpful in dealing with apprehensions.

A worker in a similar situation with gay men may want to move more slowly in developing interactional experiences between them. For those who have had little opportunity to interact socially with other gay men, the worker may even suggest fictional and non-fiction readings to begin easing the feelings of isolation. Or the worker might accompany the person to a gathering of gay men. This allows the client to begin to bring his expectations into a more reality based perspective. As the gay man begins to feel more comfortable with his own gayness he will be better able to risk interaction. As was described in earlier chapters, this is basically a re-socialization process and there is much to unlearn and relearn.

If the worker is familiar with a number of gay men who are ready for interaction but do not know how to go about getting together he/she may been to serve as mediator and resource person. As with the earlier example for lesbian women, the possibilities of settings for such gatherings is limited only by the worker's imagination. The remainder of this chapter may also give the reader ideas for building more formal social networks.

Social Worker as Consultant in Developing New Action Systems

Since social workers are experts in group and organizational processes they are in a position to be valuable resources in developing new organizations or helping modify existing resources to better serve their intended population. Since helping agencies have not traditionally been approachable by lesbian women and gay men it may be necessary for the social worker to reach out to offer organizational assistance to this population.

Lesbian women and gay men may need assistance in how to get started (definition of purpose, goal setting, or activity planning), or they may be able to benefit from exploring options in organizational structure, fund raising, communication, or just information about the ramification of their existence.

Relative to definition of purpose, basic questions are: why does the group or organization exist or why is it needed? Assisting gay and/or lesbian people in an exploration of need can be fruitful and rewarding. It allows a group to establish verbal interaction and narrow its focus so that it may be manageable given the existing resources and attitudes of the larger community as well as this group's own motivation. Many groups in their initial stages have an impression that organizations or groups should serve the whole gay population in a town or region. They may need to be reminded of the tremendous diversity which exists among gay and lesbian people (Jay & Young, 1977; Bell & Weinberg, 1978) and recognize that, until they have a better sense of the balance of supports and resistance, a narrow focus may be beneficial. This will also help them deal with the reality that some gay and lesbian people oppose organizations and not only resist their development but may work to prevent or sabotage them once they are begun. Such people are highly threatened by any signs of community visibility and fear its impact personally.

In communities where no other gay and/or lesbian groups or organizations exist, the pioneering efforts may be slow and frustrating. As with all groups or organizations, a small core of active participants is the rule rather than the exception. The workers will need to help this small core see this reality and avoid the conclusion that just because it is a gay/lesbian organization "no one is going to become involved."

If the worker has a good understanding of the impact of social oppression on gay and lesbian people (Altman, 1971), he or she will be better able to deal with the resulting hostility (unfocused anger) that may be exhibited by some gay or lesbian people. In an organization, this hostility may be manifested by behaviors that focus anger on other group members or the organization. It is safer and more tangible than putting it where it belongs - social structure and values. It may also be seen in attitudes that indicate hopelessness and perceived powerlessness: "that won't work;" "nobody really wants to bother;" "it will never happen in this town." These people become blockers in a group or organization and may need group experiences that give them specific responsibility which can lead to short term success, thus, providing rewarding experiences.

The worker will want to maintain a positive approach in work with this population. Gay and lesbian people, like most populations, will need to borrow from the worker's enthusiasm. In locations that have a variety of resources for gay men and lesbian women, the worker will want to help organizations explore ways they can coalesce on certain issues or events. This creates a stronger sense of community and appreciation for organizational efforts plus the reality of more strength in numbers. Time-limited, specifically focused coalitions may be the most functional with gay and lesbian people. Again, various groups and organizations may need to protect their independence in order to serve the diversity of this population. For instance, in some communities it may be beneficial to have organizations for only lesbian women and/or organizations for gay men. Membership exclusion may be positive for purposes of identity formation, comfort, exploring issues of gender based social expectations, appreciation of shared history, etc. There are, however, issues which call for unity. Social workers may be helpful in serving as initial coordinators of such coalitions and in teaching leaders necessary roles and skills to assume this task.

Another example of how social workers can serve as consultants or initial organizers is in the development of recreation, leisure, or religious organizations. For example, recreation and leisure activities may focus on sports, regular potluck suppers, cards and games, the arts, travel, camping and hiking, etc. A group may decide to focus on one activity or plan a calendar of different events. If the group is located in a city with few resources they may want to plan trips to other places where they can go to gay owned or oriented businesses, restaurants, dances, theatre programs, sports events, and other social activities.

Religious organizations may range from informal discussion groups to caucuses of organized religious bodies, new churches, synagogues, or other spiritual bonding. Historically, in tradition, Judeo-Christian societies, the spiritual needs of gay and lesbian people were seen as nonexistent. Members of this group were viewed as heathens or damned. Lesbians and gay men have had to struggle on their own to insist they have a place in the greater universe of spirituality.

To begin the development of recreational, leisure or religious groups, a social worker may only need to plant the idea and encourage organizational efforts. In other cases, the worker may need to serve initially as the organizer, particularly in locations where few or no formal organization exists. Again, any social worker is professionally obligated to see that resources are offered through humanely operated services. The NASW Code of Ethics provides the rubric for the use of time and agency resources (such as space) to facilitate such organizational work. A worker may find that initial "feeling out" meetings may consist of themselves and two or three other people. Meetings may occur over lunch, at the office (providing it is not too threatening for initial planners), in someone's home, at existing public recreation facilities, at a church, etc.

The worker may find, if resources do not exist within their community, that they can call on gay and lesbian groups who are organized in other localities to come in as consultants, supports or resources. These people could share their experiences with an initial planning body. This may also give the group a feeling that success is possible.

Many lesbian women and gay men have highly developed organizational and planning skills. They may not be aware of them or they may never have used them in work with other gay and/or lesbian people. The worker needs to keep an eye out for such experience or talent and encourage its growth. It should be noted that gay and lesbian people, like other oppressed people who have never worked together on such a project, may feel a sense of hopelessness and may appear negative about the feasibility of such work. The worker has to be sensitive to this and make the planning itself a fulfilling socio-emotional experience. Make each encounter fun, focusing on at least one tangible idea to accomplish, pointing out success in other places, and making sure there is enough time for social interaction. Remember that years of unsuccessful efforts in one's personal experiences are not easily overcome. On the other hand many gay and lesbian people have blossomed under extreme adverse conditions to become very creative and crisis competent. A worker will want to encourage every opportunity for that creativity to manifest itself.

As these recreational, leisure and religious organizations develop and grow, new leaders will emerge. The worker will need to encourage and enhance the potential of these leaders and begin to relinquish the reins. This needs to be done gradually and skillfully to insure the continued success of the group. The worker who has served as organizer and moves away from that role will, during the initial withdrawal, need to remain available on a consultant basis. The worker may choose to remain involved with the group as a member or move on to another project. The gay or lesbian worker may decide to remain in various leadership roles at the same time they are purposefully enabling new leaders.

Groups that initially organize for leisure purposes frequently become interested in broader community needs and either expand their focus or some members create new groups or organizations to address other concerns. The social experience, support, and comradery received through leisure activity builds strength and self-esteem which may lead to efforts that focus on enrichment for the whole community. Workers should never minimize the importance of opportunities for social gatherings. Organizational work is difficult without the benefit of successful social interactional experiences.

Establishing a "Phone Help Line"

The development and maintenance of a phone help line may be an example of a further service which grows out of leisure or social organizing. Help lines can be an information and referral service as well as a way of making initial contact with the population. Workers may find that their agencies or programs can even contribute the use of space and phone already in existence. In this way no extra staff or money is necessary except the worker's time to develop procedures and train volunteers. This may sound like a simple process but it frequently takes a number of months for organization and implementation.

The social worker, together with a few volunteers can develop goals and set limits on what a phone service can do by starting in a small way. Objectives of having someone to talk to and making referrals are a reasonable beginning.

The volunteer personnel will need to be trained in the following areas:
- basic helping skills
- how to respond to crank calls
- active listening
- the professional rules of conduct e.g. no dates ever made with callers, do not give location of phone service (could lead to abusive behavior by homophobic caller).
- how to select appropriate referral source
- laws that could create problems. (For example, painful as it is, personnel may not want to extend service to adolescents since this could in some locations be interpreted as contributing to the delinquency of a minor.*)

Other tasks this small planning body would need to consider are:
- establishing hours— begin slowly (maybe three nights a week)
- scheduling hours and volunteers
- developing referral files: legal, recreational, counseling, medical, social welfare, religious
- establishing relationships with other helping agencies. This helps establish credibility.
- scheduling regular phone personnel meeting for further training and discussion of problem and issues.

Such a service could well begin in a social service agency. As it grows and becomes more secure it could expand, move to another location and extend its hours. Some groups have found it beneficial to purchase a machine which will allow the volunteers to transfer calls to their home phones. This is more convenient for busy people, plus it is less expensive than having to rent a space for the phone. The structure for

---

*In most locations, offering referrals to professional services for any age person is perfectly acceptable. However, in other locations for self-identified gay or lesbian adults just to talk with minor can be open to wide interpretation.

the service could remain rather loose or could be formalized with by-laws, a board and officers.

Throughout the developmental process, the worker would be training volunteers to take over leadership roles.

Organizing for Community Education and Advocacy

Community education is an area in which the social worker, regardless of sexual orientation, can be involved as an organizer and advocate. One problem that continues to prevent gay and lesbian people from realizing their full potential as citizens is their exclusion from mainstream public life. Major rationalizations for this exclusion are the myths and half-truths which have been promoted by many religious establishments. These myths have now proliferated into all social institutions and are manifested in homophobia and heterosexism. Efforts to eradicate this social problem and reeducate the populace have been taken by gay and lesbian individuals, groups, and organizations. Valuable contributions in this area have also been made by non-gay people.

The process of organizing for the purpose of community education can have many beneficial effects. Gay and lesbian people build informal supports through the people they meet and work with on such projects. They also learn more about their own responses to socially oppressive forces, including the impact it has had on them individually and collectively. They learn valuable skills in interacting with various segments of the larger community. A new sense of pride may also develop because of new learning and realizations or a newly developed confidence. Direct participation in the education efforts can also lead to an enhancement of self esteem and self image.

The social worker may recognize the need for community education simply because of daily interaction with other people. It might be brought to light by a single incident in a community or by a series of incidents that result from an obvious lack of knowledge. If gay and lesbian oriented resources exist in a community, a worker can help such organizations add community education efforts to their services. If no resources exist, the worker may again begin with a small planning group - which may or may not be all gay and lesbian people - and move in snowball fashion to a larger planning body. This body would have to decide what basic information seems to be lacking within a population they wish to encounter, what information needs to be presented, the method of delivery, how to prepare themselves to deliver information, publicizing the service, and an organizational framework for the new action system.

A number of organizations have developed what they call speakers bureaus - a cadre of people who can be called upon to go to classrooms, club meetings, churches and other organizations and speak about the experience of being a gay or lesbian person. The information covered is usually rather loosely structured with plenty of time left for questions and answers. These speakers are usually encouraged to share their own personal stories of coming-out, familial experiences, personal life style issues, and social and civil problems encountered. To insure a diversity in perspective, a panel can be used for these engagements. The social workers can assist in assessing the prospective audience and developing strategies that best communicate with that group. Non-gay workers can also serve on these panels and share their perspectives of obstacles faced by lesbian women and gay men. They can also serve as resources in researching and locating information and material aides for better presentations - i.e. films, video, slides and pamphlets. (Commission on Gay/Lesbian Issues of the Council on Social Work Education, 1984; Task Force on Gay and Lesbian Issues, 1983).

A group or organization interested in community education could also present workshops and seminars covering various topics. The gay and lesbian community may be well served with workshops on legal issues, e.g., how to handle job discrimination, custody situations, wills and legal agreements etc. The whole community, regardless of sexual orientation, can certainly use a series of seminars on AIDS and AIDS related issues. Social workers could be especially useful in locating infectious disease specialists, STD personnel, mental health specialists, or could conduct workshops themselves if they have the needed expertise. Workshops on gay and lesbian parenthood could lead to the development of new organizations— e.g. Dykes and Tykes or Gay Fathers.

Workshops and seminars may also give an opportunity to go into more detail with certain groups in the larger community. For example:

- Social service agencies may need assistance in how to better provide services to this special population.
- Children's services need help in understanding and working with gay youngsters.
- Police departments need assistance in seeing that the gay and lesbian community is diverse in membership as well as knowing some of the problems encountered by gay and lesbian people in so far as law enforcement is concerned.
- Medical professionals need help in how to approach subject matter that is important in understanding the gay and lesbian person as a whole person.
- Teachers and education personnel need help in reviewing education material and its impact on gay and lesbian students.
- Ministers and religious leaders need help in knowing how to effectively address spiritual issues.
- Media resources need help in assessing their approaches to coverage of gay and lesbian events as well as ways they perpetuate myths and half truths.

One of the basic educational and communication tools for any grass roots effort is the newsletter. Local lesbian and/or gay newsletters can be a method of informing the gay and lesbian community of events, news stories, and meetings as well as an instrument of support and pride. These newsletters can also contain fiction, poetry and art work. Some of the better local lesbian and/or gay newsletters are published on a regular basis, professionally printed, supported by advertisements, contain a detailed calendar of events, and use a variety of communication styles. They did not start out that way. The beginning newsletter may be one page of announcements which is reproduced on a mimeograph machine. A worker can be helpful to a group which wishes to begin a newsletter by helping to: obtain copies of similar newsletters; locate printing sources; donating work space; develop policies concerning publishing material; develop distribution procedures (mailing list, drop offs, hand outs); and locate funding sources.

Some groups have found the use of art forms to be very effective in educational efforts. Certainly the use of video is an example. Groups can produce their own educational tapes to help with speakers bureau engagements or workshop presentations. A simple interview format could allow audience exposure to a wide variety of gay and lesbian life styles. The use of scripts and planned scenarios could also be used. Music and dance are also charismatic methods of getting information across to particular audiences. There is a large body of lesbian music available, performed by some of the nation's most talented musicians - Holly Near, Chris Williamson, Marge Adams, Meg Christian, and Sweet Honey and the Rock to name a few. Much of this music can be used to set an atmosphere for verbal presentations and discussions. There are also a few commercial films that may be useful with carefully selected audiences. The Commission on Gay/Lesbian Issues of the Council on Social Work Education (1984) has published an annotated filmography which is a useful starting point to explore this medium.

Community education efforts may also include the use of public and private media:

- Public access channels in some communities give groups or organizations an opportunity to present entertainment and educational programs.

- Guest columnists in local newspapers are a popular means of addressing specific concerns. (This is not the best place to address broad or vague issues.)
- Developing working relationships with feature writers may be a way of getting newspaper coverage of events as well as a series of articles concerning gay and/or lesbian issues.
- Press conferences can be helpful if used sparingly. Press conferences, because of limited time and no control over editing the material, must be very focused and short.
- Press releases or public service announcements can be helpful in publicizing events, meetings, and new developments of an earlier news item.

The social worker who is assisting a group or organization interested in community education needs to realize that many local communities will have gay and/or lesbian people who have expertise as writers, speakers, musicians, artists, dancers, actors, videographers, photographers, and a host of other vital specialties. Locating these people and persuading them to be involved calls for workers to use all of their social work foundation skills.

In all of these community education efforts non-gay/lesbian social workers can be valuable by being active participants. In some areas, particularly where heavy resistance may be expected, the non-gay/lesbian worker may mediate with the potential audiences. This would be true in cases where it is clear gay and lesbian people have little credibility.

Organizational Roles for "Closeted" Individuals

Particularly in small communities, workers will need to realize that some people have a lot to lose by being involved with any gay and/or lesbian organization effort. However, this does not mean that they do not want to contribute to such an effort. It seems particularly easy for some workers to forget the pain and stress experienced by the gay or lesbian person who feels, for whatever reason, they can not be open. These people can make valuable contributions to any organizational effort. There are always behind the scenes tasks such as stuffing envelopes, doing research, writing by-laws, phoning, drawing charts, developing videos, child care, baking, or a thousand other important nitty-gritty efforts which these individuals may gladly perform. Finding, encouraging and using people's talents are tasks for social workers.

Some people who can do nothing more than donate money or other material resources will gladly do that if their contribution is recognized and encouraged. In some communities, workers will find that there may be a rather strong network of "closeted" people who can risk interactions on a network level but not on any public level. The author has seen these networks used as very successful fund raising mechanisms for groups or organizations who are more visible.

Everyone in the gay and lesbian community can play important roles in local organizational efforts. The development of elitist attitudes within gay and lesbian groups is possible when the group forgets the larger picture of things. Professional social workers can be valuable if they assist groups in gaining and maintaining mutual respect for varied abilities. Non-gay and lesbian people can be helpful in promoting a real sense of interdependence and appreciation for diversity. They may also be of measurable assistance as initial contact persons in arenas where open gay and/or lesbian people would be rejected.

Summary

To be effective in local community organizational efforts with lesbian women and gay men, it is imperative that social workers have a good understanding of social oppression and its impact, individually and collectively, on gay and lesbian people. They must also have skills in working with different size systems - individuals, couples, families, groups, networks, and organizations. All traditional social work methods are effective with this group when applied with an appropriate knowledge base.

Any of the groups or organizations mentioned in this chapter may choose, when the time, resources and motivation are present, to expand their focus or formalize their structure. The author has seen a gay men's softball team become the core of a new political organization and a group move from a muddled focus of attempting to represent a whole community of gay and lesbian people on every possible front to a formalized community service program with clearly established goals and objectives.

Looking across the United States, social workers can see that local organizational efforts by and for lesbian women and gay men have mushroomed and have a broad scope of intent. The author lives in a medium size Southern city which has gay and lesbian groups and organizations which are by nature of purpose political, community service, arts and entertainment, recreational, religious, business, and social service. All of these have sprouted over the past ten years. One of these organizations has moved, almost metaphorically, from a small group which stored its materials and records in a member's closet to an incorporated non-profit organization with an office in a major downtown complex, complete with filing cabinets and a budget consisting of money raised locally as well as grants from foundations. All of this occurred over ten years of ups and downs, disappointments and successes, internal struggles and external pressures.

It is to the credit of the profession that many social workers, despite inconsistent education and training, have been in the forefront of this growth. The profession still has far to go to honor its commitment to socially oppressed and disenfranchised groups, particularly lesbian women and gay men. This commitment can be advanced when all programs and schools of social work incorporate information and skills training that is consistent with social work values, traditions, and espoused accreditation standards.

References

Altman, D.(1971). *Homosexuality: Oppression and Liberation*. Outerbridge: Dutton.

Bell, A. P. and Weinberg, M. S.(1978). *Homosexualities: A Study of Diversity Among Men and Women*. New York: Simon and Schuster.

Commission on Gay/Lesbian Issues in Social Work Education (1984). *Annotated Filmography of Selected Films with Lesbian/Gay Content*. Washington, D.C.: Council on Social Work Education.

Cooper, S. (1974). A Look at the Effects of Racism on Clinical Work. In J. Goodman (ed.), *Dynamics of Racism in Social Work*. New York: National Association of Social Workers.

Harry, J. and Devall, W. B. (1978). *The Social Organization of Gay Males*. New York: Praeger Publishers.

Hunter, F. (1952). *Community Power Structure*. Chapel Hill, North Carolina: University of North Carolina Press.

Jay, K. and Young, A. (1977). *The Gay Report*. New York: Summit Books.

Kramer, R. M. and Specht, H. (1983). *Readings in Community Organization Practice* (3rd ed.). Englewood Cliffs, New Jersey: Prentice-Hall, Inc.

Levine, M. P. (ed.) (1979). *Gay Men: The Sociology of Male Homosexuality*. New York: Harper and Row.

Martin, D. and Lyon, P. (1972). *Lesbian/Woman*. San Francisco: Glide Publications.

Pleck, J. H. and Sawyer, J. (eds.) (1974). *Men and Masculinity*. Englewood Cliffs, New Jersey: Prentice-Hall, Inc..

Ross, M. (1955). *Community Organization Theory and Principles*. New York: Harper & Row.

Rothman, J. (1971). Three Models of Community Organization Practice. In F. M. Cox, J. Erlich, J. Rothman, J. Thropman (eds.), *Strategies of Community Organization*. Itasca, Illinois: Peacock Publishers.

Schwartz, W. and Zalba, S. R. (eds.) (1971). *The Practice of Group Work*. New York: Columbia University Press.

Task Force on Lesbian and Gay Issues (1983). An Annotated Bibliography of Lesbian and Gay Readings: 1st Edition. New York: Council on Social Work Education.

Towle, C. (1965). *Common Human Needs*. New York: National Association of Social Workers.

Warren, R. L. (1978). *The Community in America* (3rd ed.). Chicago: Rand McNally.

Wolf, D. G. (1979). *The Lesbian Community*. Berkley: University of California Press.

PART IV

SOCIAL SERVICES AND POLICIES

Introduction

In Chapter 11, Pierce identifies the interrelationship between policy, resources, and service. The customary links among legislative policy, agency procedures, and service delivery are included. However, the author has expanded this view to include personal policies, policies of small groups, organizational policies, social policies, and policies of social welfare institutions. He then proceeds to demonstrate the impact of each of these on access to and implementation of services which enhance the lives of lesbian women and gay men, as well as illustrating the gaps in policies of concern to this population. Homophobia at each level of policy determination is exemplified, particularly in reference to resource allocation and utilization. Throughout his work, Pierce uses a systems approach, providing the reader with alternative avenues for action. The need for attention to formulated social work policies as prescribed in the Code of Ethics and other documents is specified with suggestions for social action.

Chapter 12 offers an analysis of current developments in services to lesbian women and gay men. Pierce provides a perspective on the development of self help organizations to meet needs not provided by traditional resources. He then proceeds to demonstrate the process by which services become part of the "mainstream" of professional service organizations. Examples of both types of resources are detailed, concluding with ideas for community development of needed social welfare services.

11

Policies of Concern for Practice With Lesbian Women and Gay Men

Dean Pierce, Ph.D.

Introduction

One way to identify policies of concern for practitioners who work with lesbians and gay men is to do so from the perspective of direct practice, the clientele served, and the systems that provide resources for a social worker's practice. In this approach, policies of concern become somewhat broader than and even different from those contained in the institution of social welfare. They are, however, much more specific than policies contained in an all-encompassing definition of social policy. The number of social entities or units that could potentially serve as sources of policies for social workers is quite extensive. In any given practice situation, professional purpose, the resource system or systems being used, and the nature of the client can be used to pinpoint policies of concern. This approach identifies potentially important policy areas for the worker's attention, provides a way to focus them in a given practice situation, and establishes an attitude for the worker to use in practice.

The threefold professional purpose includes enhancing the problem-solving, coping, and developmental capacities of people; linking people with systems that provide them with resources, services, and opportunities; and promoting the effective and humane operation of the systems that provide people with resources and services. Each has relevance to particular aspects of policy used in practice. Focusing on the enhancement of people's capacities includes policies that do the following:

- Recognize and support cultural and lifestyle differences
- Promote natural helping and support networks
- Provide support to persons who find themselves in transitional situations
- Teach or inform others about new information and skills
- Further people's involvement in decision-making and developmental opportunities
- Encourage self-help activities

Policies that oppose such enhancement should also be of concern, since they make it more difficult for social workers to help people attain their life goals.

Policies covering a system's available resources, services, and opportunities have received much more attention than those concerned with the enhancement of people. This second area involves many of the polices of the social welfare institution. However, policy also governs opportunities and access to resources, and this must also be a concern of social workers in each resource system. Services that are inaccessible, or that promote dependency rather than enable growth and decision-making, are not fully supportive of the purposes of social work. Therefore, social workers need to understand policies in the third area of professional purpose which: affect access to and guide procedures for obtaining information about a system's operation; describe an agency's or organization's procedures, communication channels, professional roles, and operating rules; and determine fund raising and expenditures. Being concerned with what services are available as well as how they are made available to people flows from the second and third part of the three-fold professional purpose mentioned above.

Many would define policy as those abstract guidelines made at the highest level of society and would dismiss other policy as being insignificant. Such abstractions are the policy concerns of scholars. For the practitioner, policies of more immediate concern cover a wider range and deal with policy or procedures that implement policy made at the highest level of society. For line workers, the implementation role is critical to practice as is the use of policy made in smaller units of society. With the broadening perspective of professional purposes in mind, an examination of resource systems provides the range of places in which policies of interest must be sought out and understood by the worker. These resource systems are those that the line worker should routinely draw upon in meeting client need. Some systems may lack specific policies dealing with one of the three parts of professional purpose. In others, policies of one type may be less clearly developed than those of other types. For some systems, policies have been worked out and analyzed in great detail. For others, however, the place of policy has not been conceptualized as an important part of their operation. Using professional purpose and the resource systems as the basis of a policy definition helps redirect the nature of policy concerns from those of scholars to those of workers.

Resources facilitate interactions between people and social institutions. They support people who need help in utilizing societal institutions, including family, religion, politics, the economy and market, or even social welfare. Resources that are basic to human life, those that help people develop problem-solving skills, and those that enhance human dignity are but a few of many types that meet human needs. Social workers are specialized helpers who identify resources and link people to them, as well as monitor and modify the procedures for allocating resources. Resources, then, are the many kinds of assets or other strengths that are or should be available to people to help them negotiate their social environment.

Baer (1979, 1981) identifies the following as systems of resources:

- the social worker
- colleagues and other helping professionals
- the client system
- the profession of social work
- the organization or agency setting
- the local community
- society at large
- the social welfare institution

Our discussion will begin with systems focusing on individual characteristics as the basis of that system's resources and policies, and proceed to an examination of larger units. In grouping the eight systems according to size and the nature of policy formulation process, five clusters emerge:

I.   Personal Policies
         social worker
         colleagues
         (individual) client systems
II.   Policies of Small Groups
         (family or small formed groups as) client
           systems
         (small formed groups as part of a) local
         community
III. Organizational Policies
         professional associations
         social service agencies
IV.   Social Policies
         (government of) local community
         society at large
V.   Policies of the Institution of Social welfare

Sorting out the resource systems as entities unto themselves helps focus attention on the details of their policies and policy formation processes. It calls for a different point of departure in defining the social welfare institution.

By breaking down the larger system into its major social work related parts, and in identifying policy within the small units, this approach becomes helpful in managing the scope, specificity, and complexity of the entire range of policies of concern to social workers.

Individuals, whether they are social workers, their colleagues, or their clients, possess policy that directs their actions and affects the utilization of resources in the systems of which they are a part or with which they work. An individual's policy results from the interaction among that person's values, experiences, and knowledge. That policy is part of the individual's guide to deciding and acting. It is usually thought that knowledge is less used than values and personal experiences in the formulation of personal policies.

On the other hand, for decision makers in agencies and institutions, the role of values and knowledge in setting policy is frequently discussed in the social work literature. In other words, it is commonly believed that individuals in agency settings use values and knowledge to set policies for agencies, but that they are less likely to set personal policy this way. What is being suggested is that a similar, somewhat less formal process is employed by individuals to set their own personal policy. This personal policy in turn affects resource allocation in systems for which an individual and the individual's professional or personal characteristics serve as the primary base of resources: the resource categories of social worker, colleague, and (individual) client systems.

Personal Policies

The social worker is one primary resource available to the client. The resources that workers can provide are based on professional knowledge, values, and skills they possess. Some of the available resources include support for self-determination by and social justice for all clients; problem solving skills, including communication, problem identification, involving and planning with others, assessment, carrying out plans, and evaluating results; knowledge of resources, policies, and human behavior; access to other needed resources; and collaboration with members of related helping professional groups.

Ideally, the professional would make all these resources available to clients. The worker's personal policy regarding the allocation of these resources modifies their availability and usefulness to the client. The worker's individual limitations and interests, including level of competency, interact to affect the client's full receipt of resources from social workers. The significance of such worker policy and its impact on professional practice either as a positive or a negative influence, has received scant attention in the literature.

Consider the following examples:

I.   Personal Policies of Social Workers:
    a. Refusal to share access to certain agency or related system resources
    b. Work a "fifty minute hour" in an agency
    c. Not involve certain clients, such as lesbians/gays, in their practice
    d. Use certain theories of human behavior, such as psychoanalytic perspectives on sexuality
    e. Consistent selection of certain kinds of interventions, to the exclusion of others, in their practice
    f. Job security above all other considerations, to the point that agency guidelines regarding practice and resources never questioned

II.   Personal Policies of Social Work Colleagues
    a. Medical doctors who refuse to refer clients to social workers
    b. Administrators who establish new discharge planning units in hospitals to the exclusion of social work input
    c. Psychiatrists who assign social workers only certain "therapy" duties

        d. Health agency director who includes the BSW practitioner as a "professional" worker along with MSW staff

III.   Personal Policies of Individual Client Systems

        a. To be free of parental influence

        b. Refusal to leave the neighborhood in order to seek needed resources.

Whether or not professional values support dignity and development, and regardless of the existence of a pro-lesbian/gay policy within the NASW, a worker with a personal policy not to serve lesbian women and gay men would not make available to clients all the resources they potentially could expect to receive. Also, because the social worker possesses the invaluable resource of access to other resource systems, worker policy not only directly affects the allocation of or linkage to available resources with clients in the worker's own system, but indirectly affects linkage with resources in other systems. Moreover, the purposes of social work activity extend beyond linkage and people enhancement tasks to those that promote system effectiveness. As a result, client linkage with other resource systems and worker change efforts in them would be affected. Worker policy could thereby either serve to block the availability of resources or lead to the expansion of available resources.

Other types of examples readily come to mind. A worker with a personal policy that would support a feminist orientation would be more likely to enhance the developmental and coping skills of women clients. Or, if the worker's policy supports her or his job security above all other concerns, he or she will probably never oppose agency policy or procedures. As a result, client concerns about the effective and humane operation of related resource systems would be unattended. On the other hand, a worker with a commitment to social change would be sensitive to issues in the functioning of self, colleagues, agency, and social welfare systems and would act to alter and improve the functioning of all these resource categories. A worker who uses only certain stock interventions or one without a policy of professional development would deny their clients the fullest range of social work practice knowledge and skills, one of the critical resources of workers. Indeed, of primary importance would be the establishment of a worker's personal policy that calls for lifelong self-development as a professional. This would assure clients' access to the best available resources.

Similar in effect is the role of personal policy held by a social worker's colleagues and other helping professionals. Although overlooked by most scholars, such policy directly affects the availability of resources to social work clients and is thereby of primary concern to the social work practitioner. The personal policy of these professionals affects the resources available in this resource system. As a system it offers resources to clients that are similar in nature to those found in the social worker resource category. These include the expertness, knowledge and ethical standards of allied professionals such as physicians, nurses, rehabilitation workers, mental health workers, child care personnel, ministers, social agency administrators, and lawyers.

For example, the policy of social work colleagues concerning access to and the status of related professionals is crucial to resource allocation. Physicians or other professionals who have a personal policy against including social workers in the mental health arena effectively block the access of social work clients to resources contained therein. The client of a social worker gains access to resources in a colleague's system through the intervention and connections of the worker. The crucial role of the social worker in client access to resources, of course, is evident for many resource systems. When the social worker's access is blocked by the personal policy of another helping professional, social work clientele lose access to resources as well.

With colleagues, the impact of personal policy plays out in terms of teamwork. The primary resources available in the social worker and colleague resource systems are those to be derived from the professional personnel themselves and from their interaction. This interaction is carried out according to some conception of teamwork, whether of a formal or informal nature. The social worker serves both as a bridge between professionals on the team and also as the team's connection to the client's environment. The social worker has responsibility to provide other team members with information about clients for professional uses. If the personal policy of a colleague excludes or diminishes social work access and expertness in the team, then clients receive considerably reduced professional resources.

In addition to non-social work colleagues, other social workers have personal policies that affect the availability of resources to one's own clients. The personal policy of other social workers in such areas as enabling clients to solve their own problems, making service delivery structures more accessible and effective, and cooperating with other social workers will affect not only their own clients, but also those of other social workers with whom they interact. Because service delivery structures operate as systems, one part, including individual people, affects other parts. For this reason, social workers need to analyze and influence the personal policies of colleagues within and outside social work.

For the individual client as a resource system, the role of personal policy has been even less explored than the personal policies of social workers and social work colleagues. This is so partly because many workers seldom consider the client system as a place to find resources. This shortcoming, when connected with the belief that individuals are not a source of policy, makes it quite unlikely that the policy of individual clients will be considered. When groups or organizations are client systems, policy has more frequently been taken into account. However, the line social worker usually deals with individual clients or with small groups: the family, small formed groups, or segments of community groups. Direct service professionals are less likely to work with organizations. As a result, line workers have not been encouraged to see the people and small groups with whom they work as having their own policy.

Regardless of the size of a client system, it should be considered as a resource and, as such, examined for its policy implications. If the client is an individual, personal policy

would determine how the resources under control are allo-
cated, or how other actors in the client's resource system
influence the available resources. An individual client's
resources are the personal characteristics, external connections, and access to formal or informal help in her/his
environment that enable clients to meet the need for help.
The worker, in the assessment process, must focus on client
resources, including coping skills, motivations, support
systems, cultural and social factors, and family or friend
relationships.

Policies of Small Groups

Small groups differ somewhat from individuals in their
policy setting mechanisms, but are similar in the kind of
resources they control and in the implications for social work
practice. Small groups as client systems may include families, specially formed groups such as therapy groups or self-
help groups, and certain elements of the local community. If
the local community is defined as a social, cultural, ethnic,
religious, or neighborhood community, the interaction of the
group itself is a resource to the worker.

The worker would view the characteristics of group
members, as for any individuals, as a resource for use in
meeting needs. Moreover, characteristics of the group itself
are important, such as group support, communication
patterns, problem solving approaches, and access to other
resources. Group policy related to the allocation of such
resources must also be considered when working with its
membership.

Organizational Policies

The resources available to clients from within the resource system of the profession of social work are those
available to the social worker as a member of the profession,
especially as a member of professional associations or organizations. Professional organizations provide members
with access to specialized knowledge and skills through

publications, journals, workshops, meetings, and educational travel. Formal and informal contact with or access to other members of the profession is facilitated during meetings, through committee work, and in the form of professional directories. Professional organizations not only supply workers with a code of ethics, but also with legal and other support structures to assure its application and practice. A variety of job-related services are provided to members, such as life, disability, and malpractice insurance. Most importantly, the professional organization promotes the interest of its members and of the entire profession in a variety of ways: finding, developing, and protecting professional employment; licensing and other standard-setting measures; lobbying policy influencing activities in other resource systems; and the setting of organizational policy designed to support the interests of social work clients.

The resources available to the client from this system are provided somewhat indirectly. They basically serve to protect, enhance, or make more effective the work of social work professionals themselves. Nonetheless, a worker's understanding and use of these resources is critical to the client's best interests. Utilization of and involvement in the policy-setting processes that guide the allocation of the organization's resources are likewise crucial to the line worker's clientele. These policies determine how different categories of professionals (BSW or MSW or other) are supported and protected by the organization. The lobbying and licensing stances of professional associations similarly have impact on what resources, transmitted through which workers, are available to clients. The nature of policy-affecting opportunities for professional development and related programs also ultimately affects clients.

For example, if a division of the NASW, a major professional association, establishes a policy to use part of its annual resources to upgrade worker salaries, how does this policy translate as a resource to clients? If a national social work organization sets a policy to support the civil rights of lesbian women and gay men, what impact might this policy have on the profession in terms of support from allied groups? If the policy at the chapter level of the NASW is to lobby against budget cuts rather than lobby in support of the so-called New Federalism, what does this allocation of organizational resources mean for clients?

Similar in policy-setting mechanisms, but dissimilar in the nature of available resources, is the agency where the social worker practices. Such agencies are similar to other organizations in their use of policy-setting mechanisms, both formal and informal. However, they are dissimilar in that they make a range of resources directly available to social work clients. What they offer are tangible resources for the client, such as services and programs to meet financial, emotional, health or other needs. They also provide intangible resources to help clients, such as access to other agencies and other professionals, the stability and sanction of a position in an accepted community agency that is accorded the social worker employed there, and a structure for social workers to use in developing resources that the client may need.

Social workers need to be thoroughly familiar with how their agencies set policy to allocate resources directly to clients and how they establish guidelines and procedures that affect the worker's practice. The first deals with tangible resources, services and opportunities made available to the client by the agency. The second addresses the way the agency manages worker access to clients and the kinds of practice strategies workers are expected to use. When regulations impede service delivery, the worker may have to try to make the agency's delivery of services more effective and humane.

Social Policies

This grouping of policies and related resource systems focuses on the public (or governmental) development of policy in legislative or other related bodies and in large-scale private welfare funding groups. Aspects of two resource systems, the local community and society-at-large, exemplify such policy making. The local community, as noted above, refers to more than just local government and its legislative processes. Communities also have geographical, cultural, social and religious boundaries. If the boundaries are formal geographical ones, such as a town or city or neighborhood, a formal or legal policy making process may exist. If the community is a cultural, social, ethnic, or religious one, the policy-setting mechanism may be more informal. In this case, the nature of its policy is likely to be similar to that of the small group, such as a family or a specially formed group or organization.

The geographic boundaries of the local community often encompass another policy making body, such as a United Way. This entity is responsible for allocating the private funding resources of the community. The local government deals with the area's policy for its economic and social resources and opportunities.

These governmental units of the local community share with society-at-large a legal, political, and economic policy-setting mechanism and related funding structure. Social policies are the broad social guidelines that determine who qualifies for society's allocation benefits. For the social worker, the basic resource in society-at-large, as in the local community, is the "social" policies they develop.

Resources utilized in society-at-large include elements of the legislative process: elected bodies, political parties, lobbying or interest groups; a range of professional, educational, and other informational groups that aim to influence social policy; and printed sources of information that influence policy. In the sense used here, social policies that deal broadly with the allocation of an extensive range of resources occur at several levels, ranging from the local community to the largest national grouping. Resources are available to workers, directly or indirectly, which enable them to influence societal policy. These range from members of the decision-making bodies to the factors used by others to understand and influence the decision makers.

Generally speaking, this is the policy making realm of the so-called informed citizen, of political careerists, and of political activists. It is more removed from the direct service

worker than policy making in the other resource systems.
Although societal policies are more distant from the line
worker's world than are other resource systems, they nonetheless have an enormous impact on line workers and on
their clients. Consider the federal legislature's cutting of the
social service budget, or a local united funding group's
allocation of money to a new service. Workers must constantly view the resources of these systems as a critical
element in policy related practice activities.

Policies of the Social Welfare Institution

Volumes have been written about the general nature and
the details of the policies and resources of the social welfare
system. The resources available to the line worker from social
welfare are all of those beyond the worker's own professional
expertise, agency, and collegial and professional network.
The remaining resources of the social welfare system, of
course, are quite extensive in scope. Some examples would
include major medical programs such as Medicaid and
Medicare, retirement benefits such as social security, un-
employment funds, job training and development programs,
housing subsidies and programs, and civil rights legislation.

The broad objective of social welfare is to provide resources and mutual support to help people with needs they
have not met in other social institutions, such as the family
or the economy. The range of services, programs, and opportunities provided by social welfare covers financial, social,
health, or emotional needs. Programs, opportunities, and
services may focus on individuals, groups, or communities.
The structural characteristics and administrative sources of
the programs in the welfare system are also resources. The
policies of the social welfare institution emerge from statutes
and court decisions as applied by private and public bu-
reaucracies implementing regulations and programs.

It should not be overlooked that the various systems are
interdependent. They form a network or over-arching system
of resources, with gaps and overlaps. They have been considered separately to facilitate understanding their details, and

to help highlight differences in the nature of their policies and their policy-formulating processes. In the broadest sense, however, the social worker is part of a vast resource network including clients, local communities, as well as formal programs. It is composed of allied helping professionals, all of whom work in agency structures of some sort, most of whom relate to one another through professional associations, and for whom there exists the institution of public social and social welfare policy making bodies.

Policies Concerning Social Work With Lesbian Women and Gay Men: An Example

Examples will be drawn from each of the resource systems to illustrate policies a line worker might identify as potentially useful for practice with lesbian women and gay men. In an actual practice situation, the worker might be dealing with a specific person or with a client group focused on such issues. In that case, the need or problem would point the search for policies of concern in one or more specific directions. For purposes of the following illustration, think about a worker who, upon discovering a lack of resources for lesbians and gays in the family service agency where the worker is employed, has decided to make an assessment of policies that control resources related to the needs of these populations.

Such a person would consider his or her own personal policies as a worker that: relate to enhancing the problem-solving and coping capacities of lesbian women and gay men; would deal with the kinds of resources they need and should receive; and that govern their stance on making service delivery systems more effective and humane. The worker would also examine the personal client system itself, evaluate existing agency policy, and determine what policy her/his own professional association has in the area of homosexuality. Then she or he would analyze policy outside the agency that controls social welfare resources for lesbians and gays. In each resource system, the worker would focus on identifying policies that deal with the rights of lesbian women and gay men to develop more fully and to participate more readily in all areas relating to their lives. He or she would also explore policies that allocate specific resources needed by lesbians and gays to meet their needs and that guide the structures that deliver needed resources to them.

Any such listing of policies will not exhaust the possibilities. To compile such a list suggests the need to know where to locate details of policies of concern. Sources of knowledge about policies of concern exist in a variety of forms. A worker's self-assessment, feedback from colleagues, and data collection with clients would give information on personal policies. Written policy priorities and program plans of professional associations, and material on policy and procedures and annual plans from an agency offer insight into existing organizational policy. Proposed and existing ordinances and legislation, funding plans, and interest group documents provide leads for social policy. For the social welfare institution, bureaucratic regulations, published program guides, and service directories yield policy detail.

One example of such a policy inventory by a social worker might look like the following. First, the worker might have a policy that views individual development and change as stemming from client self-motivation. In this case, such a personal worker policy would slow or cancel the allocation of worker resources until the client either actively sought help or showed initiative. Our hypothetical worker might have a policy that relies on family resources. This personal policy is, of course, in conflict with the needs of many lesbian women and gay men and would profoundly affect working with them. Couple those two personal policies with our imaginary worker's other policy orientation that supports the agency status quo. Lesbians and gays coming to the supposed agency would undoubtedly fail to receive needed access to additional resources from the social worker.

The potential personal policies of colleagues would be those of all workers in health, mental health, employment programs, public social services and supportive services. Our worker might have discovered that colleagues use only psychoanalytic perspectives in assessing problems and that the outreach unit will not enter certain areas, including one known as containing a large lesbian and gay population.

In investigating professional social work associations in which the worker is involved, national NASW and the worker's chapter have taken pro-lesbian and gay policy stances. The NASW adopted a policy statement in 1977. It views discrimination as inimical to the mental health of lesbian women and gay men and of all members of society. Social workers are called upon to create system change and lobby for legislation to end unequal services to and treatment of lesbians and gays and to create effective services. The statement concludes that all should be encouraged to achieve their fullest potential within a lifestyle of their own choosing. NASW, nationally and within chapters, has established committees and task forces on lesbian and gay issues. These groups develop programs and work to implement and interpret NASW's policy position.

The worker's family service agency has a policy that its programs are made available to parents and/or their children. It does not define lesbian or gay couples as an alternative family type. This policy reinforces those of the outreach unit.

The local lesbian and gay communities, on the other hand, offer a variety of services. There is a lesbian and gay services center that offers a variety of educational, counseling, and support group programs to enhance the lives of lesbian women and gay men. In addition, it provides an informational hotline and free space to the community. It is directed by a trained professional who is lesbian identified and uses only lesbians and gays as volunteers and staff.

Although a local lesbian or gay community may provide numerous resources and have policies that are sensitive to lesbian and gay needs, this is not necessarily the case of the larger society. A few examples suffice. The court decision making illegal certain gay sexual activities, even when conducted in private, is a major anti-gay social policy. The failure of insurance companies to include lesbian and gay couples as a unit represents another failure. Some cities, however, have passed ordinances prohibiting discrimination against lesbian women and gay men in housing or employment.

As defined for our purposes, the institution of social welfare is devoid of policies to protect or service lesbians or gays.

The following table summarizes the policies discussed above. Blank spaces in the chart indicate that clear policies have not been developed or cannot be readily identified. Frequently, as the table indicates, policies that aim to develop people do *not* enhance lesbians and gays. Public systems do *not* provide resources. Most resources come from lesbian and gay communities themselves, often in the form of self help programs and services. Social work educators and students should ask themselves why this is the case. Moreover, they should attempt to complete a "policies of concern chart" covering the policies they and their area have developed to enhance lesbians and gays and to provide them with resources and rights.

POLICIES OF CONCERN FOR SOCIAL WORK WITH LESBIANS AND GAYS

Types of Resource Systems

Policy Designed To:	Social Worker	Colleagues	Lesbian or Gay Client	Profession of Social	Worker's Agency Work	Local Community	Society	Social Welfare
1. Enhance People	Policies that all clients need to demonstrate self-motivation toward change	Policy to use psycho-analytic theory in making client assessments	Policy to lead an openly gay lifestyle	Policy to to work to enhance opportunities and lifestyle freedom for lesbians and gay men		Counseling services and support groups in gay service center	Court decision excluding certain gay sexual practices as being legal, even if done in private	
2. Link Them With Resources	People should rely on family based resources		Policy to seek only emergency help from family			Hot-line providing information bout services to lesbians and gay men	Policy of no shared health or insurance benefits for same sex partners	
3. Deliver Services To Them	Status quo policy orientation regarding agency change	Refusal of outreach workers to enter well-known lesbian-gay		Policy to work to remove discriminating laws	Policy that services be offered only to parents and/or their children	Operating procedures of lesbian-gay services center; staff must be lesbian or gay	Ordinances prohibiting discrimination in housing and employment	

References

Baer, Betty L (1979). "A Conceptual Model for the Organiza-
    tion of Content for the Educational Preparation for the
    Entry Level Social Worker." Unpublished doctoral disser-
    tation, University of Pittsburgh.

Baer, Betty L. (1981). "A Conceptualization of Generalist
    Practice." Westchester Social Work Education Consor-
    tium.

Baer, Betty L. and Ronald C. Federico (eds.) (1979). *Edu-
    cating the Baccalaureate Social Worker: A Curriculum
    Development Resource Guide*. Cambridge, Mass.:
    Ballinger.

Dolgoff, Ralph and Malvina Gordon (1981). Educating for
    policy making at the direct and local levels. *Journal of
    Education for Social Work*, 17(2):98,1-5.

Federico, Ronald C. (1980). *The Social Welfare Institution: An
    Introduction*. 3rd ed. Lexington, Mass.: D. C. Heath.

Pierce, Dean (1984). *Policy for the Social Work Practitioner*.
    Longman: White Plains, New York.

12

Lesbian and Gay Social Welfare Services

Dean Pierce, Ph.D.

Introduction

The discussion in Chapter 11 of the range of policies of concern to lesbians and gays draws a blank regarding the formal, public social welfare system. Although there are a few policies addressing the needs of lesbians and gays in the social welfare system, most of the programs appear to be based on resources from local lesbian and gay communities and the work of volunteers from these communities. There are signs that a possible trend is developing whereby the public will fund social welfare services for lesbians and gays.

Some authors have attempted to outline the *services of* lesbians and/or gays in the development of social welfare services. Jane Addams' work is a case in point. On the other hand, less attention has been paid to understanding public social welfare *services for* the development of lesbians and gays. It is in this area that last chapter's discussion drew a blank.

This chapter will offer an analysis of current developments in social welfare services for lesbians and gays. It will:

- offer a perspective to describe why social welfare services are provided to and created by lesbians and gays themselves and how this approach is changing,
- detail a few of the accomplishments of lesbians and gays in developing services for their communities,
- suggest a way in which teachers/learners can develop their own knowledge base in the area of lesbian and gay social welfare services.

From Self Help to Mainstreaming

Services, in the area of civil rights and social resources, have begun to emerge in the last decade. These developments, of course, are an outcome of the new lesbian/gay rights movements in this country. That movement began with protests and self-help efforts and has now been extended to the protection of public policy and the mainstreaming of social services for lesbians and gays.

Following and/or guided by the protests of the initial stage of the gay pride movement, some public social welfare programs in the area of civil rights protection have been developed by municipalities and states. In some cases, the struggle to create policies to protect the housing, employment, and privacy rights of lesbians and gays have extended for a decade or more and have been marked by many setbacks. National legislation is still pending and must be understood in relation to recent negative court decisions.

While efforts to protect the civil rights of lesbians and gays have moved into public arenas, parallel initiatives to provide social services to lesbians and gays still take place within the communities themselves. The lesbian and gay rights movement has led to the creation of a range of self help, grass roots organizations designed to meet a variety of needs and handle a number of common problems. The more "sophisticated" and mature are turning to public funding sources to supplement the resources provided by the local communities.

This movement has been spearheaded by large urban service centers, such as the one in Los Angeles, and by some of the AIDS organizations. The latter organizations, because of the relatively greater recognition by public funders for this problem, are more likely to be eligible for public funds. They are being "mainstreamed."

Mainstreaming, in this sense, refers to service organizations turning to the public for funding and support to create high caliber, professional services. The danger of mainstreaming is to lose the total gay orientation of services and the grass roots funding and volunteerism that have marked much of the alternative lesbian and gay health and social services structure (Vandervelden). The other side of mainstreaming, of course, is the implicit recognition by public policy makers and funders of the "normalcy" of the needs of lesbians and gay communities.

At this stage in the development of social welfare services for lesbians and gays many communities in this country are still in the grass roots stage and others are receiving public support. Some needs are covered only by grass roots activities, others by public sponsorship. How do social workers develop a current, comprehensive knowledge base about services to lesbians and gays? Some printed material is available and will be examined. In addition, a survey of programs in one community will be offered.

Sources of Information on Social Work/ Social Welfare and Lesbians and Gays

The available social work materials dealing with lesbian and gay issues are more likely to discuss the lifestyles and needs of lesbians and gays or how to work with them. For example, a 1984 edition of the *NASW Practice Digest* was devoted to articles discussing how to work with lesbians and gays in direct practice. Topics included the needs and concerns of the elderly, couples or partners, young lesbians and gays, and of people with AIDS. The common themes of discrimination, fear, isolation, and coming out were stressed in many of the articles. The articles included the practice of those in alternative as well as mainstream agencies. That many lesbians and gays will receive services from nonlesbians and non-gays highlighted the necessity of all social workers to understand and deal with homophobia.

Resources, either to help understand the lives of lesbians and gays or issues in working with them, have been provided in a few social work publications. One example is *Lesbian and Gay Issues: A Resource Manual for Social Workers*. In the appendix of this book are lists of resources such as directories, clearinghouses, and support groups. Special material on legal rights and organizations is included. In a section on resources related to special issues a number of social service organizations are listed. Topics include aging, alcoholism, drug abuse, disabilities, health, legal issues, and third world organizations. Examples of organizations include a center for the disabled in San Diego, counseling centers in Los Angeles and San Francisco, and programs for the gay aged in San Francisco and New York.

Examples From One Community

Our examination of the resource listing in Hidalgo, *et al.*, provides a lead to pursue in gaining a greater understanding of the social welfare services and programs provided for the development of lesbians and gays. Looking at the response made by one community and some of its programs can enrich our understanding and help answer the question regarding how much the services are coming under public support. It also provides a framework for learners to use in developing their own knowledge base regarding social welfare services to lesbians and gays.

A lesbian and gay services center has been established in New York City. It houses a wide range of social, recreational, legal, and social service programs. The building symbolizes the growth of one community's services. The New York City center represents the broadest usage of the notion of social welfare. Although not all of New York City's services to lesbians and gays are housed in this space, examples to be found there include:

- services to the elderly
- support groups
- recreational associations
- political organizations
- social groups
- counseling
- ethnic oriented organizations
- hot lines
- physically challenged
- music
- sports
- religion
- sexual minorities
- archives

Let's consider two New York City organizations— one from this list, SAGE (Senior Action in a Gay Environment); and another that exemplifies "mainstreaming" GMHC (Gay Men's Health Crisis).

SAGE is a large agency that provides comprehensive services in New York City and one that also has a strong social services component. It uses about 250 volunteers in a number of ways which include a friendly visiting program for the homebound, as office workers, to organize and conduct monthly social events, as hosts in a drop in center, to help record reminiscences for an oral history group, and as speakers in the larger community. Social services, under the coordination of a social worker, offer a range of support, outreach, and resource programs.

The agency operates with a small staff of an executive director, social services coordinator, coordinator of public education, volunteer support coordinator, and office and support staff. Each coordinator also uses and supervises volunteers (Cinnetar, 1987).

Special workshops on topics as varied as health, exercise, writing, and assertiveness training are provided. Weekly rap groups are sponsored and SAGE arranges a number of special events, dances, parties, trips, and other entertainments. Legal, nutrition, and health clinics are also scheduled. SAGE produces a number of newsletters and "contact" publications, aimed at providing information to select groups about their special needs.

GMHC is a large agency and one that exemplifies a great degree of mainstreaming. Overtime GMHC has received government funds from: New York State's Department of Health, New York City's Human Resources Administration and Department of Mental Health; and the federal Centers for Disease Control and Public Health Service. More than one-third of the agency's funding has come from non-grass roots fund raising. This, of course, offers strong indications of mainstreaming. GMHC provides a comprehensive range of services with this money. Legal services, financial advisement, support groups, recreation, and crisis intervention services are supplemented by a range of education, hotlines, prevention, research, outreach, and community awareness programs (Behrman).

Developing Knowledge About Lesbian and Gay Social Welfare Services

The discussion in this chapter indicates some of the approaches and types of social welfare programs and services to assist in the development of lesbians and gays and to help them with their social functioning. The discussion was not comprehensive but does point to ways to develop a sizeable knowledge base.

Two questions remain:

- why do services to enhance the lives of lesbians and gays and to deal with issues of primary concern to them come from their communities?
- how can social workers develop an accurate and in-depth knowledge base about social welfare services for lesbians and gays?

The answers to these questions have to be developed by social workers themselves.

The answer to the first, of course, can be answered through the worker's understanding of homophobia. That issue has been covered elsewhere in this book. Its impact on public support, or non-support, for lesbian and gay social welfare services should be obvious to those who recognize the destructive power of homophobia.

Workers also must develop their own knowledge base about social welfare services in their own geographic areas. The first thing to do is to identify local lesbian and gay leaders in politics, religion, and social services. This can be done by identifying and reading newsletters and other publications from the local lesbian and gay communities. Also, pursuing some of the suggestions identified by Burnham in Chapter 10 will facilitate this process. The second is to develop a comprehensive resource list of community programs and services designed to support and develop lesbians and gays, including therapy and counseling services, regulations to protect the civil rights of lesbians and gays, support groups, and programs to meet the needs of special groups. Only by proactive social work practice will the profession respond to the needs of lesbian and gay persons and communities.

References

Behrman, Lori (editor) (1987). *The Volunteer: The GMHC Newsletter*, 4 (2), entire issue.

Cinnater, Nan (editor) (1987). *SAGE—Monthly Calendar*, April.

Hidalgo, Hilda, Travis L. Peterson, and Natalie Jane Woodman (editors) (1985). *Lesbian and Gay Issues: A Resource Manual for Social Workers*. Silver Spring, Maryland: National Association of Social Workers.

Lopez, Diego and George S. Getzel (1984). "Helping Gay AIDS Patients in Crisis." *Social Casework*, 65 (7): 387-94.

Lopez, Diego and George S. Getzel (1984). "Strategies for Volunteers Caring for Persons with AIDS." *Social Casework*, 68 (1): 47-53.

Sancier, B. (editor) (1984). "Working With Gay and Lesbian Clients." *Practice Digest*, 7 (1): entire issue.

Vandervelden, Mark (1987). "Gay Health Conference: Gays
    Call for Nationwide Civil Disobedience." *The Advocate*,
    April 28, p. 12.
White, E. John (1987). "How GMHC Spends Its Money." *New
    York Native*, March 2, p. 10.

PART V

RESEARCH

Introduction

Brooks introduces this section with abuses which contribute to reluctance in engaging in research and/or creating truly viable studies of lesbian and gay populations. A primary factor in the dearth of meaningful gay research has been what the author identifies as emphasis on "heterosexually defined research." Brooks discusses the effects of "a nonconscious ideology in research about gay people" and suggests topics or areas for study by helping professionals. Included in the part of the article addressing problems and issues are: critiques of problem selection and formulation (with particular attention to stereotypical assumptions and heterosexist attention to etiology); bias in interpretation and results (citing over-generalization from non-representative results); and "majority versus minority frames of reference." The breadth of topics for possible future research provided by Brooks can assist the educator, practioner, and student in addressing needed areas of study related to lesbian women and gay men.

Berger, in Chapter 15, demonstrates how rigorous research endeavors can contribute to our knowledge. By addressing the populations of older gay men, the author provides the reader with data that, more often than not, refutes the stereotypes related to this group. Particular areas covered include: loneliness and isolation; lovers and friends;

participation in the gay community; feelings about aging; over-all adjustment; sexuality; and attitudes about being closeted. As Berger points out, most of the data were collected prior to the AIDS epidemic. He also joins all of the authors in this book (and many others who deal with lesbian and gay issues from a non-homophobic perspective) in pointing out the degree to which institutionalized homophobia creates repressive forces. However, he then identifies the fact that concerns about sexual behaviors should not be an impediment to continued research. Indeed, he provides ideas for further study in just the one area of gay male aging, indicating that pursuit of such research may well have to come from within the gay community itself.

Tully's article complements Berger's by addressing lesbian aging. As in the previous chapter, review of the literature provides the reader with a picture of "what is known" to date and then proceeds to discuss "what is not known." Areas covered are comparable to research relative to gay males. However, as the author indicates, more needs to be learned than what has already been documented. She then expands on Brooks' chapter by citing research problems as they relate directly to the study of lesbian elders. Tully compares and contrasts the theoretical perspectives and research methodologies affecting gerontological study and studies related to older lesbian women. The identification of weaknesses and limitations expands upon the material presented by Brooks and Berger, thereby providing the reader with further challenges for learning and writing.

13

Research and the Gay Minority: Problems and Possibilities

Winn Kelly Brooks, Ph.D.

The purpose of teaching research in social work education is to prepare social workers for both the consumption and production of empirically-derived knowledge, which in turn is expected to contribute to more effective practice. As a profession, however, social work has been more reluctant than other mental health professions to embrace scientific methodology as a primary means to acquire practice knowledge. The reasons for this reluctance may be as varied and diverse as our profession, but to some degree they may reflect a healthy skepticism toward the uses and abuses of research.

The abuses, paradoxically, are not apparent until we learn the fundamentals of research methodology. A research study may be technically in order as related to data analysis and statistical procedures, and yet be irrelevant or misleading in its conclusions about a particular problem or population. Just as we cannot solve problems if the definition of the problem has been inaccurate, research cannot contribute to our knowledge base if it is formulated around faulty premises. To the extent we proceed from non-conscious ideologies, unfounded theories, or unchallenged assumptions (as research has done frequently in regard to minority or marginal groups), our research and its conclusions will add to existing distortions rather than generate new knowledge. In computer lingo, garbage-in yields garbage-out.

Bem and Bem (1970) defined a nonconscious ideology as a set of beliefs and stereotypes about which one is unaware because of a failure to imagine any alternatives. They employed the concept to describe sexist bias, stating that, "We are like the fish who is unaware that its environment is wet. After all, what else could it be?" Over the last two decades, women scholars have analyzed the patriarchal ideology that has long dominated research questions about women, and have demonstrated the negative effects of this ideology on women's mental health (Broverman, et al., 1970; Weinstein 1976). Similarly, minority scholars have made us aware of the negative impact of research which has been based on a white cultural ideology (Billingsley, 1973; Montiel, 1973; Staples, 1971). To date, however, there has not been an equivalent challenge to the heterosexual ideology that has dominated research with the gay minority.

The central problem that is common to research with women, racial and ethnic minorities, and gay people is that the assumptive world of allegedly "majority" norms - that is, white, male, or heterosexual - is utilized to inform and define the major research questions. The use of majority "norms" is too often synonymous with presuppositions about non-majority groups that infer some degree of defectiveness. As Murray (1973) noted, "The contemporary folklore of racism in the United States is derived from social science surveys in which white norms and black deviations are tantamount to white well-being and black pathology." Similarly, Johnson (1978) observed, "Along with the sexism against women goes an equally non-conscious and sexist set of assumptions regarding the positive, normal, and natural character of the male world."

Heterosexist bias in mental health research has remained largely unexamined, and, in general, both gay and non-gay researchers remain unaware that their belief systems reflect a heterosexist ideology. After all, what else could it be? Just as sexist bias resulted in the creation of a "psychology of man," heterosexist bias has resulted in the creation of a "psychology of heterosexuality" that is so deeply embedded in the assumptive world of mental health research that it is as the water is to fish, wholly nonconscious and relatively unchallenged.

This article is intended to increase awareness of how heterosexually-defined research about gay people keeps potentially interesting topics regarding this population from emerging. It is in that sense polemical, according to Webster's (1971) definition of the term, "any controversial argument, particularly on attacking a strongly-held belief, principle, or doctrine." I have presented an extensive literature review and critique, as well as the results of my own large study of lesbian women in another work (Brooks, 1981), and this chapter is to some extent predicated on the viewpoint gained from completing that work. If any of us are to succeed at the task of cognitively restructuring cultural perceptions of gay people, our research must break out of the framework that yields only more-of-the-same results. This article, then, is limited to a discussion of the effects of a nonconscious ideology in research about gay people, and to some suggestions of topics or areas that might move research efforts out of the majority-defined framework.

Research Problems and Issues

Just as with sexist or racist bias, heterosexist bias can be exhibited in any of the major components of research methodology, but most importantly in those of problem selection and formulation, selection of population and sample, and interpretation of research results. While these tasks in the research process obviously overlap and are interrelated, it is clear that the assumptive world regarding lesbian and homosexual populations is the major precipitator of heterosexist bias in research with gay populations. If research questions are based on faulty assumptions that have been reinforced by psychological postulates of no empirical validity and which are reflected in pervasive cultural stereotypes, any results will serve to merely perpetuate the original bias.

Problem Selection and Formulation

Four major assumptions about lesbian women identified in the author's previous work that apply equally to gay men typify the stereotypical premises on which most research with gay populations has been based: 1) lesbianism and homosexuality have to be explained, 2) adult sexual orientation is determined by early childhood experience, 3) lesbianism and homosexuality are negative outcomes of childhood socialization, and 4) lesbian women are "masculine" and "masculine" women are pathological, or gay men are "effeminate" and "effeminate" men are pathological. For present purposes, research that incorporates these aspects of the nonconscious ideology about gay people is the primary focus.

Until recently, the focus of most research with gay people has been etiological questions, the inference being that if we can find out what "causes" it, we can "cure" it. Attempts to validate clinically-derived judgments of "pathology" were blatant, and the notion of value-free objectivity in research was often made a travesty, as a subsequent example will illustrate. A related research focus was on the sexual behavior of same-sex pairs, generally inferring that this behavior was aberrant and the result of a defective childhood socialization. Undergirding both preoccupations has been the unchallenged assumption that lesbianism and homosexuality have to be explained in human beings, in spite of its existence throughout the animal kingdom, increasing as one ascends the taxonomic tree toward the mammal (Denniston, 1965), or the fact that it has existed throughout human history in virtually every culture (Ford, 1951).

Modern psychology has convinced us, nonetheless, that if we can find the cause, then the "negative outcome" of being gay could be eradicated. Further, "causative" theories have a way of blaming the victims by blaming parents, often convincing parents that they are guilty of too much or too little love and are accountable for this "defective" product. As these theories were shown to be erroneous (Armon, 1960; Bene, 1965; Hooker, 1952 & 1957), the medical model approach - that is, find the "cause" and "cure" it - reverted to biological theories, continuing the notion that the existence of gay people in human society requires an explanation, as opposed to accepting it as a normal variant of human behavior, no more remarkable than having blue eyes in a predominantly brown-eyed species, and behaviorally, no more unusual than choosing celibacy in a sex-obsessed culture.

The second wave of research with the gay population attempted to refute the stereotypes produced by the first, that is, seeking the null hypothesis confirmation of no significant differences between non-gay and gay groups in various behavioral or personality characteristics (Oberstone & Sukoneck, 1976; Thompson, McCandless & Strickland, 1971). These two directions that previously accounted for most research about gay people are comparable to the "normality" and "deviant" perspectives described by Sawyer (1973):

> People in general tend to think in terms of a set of abnormal deviant persons who possess certain characteristics that separate them from the normal members of society; and they are likely to perceive the entire lives of these persons or groups as centered around that deviance...In his concern with deviance, the researcher often ignores more conventional forms of behavior...There is, however, not only a deviant perspective but also a normality perspective— one that holds that there is little or no difference between and among groups of people. I think the challenge...is to break through these two perspectives and see life as a whole, as an entity.

The main point to be emphasized here is that gay people are locked into the heterosexual paradigm the moment they are expected to explain *why* they are gay. The majority culture's initial premise is rarely challenged. If lesbian women and gay men are ever to achieve equality of lifestyle, the means test for research questions needs to be - Would this question be asked of a heterosexual person? And if not, why not? Additionally, premises should be examined that: infer states of mind such as guilt or negative self-perceptions; delve into one's childhood socialization processes; presuppose that traditional sex roles are "normal" and "healthy" and ignore findings relating to androgyny and mental health; or assume any degree of monochromatic behavior or belief system among gay people.

This last point needs to be emphasized particularly in regard to the lumping together of issues pertaining to lesbian women and gay men. This methodological error is most evident in reviews of previous research which failed to note that samples were single-sex or had highly imbalanced sex ratios, and in reference to validity issues, scales were sometimes employed that were validated on a single sex but then applied to both men and women. The earlier etiological literature often carelessly transposed assumptions about gay male behavior to apply to lesbian behavior. Thus, premises need to be examined for their inherent sexism as well as their heterosexism.

Bias in Samples and Interpretation of Results

In addition to faulty premises and erroneous assumptions that have often characterized research with gay people, the selection of samples and over-interpretation of results derived from non-representative samples have served to perpetuate stereotypes as well. Obviously, to the extent that gay people remain socially and numerically invisible as a group, a random sample cannot be obtained. Although this sampling problem exists for other groups, a lack of sample representativeness in a research project would typically be noted for the reader and appropriate cautions stated as to the ability to generalize from the findings. However, such cautions are often abandoned in regard to gay and lesbian samples.

One study that exemplifies this absence of caution was based on only psychoanalysts' reports about 24 female psychiatric patients (Kaye, et al., 1967). In this small sample, 53% self-identified as bisexual at the onset of "treatment." Also, 70% were having heterosexual experiences at the time the psychoanalysts completed their reports. Not withstanding, the Kaye group concluded that, "Homosexuality in women, rather than being a conscious volitional preference, is a *massive adaptational response to a crippling inhibition of normal heterosexual development*," and that "50% of them can be significantly helped by psychoanalytic treatment (p. 633)." Given the bisexuality of the majority of the sample and the need for psychiatric attention, one could as reasonably conclude that heterosexuality in women, rather than a conscious volitional preference, is a massive adaptational response to a crippling inhibition of normal lesbian development. In fact, larger and more representative samples have indicated that 70% to 80% of all lesbian women have heterosexual histories, and some have not entered a lesbian relationship until their forties and fifties, all of which suggests that the notion of "normal heterosexual development" may need closer examination itself. In any case, this type of "sample selection" and sweeping generalization would not pass muster if it referred to a majority group, and well illustrates the degree of distortion introduced by heterosexist ideology.

Over generalizing from the results of research based on nonrepresentative samples, even if large in number, belies the myth of scientific objectivity and supports the view that science can be a handservant of ideology (McWorter, 1973). The somewhat later conclusions of Bell, Weinberg, and Hammersmith (1981) that there appears to be a biological predisposition toward homosexuality is another case in point. Any researcher, particularly one using the Kinsey Institute's auspices, who would draw an etiological conclusion based on a male sample classified as 44% "effeminate" would surely cause Alfred to turn over in his grave, or at last cause him to wish he had stayed with the study of gall wasps. In reference to Kinsey's original work on male sexuality,

Brecher (1971) stated:

> The Kinsey data...distinguish sharply between ho-
> mosexual behavior on the one hand and such phe-
> nomena, often confused with homosexuality, as ef-
> feminate appearance or behavior. The effeminate
> type of male often identified as a "fairy," "fag," or
> "queen," for example, accounts for only about ten
> percent of men with homosexual acts in their histo-
> ries.

The use, then, of a clearly nonrepresentative sample may
partially account for the subjects' frequent attribution of
"cause" to a probable biological predisposition.

Unfortunately, it is not unusual to find the assumptive
world of the majority firmly implanted in the self-perceptions
of the minority; thus, researchers have little difficulty in
finding sample populations of gay people who will confirm
their expectations. There's also something very tidy in the
biological explanation in that the proponents of this view are
relieving responsibility from everyone and are in a sense,
defining it in the manner those concerned with civil rights
and equality under the law would hope for - that is, as a part
of nature. I find two obstacles to the biological explanation,
in addition to the fact that it is still an *explanation*. One, it is
not supported by the evidence and at best, may account for
about 10% of the population identified as gay (Money,
Hampson & Hampson, 1958; Stoller, 1968). Two, it bothers
me that biological explanations could lead to the proposal of
biological "solutions." Irrespective of the popularity of the
biological explanation, the etiological focus is clearly a Game-
Without-End, and speaks more to the politization of research
than to a quest for knowledge.

Majority vs. Minority Frames of Reference

"Majority" in this context refers to those who have the
power to define the framework of inquiry into another
population group's behavior without consideration of that

group's perspective of self-definition. Just as, until recently, the majority frames of reference regarding racial and ethnic minorities and women were unquestioned and somewhat non-conscious, we, as gay minority group scholars, are still in the process of finding our own perspectives. An initial response to the problem has been to advocate that only researchers who are members of a group to be studied should conduct such research. The argument has merit in that it might prevent the grosser errors that majority-group researchers have often made, but it cannot provide assurance of impartiality or absence of bias given the possibility of having internalized majority belief systems about one's own group. In the spirit of Sally Kempton who noted, "It is hard to fight an enemy who has outposts in your head," (Cox, 1976) we must move beyond our own internalized stereotypes first, and design research that restructures the critical questions, assuming there are any.

The symbolism of transactional analysis concepts expressed as states of O.K.-ness seems appropriate to describe the stages through which minority group research has progressed. The majority framework states that they are O.K. but the minority group is not O.K.; the minority group responds that they are O.K. but that the majority group is not O.K. How better could we utilize our research efforts if we reached an I'm O.K./you're O.K. position? Unfortunately, this ideal state seems far in the future. Our cultural mandate of competitiveness relies on comparing levels of performance and striving for One-Up positions; thus, the Western psyche defines its O.K.-ness by the Not O.K.-ness of those who are different. For those majority groups who have the power to define "difference," the Not O.K.-ness of minorities becomes essential. The stages through which research about minorities seems to progress may have to be repeated during "backlash" periods in which the tenacity of the Not O.K. position of minority groups is clear. For example, we are witnessing a replay of old themes such as the pathology of the black family, the un-American habit of speaking a language other than English, and the entry of a female psychiatric disorder— premenstrual syndrome— that reinstates the women-as-Jello theme. As the old themes arise from irrational political processes, however, little is to be accomplished by rational scientific methodology or the replication of previous lines of research.

A third wave of research relating to gay issues has concerned itself with unraveling the homophobic personality. This stage is characterized by shifting from a change-the-victim approach to an analyze-the-victimizer approach, and given the current backlash climate, further research in this framework may be necessary. Studies of the homophobic personality (MacDonald, Huggins, Young & Swanson, 1973) suggest that homophobia is more prevalent among those who support a double standard between the sexes, which, in turn, supports the premise that sex-role nonconformity evokes hostility toward gay men and lesbian women more than does their sexual preference per se. This focus may be more productive, however, if put in the broader context of examining the function of sex-role identity and why it, as opposed to other identities, seems both critical and inflexible in self-definition and defining others.

In sum, it would seem more useful for minority researchers to carve out their own terrain, that is, to define their own framework, as opposed to the reactive framework of studying the racist, sexist, or homophobic personality. For the gay minority, research is needed that arises from social relevance rather than from the need to explain why we are here to others.

Possibilities in Future Research

One major difference that appears to distinguish lesbian and gay people from other groups is that we live in the majority-defined environment without many structural or institutional supports, without many recognized or respected role models, without accurate portrayal of the fabric of our lives in the media or literature, and without any of the legal or social prerogatives that heterosexual partners take for granted. Perhaps the next wave of research with gay populations should focus on the survival skills and coping strategies of gay people whose alienation from their external world is often so deep and profound that even they cannot allow it to become conscious. Gay and lesbian people live at all times in an assumptive world that negates their existence, and which directly or indirectly rewards their invisibility and punishes healthy disclosure.

However, gay people find that the heterosexual assumptive world which attempts to ascribe defectiveness to gay populations is incongruent with their own experience and observation, that is, with their own social reality. On-going analysis of the effect of these incongruities may lead to new and more insightful research formulations in relation to the gay minority. For example, the sociological concept of alienation suggests that only negative results befall individuals who do not feel that they "fit in" with the dominant mass culture. If the same phenomenon was observed from a metaphysical perspective, the separateness of one's experience might be a pathway to a higher Self by providing the detachment necessary for spiritual growth. Or, it could be a wellspring for creative endeavors that require being less invested in, and thereby less constricted by conventional structures. In any case, the psychological effects of marginal status bear examination from a neutral corner that doesn't assume that the effects are altogether negative.

In the realm of more standard psychological and social topics of research, the following questions address areas of potential interest and may serve to stimulate researchable ideas from others. Topically, the questions relate to disclosure, assertiveness, androgyny, interpersonal attraction, self-image, alienation, evaluation of social service needs, parenting, aging, intergroup relations, and "marital" lifestyles.

- Regarding disclosure, what are the effects of gay disclosure on heterosexual associates, and what variables relate to rejection or acceptance?
- Is there a relationship between general level of assertiveness and level of self-disclosure as being gay?

- Do levels of androgyny differ between gay and hetero-sexual groups?
- What are major factors in interpersonal attraction between same-sex pairs? Are these factors different from those between cross-sex pairs? More specifically, in regard to mate selection, what physical, emotional, behavioral, or attitudinal characteristics are more reinforcing in one than in the other sex for the different groups?
- How is the self-image of a gay person affected by heterosexual social milieus, in contrast to gay social milieus?
- Is there a relationship between identification with a gay community and the degree of alienation a gay person experiences? And if so, would this vary significantly with age?

To what extent are social service agencies meeting the needs of gay people? Are they offering services comparable to marriage or divorce counseling, family or single-parent services? To what extent are gay people given consideration as foster or adoptive parents, and what are the major attitudinal obstacles to equal consideration?

Does the experience of aging differ in any significant way between gay and non-gay groups? Between gay men and lesbian women? And if so, what areas are more or less stressful for the different groups?

In regard to intergroup relations, what are the barriers to more effective political coalitions among oppressed groups? Stated otherwise, what cultural stereotypes, value conflicts, or other variables contribute negatively toward the achievement of greater reciprocal support between gay men and lesbian women, between gay people and feminists, or between gay people and people of color?

Finally, with the increase of women in the labor force, resulting in more two-career heterosexual marriages, what could be learned from the adaptive styles of gay couples for whom this phenomenon has always been a reality? Similarly, what could be learned about the long-term relationships of gay people that are without legal marital status that might be applicable to heterosexual couples who are increasingly choosing this option?

The role of scientific research is to generate new knowledge, and ideally, new knowledge that contributes to human progress. Social science knowledge will benefit from the recognition and elimination of a value-laden, nonconscious ideology about gay people, and form a perspective that views sociosexual orientation as a part of human diversity. Eventually, success in eliminating heterosexist bias toward gay people in social science research may be measured by the extent to which sociosexual orientation is introduced and treated as simply another demographic variable, paralleling the inclusion of sex, race, socioeconomic or marital status. Future research should seek to reconnect the gay minority experience with that of other groups who are denied equal access to social and economic resources. Premises that undergird future research should acknowledge that gay people are one-tenth to one-fifth of the human family who live out their lives in the same social and cultural environment as do non-gays, albeit without societal sanction, and that "differences," where found, relate to qualities of this social experience more than to inherent or exotic features of being gay.

References

Armon, V. (1960). Some personality variables in overt female homosexuality. *Journal of Protective Techniques, 24.*

Bem, S. & Bem, D. (1970). Case study of a nonconscious ideology: training the woman to know her place. In D. J. Bem, *Beliefs, attitudes, and human affairs* (pp. 89-99). Monterey, CA: Brooks/Cole.

Billingsley, A. (1973). Black families and white social science. In J. Ladner (Ed.), *The death of white sociology* (pp.431-450). New York: Vintage.

Brecher, E. (1971). *The sex researchers.* New York: New American Library.

Brooks, V. (1981). *Minority stress and lesbian women.* Lexington, MA: Lexington Books.

Broverman, I. K., Broverman, D. M., Clarkson, F. E., Rosenkrantz, P. S., & Vogel, S. R. (1970). Sex-role stereotypes and clinical judgments of mental health. *Journal of Consulting and Clinical Psychology, 34,* 1-7.

Cox, S. (Ed.) (1976). *Female psychology: The emerging self.* Palo Alto, CA: Science Research Association.

Denniston, R. H. (1965). Ambisexuality in animals. In J. Marmor (Ed.), *Sexual inclusion: The multiple roots of homosexuality,* New York: Basic Books.

Grolier, (1971). *The new Grolier Webster international dictionary of the English language, Vol. 2.* New York.

Hooker, E. (1952). Comparative twin study on the genetic aspects of male homosexuality. *Journal of Nervous and Mental Disorders, 115,* 283-298.

Hooker, E. (1957). The adjustment of the male overt homosexual. *Journal of Projective Techniques, 21,* 18-31.

Johnson, P. (1978). Doing psychological research. In I. H. Frieze, J. E. Parsons, P. B. Johnson, Diane N. Ruble & G. L. Zallmen, *Women and sex roles: A social psychological perspective* (p. 13). New York: W. W. Norton.

Kaye, H., Berl, S., Clare, J., Elston, M., Gershwin, B., Gershwin, P., Kogan, L., Torda, C. & Wilbur, C. (1967). Homosexuality in Women, *Archives of General Psychiatry, 17.*

MacDonald, A. P., Huggins, J., Young, S., & Swanson, R. (1973). Attitudes toward homosexuality: preservation of sex morality or the double standard? *Journal of Consulting and Clinical Psychology, 40,* 161.

McWorter, G. (1973). The ideology of black social science, In J. Ladner (Ed.), *The death of white sociology* (p. 173). New York: Vintage.

Money, J., Hampson, J. G., & Hampson, J. L. (1955). An examination of some basic concepts: The evidence of human hermaphroditism. *Bulletin Johns Hopkins Hospital, 107,* 301-319.

Montiel, M. (1973). The chicano family: A review of research. *Social Work, 18,* 22-31.

Murray, A. (1973). White norms, black deviation. In J. Ladner (Ed.), *The death of white sociology.* New York: Vintage.

Oberstone, A. & Sukoneck, H. (1976). Psychological adjustment and life style of single lesbians and single heterosexual women. *Psychology of Women Quarterly, 1,* 172-188.

Sawyer, E. (1973). Methodological problems in studying so-called 'deviant' communities. In J. Ladner (Ed.), *The death of white sociology* (p. 363, 366). New York: Vintage.

Staples, R. (1971). Towards a sociology of the black family: A theoretical and methodological assessment. *Journal of Marriage and Family, 33,* 119-139.

Stoller, R. J. (1968). *Sex and gender.* New York: Science House.

Thompson, N., McCandless, B., & Strickland, B. (1971). Personal adjustment of male and female homosexuals and heterosexuals. *Journal of Abnormal Psychology, 78,* pp. 237-240.

Weinberg, M. & Hammersmith, S. (1981). *Sexual preference.* Bloomington, IN: Indiana University Press.

Weinstein, N. (1976). Psychology constructs the female. In S. Cox (Ed.), *Female psychology: The emerging self,* p. 103. Palo Alto, CA:Science Research Associates.

14

Research on Older Gay Men: What We Know, What We Need to Know

Raymond M. Berger, Ph.D.

Until recently almost nothing was known about older gay men. Ironically, this situation holds great promise. For the less that is known about a group of people, the greater is the potential for research to have an impact on social attitudes toward this group, and ultimately, on the lives of people. This is the case for older gay men. Stereotypes about them have been extreme, and the results of research on this group have dramatically defied these stereotypes.

In this chapter I will review what current research has taught us about older gay men and how that agrees or fails to agree with popular images of this group. The following questions will be addressed. Are older gay men lonely and isolated? Do they have lovers? Do they participate in the gay community? How do they feel about their own aging? Are they well adjusted? What sort of sex lives do they have? Are they more concerned than younger gays about concealing their sexual orientation? Finally, several areas for future research will be outlined.

Are Older Gay Men Lonely and Isolated?

Perhaps no image has been so well ingrained into the public image of the older gay, than that of the loner. It is said that as the older gay man ages, his company becomes unacceptable to others. He has been portrayed as follows:

The homosexual's world is a young person's one. Among men without special gifts, a man is middle-aged at thirty, elderly at forty, and unless he has unusual endowments of talent or wealth, by the time a homosexual reaches fifty, he is obliged to buy companionship. . . For the most part, though, the aging homosexual is usually his own worst problem, so desperately lonely and frightened at times that he frantically beats the walls in his anguish (Stearn, 1961).

Studies have shown that anywhere from about one-third to over one half of gay men over 40 live alone (Berger, 1982a; Friend, 1980; Weinberg, 1970). And there is some evidence that loneliness is a problem for this group. For example, when asked what specific problems they experienced, older gay men most frequently named loneliness. Over a third mentioned this as a problem (Kelly, 1974). In a study of 22 gay and straight older men and women, Minnigerode and Adelman (1976) found, that while the groups did not differ in level of morale, the gay men and women reported loneliness more frequently than the heterosexuals. However, in a much larger and more comprehensive study, Weinberg (1970) found no differences in reported loneliness among different age groups of gay men.

A consistent pattern in the research on older gay men is the decreasing participation of these men in the social and political life of the gay community. Weinberg (1970) reported a steady decrease with age, in the frequency of attending bars and clubs. Kelly (1974) also found that gay men 45 and older were much less likely to attend bars, but the level of their participation in social activities was unclear due to small sample size. Berger's (1982a) sample of 112 gay men over forty had consistently lower attendance at political/social service organizations, bars, bathhouses and social clubs than younger men in a comparable study.

These figures can, however, be deceptive. The general decline in community participation with age should not obscure the fact that, at least for older gay men, community outlets are an important aspect of life. Most gay men, including those over 40, do participate regularly. For example, 59% of older gay men in Berger's (1982a) study attended bars or bathhouses about once a month or more often; over a third visited a political or social service organization with the same frequency.

But that is not the whole story. In a provocative paper based on interviews with ten older gay men, Francher and Henkin (1973) suggested that older gay men are well equipped to deal with loneliness because they have had to develop, early in life, skills for dealing with loneliness and alienation from the traditional male role. Moreover, Francher and Henkin also argued that older gay men are not likely to be isolated because they have replaced family supports with support from friends. (Wolf [1978] made the same point for older lesbians. She argued that the older lesbian uses friends as "fictive kin.")

In a study of 43 gay men (most of whom were over 40) Friend (1980) found that most had many high quality friendships; 86% had at least three close friends. His respondents reported that they did not lose family support when they came out as gay, but rather they acquired additional support from friends. In fact, their closest emotional support came from friends.

One consistent stereotype is that unwillingness of younger homosexuals to associate with their older counterparts forces the older gay man to associate primarily with heterosexuals. This may not be true. Weinberg (1970) did find that older gay men were more likely than younger gays to associate with heterosexuals, and less likely to associate with other gays. Kelly (1974) on the other hand, found that with increasing age, gay men associated less frequently with both gays and heterosexuals. But Kelly noted that his older respondent's self-reported level of social association was generally moderate to high in any case, debunking the notion of social isolation. The same was true of the Weinberg (1970) study in which well over half of older gay men scored high on amount of association with other homosexuals and with heterosexuals as well. Berger (1982a) reported that the great majority of gay men over 40 chose friends primarily from among other homosexual persons.

If the evidence on association with heterosexuals is mixed, there is little question about the preference of older gay men to select friends of similar age. In Berger's (1982a) study, 80% spent half or more of their leisure time socializing with people within ten years of their age or older; over half had few or no friends twenty or more years their junior. It appears that older gay men, like older people in general, choose friends from within their own age cohort (Atchley, 1977, p. 309).

Do Older Gay Men Have Intimate Relationships?

Having an intimate relationship is of central importance to most people. While gay men cannot be assured of an intimate relationship in old age, many do achieve such relationships. Berger (1982a) found that 43% of gay men over forty lived with a lover, and almost three-fourths had had a primary sexual relationship with another man at some time in the past. In Kelly's (1974) study of 193 gay men, the proportion of men who were currently in a "gay marriage" of at least one year's duration increased steadily with age; 59% of those in the 46-55 year age group had such a partnership. (Results for the over 55 age group were unclear due to small sample size.)

What were these relationships like? Berger (1982b) identified three types of relationships among older gay men. *Committed* gay men maintained a long-term same-sex relationship, each lasting a number of years. Among these men relationships often occurred in serial fashion. They may or may not have been monogamous, and the relationship sometimes began with sexual involvement but changed into a non-sexual relationship over the years. The level of commitment of the partners remained high.

Independent gay men limited their relationships to close friendships and brief affairs. Not really loners, most had at least a few close friends, and many lived with other gays.

Ambisexual persons had relationships with both men and women for substantial portions of their lives. Typically, an ambisexual was married for at least several years, and often had children. At some point he withdrew from heterosexuality and began homosexual relationships. Some remained married and led a "double life" in that they hid gay activities from their wives and from heterosexual friends. Others separated from their wives and assumed completely gay lifestyles. Kimmel (1977) reported a similar typology of relationships among fourteen older gay men.

There is an important point here about intimate relationships. It is often assumed that an intimate relationship, especially in old age, is essential to avoiding loneliness and isolation. Many mental health authorities view an exclusive intimate relationship as a criterion of mental health.

The situation of many older gay men challenges this view. As Francher and Henkin (1973), Wolfe (1978) and others have noted, friends can be used successfully as an alternative to a single intimate relationship. Bell and Weinberg (1978) found that non-coupled gay men and women (of all ages) spent less time at home, suggesting that gays use friends and social outlets to prevent the isolation that might otherwise result from lack of an intimate partnership.

How Do Gay Men and Women React to Aging?

As I indicated above, one of the most prevalent stereotypes is that older gay men face a horror-filled old age. It is not surprising then, that many gays have acquired negative attitudes and fears about their own aging. However, research indicates that these attitudes, although prevalent, are far from universal. More interesting is the finding in studies which compare homosexual men of different ages that older gay men are least likely to experience negative attitudes and fears about old age.

As Weinberg and Williams (1974) suggested, based on their own research, while the situation of the older gay may seem undesirable to the younger person, from the perspective of the older gay man himself things look much better. As the gay man approaches old age, the dire consequences predicted by the stereotypes begin to seem less likely. I would guess that future research will find that this holds true for lesbian women as well.

Saghir and Robbins (1973), based on interviews with 57 gay men and 40 lesbians of all ages, found that almost half believed they would "grow old gracefully with interest and involvement in social and current issues." Of course this leaves over half of respondents who expressed negative attitudes about their aging, but it is difficult to assess these results without comparison data from heterosexuals. Do as many (or as few) older heterosexuals believe they will grow old gracefully? Only 28% of the men believed they would grow old in a stable relationship and a small minority believed they would grow old feeling afraid and lonesome.

Kelly's (1974) survey of gay men of all ages showed that many had negative beliefs about their old age. When asked to indicate their beliefs about what happens to aging gays, the largest category (33%) left the item blank or didn't know. Twenty-seven per cent believed that gays adapt poorly to age. However, analysis by age groups showed a dramatic decline in negative beliefs with increasing age: 36% of those under 26, but only 13% of those over 55, expressed negative beliefs. Only about one-fifth said they were fearful of their own old age. The most frequently mentioned problems of old age were loneliness, loss of physical attractiveness, and failure to accept the aging process (each of these problems was mentioned by 27% of respondents.)

Generally, positive attitudes toward aging were reported by Jay and Young (1979) in their survey of gay men and lesbian women of all ages. However, Jay and Young noted an important sex difference: men tended to feel that age was important in choice of a partner, while this was less likely to make a difference to the women. This may lead to a more difficult acceptance of age on the part of gay men.

In comparing the responses of older to younger gay men, Berger (1982a) found that older gay men experienced less anxiety or worry about old age. Only a few older gay men reported that they worried "often" or "constantly" about growing old, or thought about dying.

Early writings on the aging of homosexual men stressed the idea of "premature aging" - given the importance that gay men attach to youth it was believed that gay men grew old before their time. Even the gay-positive researcher, Evelyn Hooker, wrote in 1965 that at the age of thirty-five, gay men were no longer considered desirable partners and fared poorly in the bars.

Three recent studies addressed to the question provide no evidence for premature aging on the part of older gay men or women. (Only Friend [1980] claimed that his data suggested accelerated aging, but this claim was based on the dubious reasoning that most of the men who responded to his solicitation for "older gay men" were under 64 years of age.) Minnigerode (1976) asked 95 gay men, 25 to 68 years of age, to describe themselves as young, middle-aged or old. Their self-assigned age labels did not differ from those of respondents in the general population. Laner (1978, 1979) addressed this question by examining "personals" advertisements for homosexual and heterosexual men and women. The only group for whom premature aging was evident, was heterosexual women. For both men and women, the homosexual advertisers were younger than the heterosexual advertisers, and were no more likely to be seeking younger partners.

Do Older Gay Men Have Poor Mental Health?

Weinberg (1970) was the first to present evidence that older gay men may actually be better adjusted than younger gay men. In his questionnaire survey of 1100 gay men, there were no differences among the age groups on loneliness, unhappiness or depression. However, older gay men were healthier on measures of worry about exposure of homosexuality, self-acceptance, stability of self-concept, negative feelings (on a psychological adjustment scale), psychosomatic symptoms, and feelings of interpersonal awkwardness. In general, there were consistent improvements on these measures as age increased. In addition, older gay men were less likely to desire psychiatric treatment.

Weinberg argues that the healthier status of his older respondents was consistent with a more general phenomenon which was documented in a large scale mental health survey of the general population. Gurin, Veroff, and Feld (1960) found that older respondents reported better mental health because "what appear to be problems or inadequacies at the time of youthful involvement may seem less serious with the passage of time" (Weinberg, 1970, p. 536).

Berger's (1982a) 112 older gay men received scores similar to those in the Weinberg study on self-acceptance, depression and psychosomatic symptoms, with most respondents scoring well on the healthy side of these measures. On a Life Satisfaction Index, older gay men scored higher than older persons in two surveys of the general population. Almost three-fourths reported that they were currently "pretty happy" or "very happy". Very few were receiving counseling for their homosexuality, or desired such counseling.

As noted above, Minnigerode and Adelman (1976) found no differences between older gay men and lesbians and matched heterosexuals on a measure of morale. The older gay men in Friend's (1980) study received high scores on a shortened version of the self-acceptance scale used by Weinberg (1970) and Berger (1982a).

Contrary to myth, older gay men did not become more effeminate as they aged. Weinberg and Williams (1974) found in fact, that older gays rated themselves as less effeminate than younger gays. Kelly (1977) also reported that the typical older gay man did not consider himself effeminate, and very few described themselves with feminine terms such as "closet queen" or "nelly."

Are Older Gay Men More Concerned About Concealing Their Homosexuality?

It is commonly assumed among younger gays that older gays are more "closeted." Having come of age in a more repressive era, and being more conservative (the thinking goes) their closeted attitudes are understandable. One of the greatest surprises of recent research is that the older gay man is actually less closeted.

Weinberg and Williams (1974) were the first to report that older gay men were less uptight about "passing," that is, hiding their homosexuality. Those over 45 were much less likely to report worry about exposure of their homosexuality.

Berger (1982a) confirmed this finding. Older gay men were less likely to report that they would not like to associate with a known homosexual, less likely to mind being seen in public with a known homosexual, and more likely not to care who knows about their homosexuality. Not only did the older men have less closeted attitudes, comparison with figures from the Weinberg and Williams age-diverse sample showed that older gay men were more likely to be "out" (known as homosexual) to a greater proportion of their friends, relatives, work associates and other homosexuals. For example, almost a third of older respondents, but only 13% of younger respondents, reported that "all" or "most" of their straight acquaintances knew or suspected that the respondent was gay.

In at least one respect it should not be a surprise that older gays are less concerned about concealment. It has been suggested that they are often less closeted than younger gays, because they are more likely to be retired and therefore freed from the worries of employment discrimination that keep many working gays in the closet (Berger, 1982b).

Have Older Gays Experienced Discrimination?

Of all groups in the gay community, older persons are most likely to have experienced discrimination in employment, housing, and other aspects of their lives. Their adult lives took place mostly in an era that was one of the most repressive anti-homosexual periods of our time (Kimmel, 1978), and they have accumulated a number of years during which they were potential or real targets or discrimination.

Unfortunately, available data are sparse. In interviews with 18 gay men and women over forty, Berger (1984) reported that half the respondents had experienced instances of discrimination in employment, housing, and child custody. Several respondents reported multiple incidents, at times due to homosexuality and at other times to age.

It is likely that most older gay men have experienced anti-homosexual discrimination at some time in their lives. However, discrimination based on ageism within the gay community itself is also a problem (Kochera, 1973). I did not find any research which attempted to measure the attitudes of younger gays towards their older peers, but in Berger (1982a) I did find a remarkably high level of belief among older gay men that younger gays have harshly negative attitudes toward them.

For example, 43% of older gay men agreed that, "In the gay/lesbian community most young people do not want to make friends with an older person." A third of older gay men scored "high" on a composite of six items from which this one was drawn, measuring "anticipated negative reaction of the younger."

What Kind of Sex Life Do Older Gay Men Have?

Anyone who tried to understand the sex lives of older gay men based on information in the popular media would be confused. The older gay man is alternately portrayed as sexually voracious or totally abstinent for lack of partners. Certainly the most damaging portrayal is the older gay man as child molester. Since the child molester image has been particularly destructive of public understanding, it is perhaps best to begin with this.

Data collected by government authorities belie the myth of homosexual child molestation. Although a small minority of gay men sexually molest children, they do so in numbers no greater than the proportion of gay men in the population. There is no reason to believe that older men molest children more frequently than younger men. (There are data to indicate that older men are less likely to use violence, at least in heterosexual molestation [Whiskin, 1967]).

The reality is that child molestation is overwhelmingly a heterosexual male problem. In ninety per cent of reported child molestations the offender is an adult male and the victim a minor female. Many molestations of male minors are committed by men who molest both girls and boys, suggesting that this problem is independent of the sexual orientation of the offender. And lest the public believe that older gays are a menace to society's children, it should also be noted that 75% to 85% of child molestations are committed by family members or close friends of the victim (Sexual Child Abuse, undated). Finally, studies show that being "seduced" or molested by a same sex adult rarely, if ever, leads a child to develop an adult homosexual orientation (Bell, Weinberg and Hammersmith, 1981).

What are the sex lives of older gays like? Although few of the "old-old"— those over 75 years of age— have been included in research studies, it is clear that most gay men continue to lead active and satisfying sex lives well into their forties, fifties and beyond. There is evidence that for both men and women, older gays have sex with fewer partners and employ a smaller number of sexual techniques (Bell and Weinberg, 1978). Subjective reports often indicate that even though the pace of sexual activity is slower in later years, it brings with it greater levels of satisfaction.

Although a number of studies report the frequency of sexual relations for gay men, only a few give any indication of these frequencies for older gay men. These studies indicate that, while older gay men are less sexually active than their younger counterparts, they nevertheless have high levels of activity on the whole. For example, Weinberg (1970) found that only a third were having sex less than once a month; so presumably, two-thirds were having sex once a month or more often. Berger (1982a) found even higher levels among gay men over forty: almost two-thirds reported having sex once a week or more often.

But in several studies (Weinberg, 1970; Weinberg and Williams, 1974; Bell and Weinberg, 1978; Berger, 1982a), older gay men had fewer partners than younger gays. For example, while 89% of gay men in Bell and Weinberg's (1978) age-diverse sample had three or more sex partners within the past year, in Berger's (1982a) study of older men fewer than a quarter had had three or more partners within the past six months; 57% of those who were sexually active limited themselves to only one partner within this period. The great majority of older gay men rated their current sex lives as satisfactory (Berger, 1982a; Berger, 1984; Kelly, 1977; Kimmel, 1978).

These data were collected before the current AIDS crisis. Given concerns about the spread of this illness within the gay community, it is likely that both older and younger gay men will reduce the number of their sexual partners, and perhaps the frequency of sexual activity as well. Younger gay men may find, as their older counterparts have already discovered, that sexual contact is not always necessary to achieve intimacy; and that getting out of the fast lane may be an opportunity to focus on the interpersonal caring that is so often lacking in genital-focused encounters.

Where Do We Go From Here?

Asking a researcher whether more research is needed in his or her area is like asking the fox to guard the chicken coop. So I am certainly not going to argue against the need for more research. However, before outlining the areas toward which I believe future research should be addressed, I would like to note an obvious but often overlooked point.

The need for more research must not be an impediment to action. At my former university, the Chancellor recently overturned non-discrimination protection for gay and lesbian students because they had not documented instances of discrimination. Explanation of the difficulties in getting students who had experienced discrimination to come forward did not seem to help, but the call for "more research" is particularly welcome, as it always is, in times of political difficulty or reluctance.

The fact is that the gay and lesbian community, and particularly the older community, is hurting right now. Right now is when we need to repeal laws which criminalize or make second class citizens of gays and lesbians. We need to revise deliberately repressive as well as unintentionally discriminatory institutional policies such as those which exclude lovers from decision-making for the critically ill nursing home patient, or make them ineligible for health insurance benefits. Now is when we need specialized services in areas where mainstream agencies are unresponsive to the needs of older gays and lesbians.

Future research must be used as a guide for action rather than its substitute. It can be used to help us shape new policies and institutions, and to document areas of need as a first step toward advocacy. What are some of the questions that need to be asked?

We need better documentation about the lives of older lesbians. We also need to include minority, low-income, and rural gays and lesbians in research, particularly research directed toward determining social service needs. The absence of minority and low-income persons in research on aging and homosexuality is remarkable. I, for one, want to know why participation rates are so low among these groups, and what can be done about that. We need to know how our conclusions about older gay and lesbian life might be different for these groups.

A great deal of energy has been spent on determining if older gay men are really "sicker" than younger gays or older people in general. The evidence has surprised us. Older gay men have many advantages in adjusting to old age: lifelong expertise in using friendship networks, knowledge of coping in the face of stigma, and so on. It is time to turn things around and ask: "What is it that older gay men do well that can be instructive for everyone?" In other words, we need to study successful coping.

Part of this may be a study of alternative relationships and living arrangements. One gerontologist has suggested lesbian relationships as one solution for the isolation that is so much of a problem for the increasing numbers of older widows (Cavan, 1973). There is no suggestion here that older people who are not homosexual should become so. But the facts are: there are more widows and widowers than ever before; old people are living longer; the end of the lengthened life span is increasingly becoming a time of dependence; and societal resources for caring for our increasing proportion of elderly are reaching a critical limit.

In short, we need new solutions and adaptations of older gay men and women should be one direction in which we look for better alternatives for the future. They have already made a contribution in showing us how survival can be enhanced even without support from families. There is also a foundling research literature on gay coupling (e.g. McWhirter and Mattison, 1984). When a same sex couple has survived the terrible odds of years of societal repression, surely they must embody lessons for successful coupling in the face of all types of adversity.

Just as young heterosexuals turn into frail elderly with time, gays and lesbians also become frail and dependent if they live long enough. But what happens to them when they are institutionalized, when they are forced to rely on heterosexually-oriented social services, when they are homebound? That is less clear. Although this chapter has talked about research on "aging gay men," in fact the research is almost entirely limited to the relatively young-old: those under 75 years of age, and those who are still relatively healthy and self-sufficient. But being homosexual may present its greatest problems when, in very old age, one is forced to rely on unsympathetic or uninformed friends, relatives, neighbors and social service providers. What happens then?

Some have suggested that the gay and lesbian community must take steps to look after its own elderly, and that is happening with the development of social service agencies like Seniors Active in a Gay Environment (SAGE) in New York City. Similar organizations have been established in several other large cities. The model is one in which younger and more healthy members of the community help those who are needy. It is clear to me that organizations such as SAGE have helped to overcome the avoidance, and at times animosity, between the generations. How have they done this? What lessons can be learned from this experience? Organizational case studies of programs such as SAGE would be useful here.

Much of what is known about aging in general has been learned from the painstaking process of longitudinal research, that is, the process of following a single "cohort" of people over time. This is a much better although more difficult method, but it has never been applied to the study of older gays and lesbians. This has left serious gaps in research knowledge. All of the comparisons between young and old gays summarized in this chapter are based on cross sectional studies: research which looked at different age cohorts at a single point in time.

For example, it has been suggested that as gays and lesbians grow older they become less concerned about concealing their sexual orientation. But is this an attitude that develops with age, or is it simply that the older generation of gays and lesbians has a more "damned with society" attitude to begin with? Older gays and lesbians have less sex with fewer partners. Is this an indication of a sex life that slows with age...or has the new sexual revolution of the 1960's really produced a different breed of sexually libertine younger gays?

Longitudinal research on older gays and lesbians has not taken place because this is a new research area. But it will never take place until substantial funding is available because this type of research is expensive. My own feeling is that the establishment— the universities, mainstream foundations and the federal government— are not about to release a flow of dollars for this purpose. So, just as the gay and lesbian community is looking to its own institutions for specialized social services, it may also have to look inward for research support.

One thing is clear: a great deal is yet to be done.

References

Atchley, Robert C. (1977) *The social forces in later life: An introduction to social gerontology*, Second Edition, Wadsworth: Belmont, CA, 1977.

Bell, Alan P. and Weinberg, Martin S. (1978). *Homosexualities: A study of diversity among men and women*. Simon and Schuster: NY.

Bell, Alan P., Weinberg, Martin S., and Hammersmith, Sue K. (1981). *Sexual preference: Its development in men and women*. Indiana University Press: Bloomington.

Berger, Raymond M. (1982a). *Gay and gray: The older homosexual man*. University of Illinois Press: Urbana-Champaign. Also published in paperback by Alyson Press: Boston, 1984.

Berger, Raymond M. (1982b). The Unseen Minority: Older Gays and Lesbians. *Social Work, 27*(3), May, 236-242.

Berger, Raymond M. (1984) Realities of Gay and Lesbian Aging. *Social Work, 29*(1), January-February, 57-61.

Cavan, Ruth S. (1973) Speculations on Innovations to Conventional Marriage in Old Age. *Gerontologist, 13*(4), 409-411.

Francher, J. Scott and Henkin, Janet (1973). The Menopausal Queen: Adjustment to Aging and the Male Homosexual. *American Journal of Orthopsychiatry, 43*(4), 670-674.

Friend, Richard A. (1980) Gay Aging: Adjustment and the Older Gay Male. *Alternative Lifestyles, 3*(2), May, 231-248.

Gurin, Gerald, Veroff, Joseph, and Feld, Sheila (1960) *Americans view their mental health: A nationwide interview study*. Basic Books: NY.

Hooker, Evelyn (1965) In Judd Marmor (ed.) *Sexual inversion: The multiple roots of homosexuality.* Basic Books: NY.

Jay, Karla and Young, Allen (1979) *The gay report.* Summit Books:NY.

Kelly, James J. (1974) Brothers and Brothers: The Gay Man's Adaptation to Aging (Doctoral Dissertation, Brandeis University). *Dissertation Abstracts International, 36,* 3130A. (University Microfilms No. 75-24, 234).

Kelly, James J. (1977) The Aging Male Homosexual: Myth and Reality. *Gerontologist, 17*(4), 328-332.

Kimmel, Douglas C. (1977) Psychotherapy and the Older Gay Man. *Psychotherapy: Theory, Research and Practice, 14*(4), Winter, 386-393.

Kimmel, Douglas C. (1978) Adult Development and Aging: A Gay Perspective. *Journal of Social Issues, 34*(3), 113-130.

Kochera, Brian. (1973) The Faggot's Faggot . . . Gay Senior Citizens and Gay S&M. *Pittsburgh Gay News, 1*(5), September 1, 6.

Laner, Mary R. (1978) Growing Older Male: Heterosexual and Homosexual. *Gerontologist, 18*(5), 496-501.

Laner, Mary R. (1979) Growing Older Female: Heterosexual and Homosexual. *Journal of Homosexuality, 4,*(3), Spring, 267-275.

McWhirter, David and Mattison, Andrew (1984) *The male couple.* Prentice-Hall: Englewood Cliffs, NJ.

Minnigerode, Fred (1976) Age-Status Labeling in Homosexual Men. *Journal of Homosexuality, 1*(3), 273-275.

Minnigerode, Fred and Adelman, Marcy (1976) Adaptations of Aging Homosexual Men and Women. Paper presented at the Convention of the Gerontological Society, New York City, October 14, 1976.

Moses, A. Elfin, and Hawkins, Robert O., Jr. (1982) *Counseling lesbian women and gay men.* Mosby: St. Louis.

Saghir, Marcel T. and Robins, Eli (1973) *Male and Female Homosexuality: A Comprehensive Investigation.* Williams and Wilkins: Baltimore.

Sexual Child Abuse: A Contemporary Family Problem. National Organization for Women, Child Sexual Abuse Task Force, San Jose, CA, and Gay Rights Chapter, American Civil Liberties Union, Los Angeles, CA, undated.

Stearn, Jess. (1961) *The Sixth Man*, Macfadden:NY.

Verwoerdt, A., Pfeiffer, E. and Wang, H. S. (1969) Sexual Behavior in Senescence. *Geriatrics, 24*, February, 137-153.

Weinberg, Martin S., and Williams, Colin J. (1974) *Male Homosexuals: their problems and adaptations*, Oxford University Press: NY.

Whiskin, Frederick E. (1967) The Geriatric Sex Offender. *Geriatrics*, October, 168-172.

Wolf, Deborah G. (1980) Life Cycle Change of Older Lesbians and Gay Men. Paper presented at the Convention of the Gerontological Society. San Diego, California.

15

Research on Older Lesbian Women: What Is Known, What is Not Known, And How to Learn More

Carol Tully, Ph.D.

There exists within the gerontological population of this country a minority group of women who face aging and old age as members of an ignored and infrequently studied cohort— older lesbian women. Demographic trends continue to demonstrate that the number of older women in the United States will expand well into the 21st century (Soldo, 1980), which implies that the numbers of lesbian women will also increase during the next decades. While no data exist to inform us of the total number of older lesbians, only limited data even describe the members of this minority. By reviewing the research in the field of older lesbian women, this chapter will address the following questions:

- What is known about the characteristics of the older lesbian woman?
- What is the nature of her social interactions?
- What kinds of sexual behaviors exist?

-     How is the older lesbian different from her hetero-
      sexual counterpart?

After reviewing what is known about older lesbians, the
chapter identifies areas for further study. Finally, using her
own research as an example, the author addresses issues
that must be identified and dealt with when attempting to
conduct research in the field.

What is Known

While research dealing with any aspect of aging emerged
shortly following World War II and continues with regularity
(Tully, 1983), research relative to women actually was discouraged in academia well into the 1970's. Additionally,
given the homophobia of prior generations, it is little wonder
that studies of lesbian elders only began in the late 1970's
when Minnigerode and Adelman (1978) reported findings
from a sample of five lesbian women aged 60-77. Research in
the area continues, although at a slow rate and with a paucity
of funding. In fact, by early 1987, only a few studies that
include data specific to lesbian aging have been generally
reported (Adelman, 1980; Berger, 1984; Kehoe, 1986; Laner,
1979; Minnigerode & Adelman, 1978; Raphael & Robinson,
1980; Tully, 1983). Not only are there few studies that
examine the existence of lesbian elders, the number of
women included in the samples is also small. The samples
have been so small that helping professionals and others who
deal with older lesbians base their knowledge on research
that has used data from a total of only 183 women. The
subjects have provided input through interviews and questionnaires but, in one study, results were compiled from
examination of older lesbian personal advertisements in a
lesbian oriented "contact" register. The findings of these
studies will be discussed chronologically.

In an effort to gain a better understanding of how
homosexual women and men adjust to aging, Minnigerode &
Adelman (1978) reported on a pilot study of 5 lesbian women
and 6 gay men aged 60-77. Through interviews that included

a 6 item morale scale, the researchers found that most of those interviewed lived alone and that men placed a higher priority on work than did women. While half of the men had lost jobs directly as a result of their sexual orientation, none of the women had, although the women felt their jobs and careers had been constrained because of their lesbianism. All respondents viewed retirement with a positive outlook and a sense of relief. While most were raised within a religious context, the majority had no current religious affiliation. Most participated in social, political organizations and none belonged to a senior citizen's center. Their friends were sex segregated and those interviewed had kept in touch with their families. While not being estranged from their families, this sample maintained closer contact with their lesbian or gay friendship networks than they did with their relatives.

Women tended to view homosexuality not in terms of sexual activity (as did the men), but in terms of a personal identification and/or interpersonal relationships with other women. The men tended to place a higher emphasis on sexual activity than did the women, yet most of the women were sexually active. All of the women noted a decrease in sexual activity with an increase in age. These women generally fulfilled their sexual needs within the context of affectional relationships and had their first lesbian experience when they were in their early 20's. The women identified themselves as lesbian following their first overt lesbian sexual encounter whereas the men defined themselves as homosexual before their first homosexual experience. Finally, all the women interviewed said that it was not proper to discuss homosexuality with either their homosexual or heterosexual friends.

In a study that sought to examine similarities and differences in the aging process of lesbian and heterosexual women, Laner (1979) analyzed 229 assumed heterosexual personal advertisements in one issue of a "single's" register and 273 assumed lesbian personal advertisements in two issues of a lesbian oriented "contact" register. She hypothesized that more older women than younger women would advertise, that there would be more heterosexual than lesbian advertisers who were in their early middle years and that no differences would exist between heterosexual and lesbian advertisers with regard to the age requirements of the advertisement respondents.

Laner found that a vast majority of both the lesbian and non-lesbian women who placed ads were younger than 48 years old and that lesbian women did not advertise for younger women. She concluded that lesbians did not seem to experience the acceleration of aging as fast as heterosexual women and that the field of potential partners may be larger for older lesbians than for their heterosexual counter parts (due to the ever increasing numbers of available older women and the ever decreasing numbers of available older men).

Adelman (1980) investigated the relationship between adjustment to a homosexual lifestyle and its effect on later life. The study took place over a 3 year period and included a sample of non-homosexual women and men in addition to the older lesbian sample (N=25) and older gay sample (N=27). Adelman found no significant differences between the homosexuals and heterosexuals with regard to sexual orientation and aging. Possible differences were sought using the following instruments: a life-satisfaction index, a psychological functioning index, and other items on a researcher designed questionnaire. A composite of the "typical" lesbian or gay subject would be a 65 year old homosexual person in good health who lived alone on an income sufficient to maintain a comfortable standard of living. This individual would have had some college and would have been professionally employed but now retired. S/he would have never heterosexually married, would have no children and claim no current religious affiliation. Adelman's study concluded that homosexual people face the same developmental crises and challenges as heterosexuals, but do so under the influence of social stigma.

As recently as 1982, the only published study that dealt exclusively with older lesbian women had been conducted by Raphael & Robinson (1980). The purpose of their descriptive study was to explore the relationship between intimacy and aging in lesbian women, to examine support patterns and to test the hypothesis that older lesbian women develop friendship networks to replace missing or weak kinship ties and that lesbians are not without support in their later years. Through a structured interview that lasted from 1 to 4 hours, Raphael & Robinson gathered data from 20 white, self-identified lesbians who lived either in San Francisco or Los Angeles. All respondents were at least 50 years old.

Of the total sample (N=20), 11 had been heterosexually married, yet most had "always known" they were lesbian. While most had their first lesbian sexual experience in their late teens or early 20's, 5 (25%) did not have their first overt lesbian sexual encounter until they were over 50 years old. Most had attended college and were or had been employed as professionals. Some (N=7, 35%) were fully retired. Slightly more than half (N=11, 55%) had no current religious affiliation (life data found in the Minnigerode & Adelman [1978] and Adelman [1980] studies), and that same number lived alone. The remaining 9 (45%) women lived in a coupled situation with another older woman.

Those sampled sought women of their own age for friends, viewed their lover as their best friend but had a need for other friends as well. They did not isolate themselves from other women and did get involved with the lesbian subculture once they knew where to find it. While 50% had close, long time heterosexual friends, these women did have a need to meet and be with other lesbian women. Although they admitted it was hard to find other older lesbians, they did meet older lesbians at older women's groups, lesbian groups and women's movement activities.

An overwhelming majority had lost a partner at some point (N=18, 90%), and slightly more than half (N=11, 55%) reported getting little or no support following the loss. What support was offered came from the lesbian subculture, not from heterosexual friends and/or family. One problem encountered following the loss of a partner was that the remaining partner who was seeking support from lesbian friends sometimes found unwanted potential lovers instead.

The pattern of love relationships for these women was serial monogamy. All had been involved in at least one major relationship, and sex continued to play a role in each one's life. Sexual frequency seemed to be a function of the availability of a new partner periodically as sex tended to get boring with the same partner year after year. Although it was hard for lesbians over 70 years of age to find sexual partners, for many their libido remained intact. Sexual experiences for these women did continue and the women sampled continued to seek and find new sexual partners. They tended to prefer relating socially and sexually with members of their own age cohort and felt a need to establish a strong emotional bond before having a sexual encounter with another woman. While sexual activity was strongly influenced by partner availability, uncoupled lesbians showed a high degree of sexual interest and had realistic expectations of finding suitable partners.

Raphael & Robinson found their sample to have weak kinship ties but strong linkages with friends. The stronger the friendship ties were, the more likely the older lesbian was to have high self-esteem. The researchers concluded that older lesbians have strong friendship ties and are not lonely, isolated women with poor self-images. Further, it was felt that these women had adapted well to aging.

In an effort to examine the social organizational structures and support systems in the social world of the older lesbian, Tully (1983) collected data on 73 self-identified lesbians who were 50 years old or older. Through in-depth interviews or questionnaires, these women provided information on their personal interactions with the economic, political, educational, religious, social welfare and familial social systems of the heterosexual culture and the homosexual subculture.

The demographic profile of a typical women in Tully's sample shows a well educated, politically liberal, professionally employed woman in her early 50's who is in good to excellent health. She tends to live in her own home with a female partner with whom she has lived for a significant amount of time. She opts to define her sexual orientation using the word "lesbian" and is predominantly both intensely emotionally intimate and physically sexually active with women. She does not totally hide her sexual orientation, but is selective with whom she shares the knowledge of her lesbianism. Her family is less likely to be aware of her sexual orientation than female friends. Her parents are deceased, but she still has living siblings. She tends to spend her leisure time with women who are younger than herself, and she has not experienced the death of a woman with whom she has been intimately involved. She was raised with some type of religious ideology, but has generally fallen away from traditional religion. She is aware of a homosexual community in her home town or within commuting distance of her home and considers herself a member of that community although not a terrible active member.

While she earns more than $15,000 annually, she does not spend much of her money within the homosexual community. She is a political liberal who supports the Democratic Party and is positively affected by a political candidate's pro-homosexual stand on issues. She belongs to politically oriented and/or professional organizations rather than hobby clubs or discussion groups, and although she is aware of homosexually oriented organizations, she may not be a member of such. She has need of and utilizes a variety of helping professionals to whom she will reveal her sexual orientation only if it is relevant to the helping process. She chooses her helping professionals based on the helper's professional expertise and her own knowledge of the professional. While she knows of emotional counseling services within the homosexual community, she had not had an emotional problem within the year of the study for which she has sought support from helping professionals.

She learned about homosexuality when she was 15, became intensely emotionally intimate with other women when she was 25 and had her first lesbian sexual experience when she was 27. She considers her formal education, her ability to earn an adequate income, her relationships with heterosexuals and homosexuals and her political activities important. In sum, she is actively involved with the world around her.

In terms of where the typical woman in Tully's study

seeks and finds support, the following picture emerges. The typical respondent gets support in times of crisis from those who are aware of her sexual orientation. This includes primarily homosexual and heterosexual women friends and some immediate family members, but rarely men. She views these homosexual and heterosexual support systems as adequate to her needs. She does not view the religious institution and the support systems it provides as a place she would seek support during a crisis situation, and she turns to family members and friends for aid in financial crises rather than the traditional financial aid sources such as banks and/or credit unions. The homosexual subculture and the heterosexual culture provide her adequate support when she has an emotional crisis for which she seeks support.

She may consider turning to the American Civil Liberties Union or a personal lawyer for help with discrimination issues, but may not be willing to take such an overt stand and thus allows the discrimination. The formal educational system provided her little support, and once she started to define herself as not traditionally heterosexual, she felt a need for some type of support from somewhere. To get the support she needed, she turned to other lesbians and female friends and not to family members or men.

Tully concluded that women in her sample are well integrated professionally into the heterosexual culture where they are educated, employed, politically active and financially supported by the traditional social order. Although the conventional world does not provide them with emotional intimacy or sexual outlets, these women tend to conform to societal norms and expectations except with regard to their emotional intimacies and sexual relationships with other women.

To examine commonly believed stereotypes of older homosexuals and to identify the unique characteristics and needs of this minority, Berger (1984) gathered data from 8 lesbian women and 10 gay men aged 40-72 by using an open-ended interview format. These in-depth interviews lasted from 1 1/1 hours to 2 hours and provided data on the older homosexual's social life, community involvement, family involvement, love relationships, sex life, attitudes, societal confrontations and perspectives on aging. However, most of the findings discuss lesbian and gay aging as though it was the same phenomenon. Yet research on younger homosexual samples has demonstrated (Tully, 1983) that some differences seem to exist between lesbian women and gay men—including lesbian and gay elders.

With this in mind, a composite of a typical respondent in Berger's sample would be a never heterosexually married, 54 year old who knew early in life of her/his same sex attraction, who conceptualized the coming-out process as a major life event and who had her/his first homosexual experience when a teenager. Currently living with a lover of several years, s/he is sexually active and satisfied with her/his sex life. The individual sees relatives occasionally and is an active participant in both the heterosexual and homosexual communities. To accommodate this, s/he maintains two distinct sets of friends—one homosexual set and one heterosexual set. Berger's typical respondent would have faced some type of discrimination on the basis of sexual orientation or age in the areas of employment, housing or child custody, and views the differences between homosexual and heterosexual aging as non-existent as long as the individual accepts her/himself. From this study, Berger concludes that the stereotypes of the older homosexual woman or man that depict her/him as lonely, depressed, child molester have no basis in reality.

Kehoe (1986) gathered data on 50 self-identified lesbians over age 65 in a cross-sectional survey where respondents completed a researcher designed questionnaire. She wanted to examine the lives of these women from a descriptive viewpoint and gather evidence to test her belief that lesbians who are at least 65 years old are survivors in more than just a physical sense—i.e. that they are better equipped to adjust to aging than their heterosexual counterparts. In her study, Kehoe looked at demographic, educational, economic, occupational and bio-psycho-social variables.

The sample included women from 23 states and Washington, D.C. Most had identified themselves as lesbian by their late teens and now ranged in age from 65-85 although 86% (N=43) were between the ages of 65-74. The sample was generally well educated, 70% (N=35) had at least a college degree and 50% (N=25) had advanced degrees. Respondents tended to own their own home and have incomes between $10,000 and $15,000 annually even though 36 were fully retired. Most were or had been professionally employed and did not view themselves as closeted even though they did not generally belong to professional organizations or lesbian social groups. Likewise, 60% (N=30) had no religious affiliation and those who attended church did so infrequently.

In terms of interpersonal relationships, 50% (N=25) of Kehoe's sample had been heterosexually married at some point and most had no children. Of those who had never married, all had advanced academic degrees. Only 9 (18%) of the sample were currently involved in a committed relationship with another woman at the time of the study although all had had at least one major lesbian relationship. They viewed lesbian relationships as more sexually gratifying, caring, emotional, sharing and gentle than heterosexual ones and 66% (N=33) had been involved in cross-generational same sex relationships where the age differences ranged from 20 to 53 years. Only half of the sample believed in monogamy. Sex was considered an integral part of a lesbian relationship by 33 (66%) although 34 (68%) were celibate. For most who were celibate, it was not by choice. While 10 (20%) felt guilty about it, nearly all had masturbated and 15 (30%) had used a vibrator for self-stimulation.

These women almost unanimously viewed themselves as well adjusted and felt positive about being a lesbian. Although their general health was not excellent (30 reported having had major surgery; 32 reported having arthritis), and 29 (58%) view themselves as overweight, 90% (N=45) reported having good self-images. They tended to see their problems revolving around issues of health, money and isolation and thought the important things they needed to age better would include companionship and places to relax and be themselves.

While Kehoe's data differ somewhat from other samples of older lesbians in terms of health, sexual activity, living companions and belief in monogamy (Adelman, 1980; Raphael & Robinson, 1980; Tully, 1983), her sample (even with the 7 self-identified bisexuals included in the study) presents data on more women 65 years old or older than has been previously presented. These findings may signal other researchers to look for similar findings with similar samples.

In sum, data on older lesbians, though scant, depict them differently than do data on older women generally. Demographically, older women have been described as poorly educated, politically conservative, religiously active, asexual, professionally unemployed, and married (or widowed) (Achenbaum, 1974; Bart, 1975; Christenson & Johnson, 1973; DeMartino, 1974; Goldberg et al., 1986; Greenberg, 1979; Lopata, 1973; Matthews, 1979). In contrast, emerging data on older lesbians tend to describe them in terms that are more congruent with the profile of younger, professional women who have been influenced by the women's movement of the past twenty years (Tully, 1973). Demographic characteristics of older lesbian samples (Adelman, 1980; Berger, 1984; Behoe, 1986; Minnigerode & Adelman, Raphael & Robinson, 1980; Tully, 1983) tend to depict the older lesbian as highly educated, politically liberal, not traditionally religious, professionally employed, sexually active, and unmarried.

Further, older lesbians have been described as generally having their first sexual experience in their late teens or early twenties although this experience could occur at any time if a strong emotional bond existed between the women (Adelman, 1980; Kehoe, 1986; Raphael & Robinson, 1980; Tully, 1983). Also, older lesbians tend to prefer to relate socially and sexually with their own age group although they do have friends and lovers of varying ages (Adelman, 1980; Kehoe, 1986; Raphael & Robinson, 1980; Tully, 1983). While older lesbians generally have been brought up within a standardized religious context, many fall away from organized religion (Minnigerode & Adelman, 1978; Tully, 1983). Finally, older lesbians have been described as not experiencing the acceleration of aging as fast as heterosexual women (Laner, 1979) and adapt well to aging with positive self-images (Kehoe, 1986; Raphael & Robinson, 1980; Tully, 1983).

What is Not Known: Weaknesses and Limitations in Research

The literature review of studies conducted in the field of older lesbians represented the bulk of what is currently known about this minority group. While more data exist that describe the younger lesbian (Tully, 1983), the older lesbian continues to be a significantly understudied group. The weaknesses and limitation of the existing research will be discussed in terms of the theories from which research questions evolve, the research questions themselves, the research methodologies employed in the studies and the conclusions of the research.

Theoretical Perspectives

A major problem confronting researchers wishing to study homosexuality or older populations is the lack of existing, unified theory. This lack of a specific theoretical base creates a dilemma for the researcher who must then formulate research questions based not on proven theory, but on theoretical perspectives which may or may not be accurate. By studying issues that evolve from a variety of theoretical concepts, researchers investigate any number of seemingly unrelated topics. Unfortunately, this pre-theoretical accumulation of data accounts for almost all of the research in the area of lesbianism and a substantial amount of the work done on older populations.

Perhaps due to this lack of a unified theoretical base, those studying lesbian women often ignore the importance of theory within their research and leave the reader to interpret the theoretical basis of the study (Adelman, 1980; Bullough & Bullough, 1977; Gundlach, 1967; Kehoe, 1986; Laner, 1979; Lewis, 1980; Raphael & Robinson, 1980). This situation has been particularly evident since lesbian research has moved away from the early etiological studies where the primary theoretical base was Freudian. Since abandoning the quest for the "cause of lesbianism," researchers have developed any number of diverse, often contradictory, theoretical perspectives about lesbians that have yet to be incorporated into a unified theory or even into a group of fairly well defined, testable hypotheses.

Although gerontology has yet to develop a well defined social theory of aging (Birren, 1971), researchers have developed several theoretical perspectives about aging which are being systematically explored (Birren & Cunningham, 1985). Thus, with the development of a fairly specific set of theoretical perspectives such as "disengagement," "subculture of old age," "socialization to old age," and "activity model" (Ibid.), gerontological researchers seem to be more directed in their study of aging than are those studying homosexuality. However, even with better defined concepts, gerontological research continues to lack any well articulated theoretical perspectives dealing with older lesbians or gays.

Research Questions

This lack of unified theory creates confusion in the design of appropriate research questions. With the absence of theory and the abundance of theoretical perspectives and suppositions, the research questions that have been asked about lesbians have had a somewhat unpredictable evolution. Research questions in the field of aging, however, seem to have evolved more predictably.

Research questions regarding lesbian women tend to cluster around questions of etiology, questions of psychological functioning and questions of lifestyles and social functioning. These topic areas tend to shift over time to respond to new information. A major weakness in the lesbian research, due to the lack of any unified theory, is that each researcher approaches the development of research questions from a different perspective which hampers the researcher from developing questions in a deductive manner.

Lesbian research continues to evolve from an inductive level where the research questions come from the researcher's own ideas, values and the abundance of unproven theoretical perspectives about lesbian women.

While research questions evolving from researchers studying aging seem to be developed at an empirically somewhat higher level than those developed for lesbians, the relevancy of research questions in the field of aging, too, relies heavily on the inductive abilities of the researcher. As the theorists in the field of aging tend to ignore homosexuality, those studying aging also ignore older lesbian and gay populations.

Research Methodology

Despite the lack of a well defined, integrated theoretical base or the relevancy of the research questions being studied, research continues in the areas of homosexuality and aging. In many of these studies, substantial deficiencies exist within the research methodologies used to study the phenomenon in question.

The overwhelming majority of all lesbian studies are descriptive, cross-sectional surveys where the operationalized key variables are frequently left to the reader's own interpretation (Abram, 1980; Belote & Joesting, 1976; Caprico, 1954; Mendola, 1980). While this is a serious limitation, other weaknesses exist as well. A major problem with the research in the field of lesbianism is the fact that what data have been collected come from primarily small, biased samples of young, white middle-class, well educated women from urban areas (Albro & Tully, 1979; Chafetz et al., 1974; 1976; Gagnon & Simon, 1973; Gundlach, 1967; *The Ladder*, 1960). Further, the data gathering procedures in the majority of studies do not provide for gathering data in any type of triangulated fashion and use researcher designed instruments. Thus, the validity and reliability of the results may be questioned. Finally, the statistical analysis in many of the lesbian studies may be ignored, leaving the reader to interpret the pages of raw data (Abrams, 1980; Beloted &

Joesting, 1976; Mendola, 1980; Trip, 1976). Only a few studies in the fields of lesbianism provide any correlation analyses (Albro et al., 1977; Chafetz et al., 1974, 1976; Brooks, 1981; Raphael & Robinson, 1980; Tully, 1983), and there is little recent experimental research dealing with lesbian samples.

Similar methodological problems exist in gerontological research as well. The majority of aging research continues to be cross-sectional surveys that are primarily exploratory and descriptive (Andrews et al., 1978; Goldberg et al., 1986; Harris et al., 1975; Matthews, 1979). While samples of older persons for research are easier to obtain for study than are samples of lesbian women, the samples used in gerontological studies tend to be dominated by white middle-class, well educated, assumed heterosexual individuals (Andrews et al., 1978; Christenson & Gagnon, 1965; Christenson & Johnson, 1973; Conner et al., 1979; Goldberg et al., 1986; Greenberg, 1979; Lopata, 1973; Matthews, 1979; Newman & Nicholas, 1960; Pfeiffer et al., 1972; Pfeiffer & Davis, 1972). As with research on homosexuality, research in the area of gerontology tends to use researcher designed instruments that are rarely well described in the published study. Also, such studies tend to gather data with only one method (generally an interview or questionnaire) which may call into question the validity and reliability of the results. While gerontological studies seem to be more rigorous in their statistical analysis of data and more frequently provide bivariate and multivariate analysis than research on lesbians, little specifically experimental research is being conducted with gerontological populations outside the field of medicine.

Research Findings and Conclusions

Because no unified theory exists from which research questions should logically emerge and because there are numerous methodological problems that exist within the current literature on lesbians and older populations, the findings and conclusions of these studies must be examined with these limitations in mind. A major weakness of homosexual research in general is that researchers may not honestly define the narrowness of their findings (Bell & Weinberg, 1978; Berger, 1984; Caprio, 1954; Kaye et al., 1967; Laner, 1979; Poole, 1970, Tripp, 1976), and others may inappropriately generalize their findings as being representative of all homosexuals (Bell & Weinberg, 1978; Caprio, 1954; Tripp, 1976). Similarly, those doing research in the field of gerontology also may fail to adequately define the ability to generalize from their findings (Andrews et al., 1978; Conner et al., 1979). Finally, the findings and conclusions from the research on lesbians and older populations tend to raise more questions about the phenomena studied than are answered, thus creating the constant need for continuing research.

Recommendations for Further Study

As noted, there is a significant need for much more research about older lesbian women. Specific questions raised by what research has been done in the field are numerous and ought not to be overlooked by future scholars. The following represent some of the research questions about older lesbians that have yet to be empirically examined:

- What are the demographic characteristics of older racially and ethnically identified lesbian minorities?

- What specific differences exist between lesbians who are older than 65 and younger lesbians?

- What specific differences exist between older lesbians and older heterosexual women?

- How do older lesbians and older gay men differ?

- What differences exist between older lesbians with a history of marriage and children and those who have never married?

- What specific variables account for the older lesbian's involvement in politics, religion, organizations, the homosexual community?

- Why does the older lesbian use informal networks for support rather than formal social systems?

- What are the specific phases of the lesbian's coming out process and have these varied for younger and older lesbian women?

- How does the older lesbian integrate her personal and professional lives?

- What do older lesbians view as problematic to them as they age?

- What role models have older lesbians used?

- What difficulties does the older lesbian face in managing a dual lifestyle where she interacts with both the homosexual and heterosexual social systems?

- What specific problems does the older, institutionalized lesbian confront?

- How are the housing needs of older lesbians different from those of older heterosexual women?

- What are the older lesbian's social service needs?

- How does the older lesbian age (biologically, psychologically, sociologically?

- What specific variables can be identified in early age or middle-age that will help the lesbian adjust to her aging?

- What differences exist between the rural and urban older lesbian?

- What are the similarities between the sexual behaviors of older lesbians and other older populations?

- How has the older lesbian's sexual orientation helped her age?

These questions coupled with countless others begin to demonstrate how little is actually known about older lesbians and how much is left to discover. For researchers wishing to gather data on older lesbians, problems and pragmatic strategies for coping with these problems will be the focus of the remainder of this chapter.

How to Learn More About the Older Lesbian Woman

When attempting to conduct research with or about lesbian elders or any population that deviates from the norm, researchers are confronted with a variety of potential problems. The majority of these occur in two of the research phases—the problem definition phase and the research design phase. Each phase will be examined and the author will use her own research as examples.

Problem Definition Phase

Probably one of the most exciting, demanding and frustrating times for any scholar is the conceptualization of a researchable phenomenon, the articulation of the study's focus and the delineation of a sound rationale for the proposed research. While these steps can cause potential dilemmas for any researcher, those wishing to study lesbian women must consider unique issues.

Researchers generally tend to study those phenomena that are of interest to them and about which they have a certain amount of prior knowledge or curiosity. For the scholar wishing to research phenomena related to older lesbians, the first issue that must be faced is that of institutionalized, personal homophobia— the scholar's fear that being interested in and wanting to study homosexuality could cause damage to her/his professional or personal reputation. For example, as both an M.S.W. and Ph.D. student who wanted to conduct research in the field of lesbianism, the author had to consider how the decision to pursue the research might be perceived by faculty, professional colleagues, students, family members and friends. The question to be considered was, "What are the short-term and long-term consequences of conducting research in an unpopular field, and is the risk of pursuing the much needed research worth the potential professional and personal price of being perceived as a lesbian?" For each scholar studying homosexuality, this question must be answered before the research study can emerge.

Assuming, as did the author, that the benefits of the study outweigh the possible consequences, the conceptualization of a researchable phenomenon within a theoretical framework can occur. As noted earlier in this chapter, a major problem confronting researchers wishing to study homosexuality or older populations is the lack of existing, unified theory. Thus, the overwhelming majority of studies on older lesbians are qualitative. In an effort to move from the purely qualitative end of the research spectrum to a quantitative-descriptive level, the author in both her thesis and dissertation utilized the conceptual framework provided by general systems theory to study the social support and interactional patterns of lesbian women. The topic was sufficiently narrowly defined so as to facilitate operationalizing key variables while also being broad enough to ensure collection of sufficient data for study.

Creating a specific focus that is neither too narrow nor too broad may be problematic for the novice researcher. In eager anticipation to explain phenomena (the experimental end of the research spectrum), s/he may overlook what exists in relation to the phenomena (the exploratory end of the spectrum) and how variables are related to one another (somewhat mid-way on the spectrum) (Figure 1: The Research Spectrum). Given the reality that so little is currently known about older lesbians, the appropriate starting point for research in this field has been, and will continue to be, exploratory research. Eventually, from beginning definitions of the phenomenon, more scientifically rigorous studies will emerge that will seek to explain the phenomenon.

Finally, scholars must present a sound rationale that will specifically articulate why their studies are needed and what new knowledge can be anticipated from their scientific endeavors. This may present problems for the researcher studying older lesbians only because providing the necessary documentation to substantiate the need for and the anticipated outcomes of the study is tedious. However, the dearth of information in the field lends credence to the need for further data collection and the anticipated outcomes of such research are easily linked to any discipline. For example, the author, a social worker, based her rationale for the need for a study on the social support networks of older lesbians within the values and ethics of her professional arena. She provided a rationale for the inclusion of such knowledge within the social work repertoire by using Bartlett's (1970, pp. 130, 148) model of the "Common Base of Social Work Practice" and the 1977 National Association of Social Workers (NASW) policy statement about lesbians and gays (NASW, 1981).

FIGURE 1
THE RESEARCH SPECTRUM

LEAST SCIENTIFICALLY RIGOROUS

MOST SCIENTIFICALLY RIGOROUS

Exploratory–	Quantitative-Descriptive–	Experimental
Descriptive	Correlational	Explanational
Qualitative		Quantitative
Univariate	Bivariate	Multivariate
	Univariate	Bivariate
		Univariate

MOST SOCIAL SCIENCE RESEARCH
          MOST PHYSICAL SCIENCE RESEARCH

With the conceptualization of a researchable phenomenon, the articulation of the study's focus, and the delineation of a sound rationale, the scholar then moves toward actualizing the research project. The research design and issues that confront the study of older lesbians will follow.

Research Design Phase

While the Problem Definition Phase begins to set the parameters of the proposed research study, the Research Design Phase becomes the blueprint from which the scholar can complete the research project. The areas to be addressed in this phase include: the methodological approach; the operationalizing variables; sample selection and procedures; the instrumentation and data collection procedures; and the statistical analysis procedures. For those interested in studying older lesbians, there are some unique areas of concern to note.

Methodological Approach: In this stage of the research process, the scholar is asked to make a judgement as to what kind of methodological approach is best suited to gather data appropriate to the focus of the study. Will the study be cross-sectional or longitudinal, will it be a survey or not, will it be exploratory or quantitative-descriptive tending more to describe and define the phenomenon as opposed to experimental or quasi-experimental? While the methodological approach is left to the discretion of the researcher, a rationale to support the choice must be provided. For example, the author's studies employed a cross-sectional, survey approach that was quantitative-descriptive and tested no formal hypotheses because the focus of the studies and the specific questions asked in the studies sought merely to describe phenomena and to see if correlations existed between certain variables. This methodological approach also was congruent with other similar studies being conducted in the field at the time.

Operationalizing Variables: How to operationalize the key variables to be studied frequently becomes a stumbling block. Basically, this stage of the research process calls for the researcher to define key variables in ways that can be empirically measured. A rationale to support the definition should also be provided. While each study will have its own unique set of variables to be operationalized, one way to assure that the variables can be measured is to see how other researchers in the field have defined their terms and use a similar approach to theirs. For example, the author's dissertation sought to identify the social organizational structures of the older lesbian's social world. In operationalizing variables the following had to be defined - older lesbian, social structure, and social world. While it is unnecessary to operationalize all these terms here, how the term "older lesbian" was operationalized will be discussed.

One significant problem confronting scholars who wish to study older lesbian women is their invisibility within the heterosexual world. Thus, some screening device is needed to assure that data collected from samples are accurate. For the author's purposes, the term older lesbian was operationalized by defining it as "any woman 50 years or older whose current overt sexual activities and/or intense emotionally intimate psychological feelings ranked "4" or higher on a modified Kinsey Heterosexual-Homosexual Rating Scale (Kinsey, et al., 1953, pp. 470-472)" (Tully, 1983, pp. 73-74) (See Figure 2). The Kinsey Scale was chosen as it accurately identifies the respondent's sexual orientation and has been sufficiently used to be considered an appropriate measure of sexual orientation. The age of 50 was chosen as it had been used in several samples of "older" populations and provided a wider sampling frame.

FIGURE 2
HETEROSEXUAL-HOMOSEXUAL RATING SCALE*

Please rank yourself on the following scale based on your *present* physical sexual experiences. (Mark the one statement that is closest to your experiences) (Circle number)

0   Sexual experiences only with men
1   Sexual experiences predominantly with men, but
    with incidental experiences with women

2   Sexual experiences predominantly with men, but with more than incidental sexual experiences with women
3   Sexual experiences with women and men equally
4   Sexual experiences predominantly with women, but with more than incidental sexual experiences with men
5   Sexual experiences predominantly with women, but with incidental sexual experiences with men
6   Sexual experiences only with women
7   Not now sexually active with another person

Please rank yourself on the following scale based on your *present* intense, emotionally intimate feelings. (Mark the one statement that is closest to how you feel) (Circle number)

0   Intense emotional intimacy only with men
1   Intense emotional intimacy predominantly with men, but with incidental intense emotional intimacy with women
2   Intense emotional intimacy predominantly with men, but with more than incidental intense emotional intimacy with women
3   Intense emotional intimacy with women and men equally
4   Intense emotional intimacy predominantly with women, but with more than incidental intense emotional intimacy with men
5   Intense emotional intimacy predominantly with women, but with incidental intense emotional intimacy with men
6   Intense emotional intimacy only with women
7   Intense emotional intimacy with neither women nor men

*Modified by C. T. Tully (1983) from Kinsey et al. (1953)

When operationalizing variables, the key is to be certain that the variable is defined in a way that can be measured using some kind of statistical analysis procedure, and that the more concrete the definition, the easier the measurement. For example, it is simpler to operationalize the variable "age" or "lesbian" than it is to operationalize the variable "creativity" because more people generally agree on what the terms "age" and "lesbian" mean. Thus, keeping key variables simple and concrete helps.

Sample Selection and Procedures: Since it is impossible for any researcher to identify the total population of older lesbians in this country due to their invisibility, there has never been a study of lesbians (or gays) that has used a random sample. There is little likelihood that this will change, so researchers must rely on nonprobability sampling techniques to get samples. This alone has made studies of lesbian women and gay men biased, yet research in the field can and must continue even with this weakness.

The most common way of getting older lesbian samples has been to use friendship networks (snowball sampling techniques), advertisements in lesbian oriented publications, contacts with known lesbian organizations and personal friends. However, it must be noted that if the scholar attempts to engage in participant observation, conduct interviews, or speak to older lesbian groups, there continues to be a reluctance on the part of many older lesbians to allow the researcher access. Women to whom the author spoke and eventually interviewed, talked to her only after months of getting to know the researcher and then only after establishing some personal relationship with her. Without exception, the women interviewed noted their unwillingness to participate in studies conducted by men, and many were unwilling to speak with young women. Thus, samples of older lesbians, while challenging to discover in the first place, may present their own dilemmas once found. That is probably why most researchers opt to collect data on older lesbians using anonymous, responder completed, mailed questionnaires.

Data Gathering Procedures and Instrumentation: Research that begins to gather data on previously unexplored behaviors or groups often does so by using researcher designed instruments and frequently uses interviews or survey questionnaires to amass information (Tully, 1983).

While questionnaires and interviews seem to be popular methods of gathering information on older lesbians (Adelman, 1980; Kehoe, 1986; Raphael & Robinson, 1980), some researchers prefer to gather data by combining various data gathering techniques within a single research project. For example, a popular triangulated data gathering technique that has been successfully used with both older populations and homosexual samples is one where information is collected from participant observation, researcher interviews and respondent completed questionnaires—or a combination of any two of these methods (Bullough & Bullough, 1977; Caprio, 1954; Matthews, 1978; Ponse, 1978; Rosen, 1974; Tully, 1983).

Gathering data in a triangulated fashion provides one method of checking the reliability of data as well as providing a wide array of data that can be compared. The author employed a participant observation phase in her research for the purpose of gaining entry to a community of older lesbians, but the primary data gathering techniques she used were researcher conducted interviews and mailed survey questionnaires. The techniques of Gorden (1969) were used for the interviews; Dillman's (1978) "total design method" was used for the mailed questionnaires. Both were successful.

Statistical Analysis: The statistical analyses for any research are dependent on the level of the data collected. For the majority of studies on older lesbians, the statistical procedures are neither complex nor difficult. Because the bulk of data on older lesbians continues to be univariate, descriptive statistics such as measures of central tendency, variability and frequency distributions with appropriate tables are appropriate. When bivariate analysis is conducted, cross-tabulation tables using appropriate measures of association provide documentation. At this point, little multivariate analysis has been conducted in the area of older lesbian research simply because so little is known about the phenomenon and the sample sizes thus far have been too small and too homogeneous to warrant multivariate analysis.

Summary

This portion of the chapter has demonstrated how problems tend to occur at two points in the research process - the Problem Definition Phase and the Research Design Phase. The issues experienced by the author in her studies with older lesbian women are presented within the context of the conceptualization of a researchable phenomenon, the articulation of a study's focus, and the rationale for the research (the Problem Definition Phase) and in the methodological approach, operationalizing variables, sample selection, instrumentation/data collection, and statistical analysis stages (the Research Design Phase).

Research on Older Lesbians: A Continuing Challenge

This chapter has examined what is currently known about the older lesbian through a review of the literature in the field that is generally available. From that data a picture of the older lesbian woman as a well adjusted, professionally employed, relatively physically healthy, politically liberal, religiously inactive, sexually active woman is emerging. Unfortunately, there are still far too few studies in the field to make any conclusions, and there is still much more unknown than known about the older lesbian. This lack of information is compounded by the lack of any unified theory dealing with either elders or lesbians and the difficulty in obtaining older lesbian subjects for study. Many further questions about the older lesbian need to be addressed. While this area is fertile for future research, it remains relatively untouched. In trying to learn more about the older lesbian researchers must confront their own homophobia and be constantly aware of the unique methodological stumbling blocks that can obstruct the scholar. Yet, regardless of the barriers, research in the field of older (and even middle-aged) lesbians is sorely needed if stereotypes and myths are ever to yield to scientifically gathered empirical evidence of the realities of this minority.

References

Abrams, M. (1980). Becoming lavender. (Doctoral dissertation, City University of New York).

Achenbaum, W. A. (1974). The obsolescence of old age in America. *The Journal of Social History, 8*(1): 48-62.

Adelman, M. R. (1980). Adjustment of aging and styles of being gay: A study of elderly gay men and lesbians. (Doctoral dissertation, The Wright Institute).

Albro, J. C. & Tully, C. T. (1979). A study of lesbian lifestyles in the homosexual micro-culture and the heterosexual macro-culture. *Journal of Homosexuality, 4*(4): 331-344.

Albro, J. C.; Kessler, B. and Tully, C. T. (1977). A study of lesbian lifestyles. (Masters thesis, Virginia Commonwealth University).

Andres, G.; Tennant, C.; Hewson, D. M. & Vaillant, G. E. (1978). Life event stress, social support coping style and psychological impairment. *Journal of Nervous and Mental Disease, 166*: 307-316.

Bart, P. B. (1975). Emotional and social status of the older woman. In *No longer young: The Older Woman in America.* Institute of Gerontology: University of Michigan - Wayne State University: 3-21.

Bartlett, H. M. (1970). *The common base of social work practice.* Washington, D.C.: National Association of Social Workers.

Bell, A. P. & Weinberg, M. S. (1978). *Homosexualities.* New York: Simon and Schuster.

Belote, D. & Joesting, J. Demographic and self-report characteristics of lesbians. *Psychological Reports, 39*: 621-622.

Berger, R. M. (1984). Realities of gay and lesbian aging. *Social Work, 29*(1): 57-62.

Birren, J. & Cunningham, W. (1985). Research on the psychology of aging: principles, concepts and theory. In J. Birren & K. W. Schaie (eds.) *Handbook of the psychology of aging 2nd ed.* New York: Van Nostrand Reinhold: 3-34.

Brooks, V. R. (1981). *Minority stress and lesbian women.* Lexington: Lexington Books.

Bullough, V. L. & Bullough, B. (1977). Lesbianism in the 1920's and 1930's a newfound study. Signs, 2(4): 895-904.

Caprio, F. S. (1954). *Female homosexuality.* New York: Citadel Press.

Chafetz, J. S.; Beck, P,; Sampson, P.; West, J., & Jones, B. (1976). *Who's queer: a study of homo and heterosexual women.* Sarasota: Omni Press.

Chafetz, J. S.; Sampson, P.; Beck, P. and West, J. (1974). A study of homosexual women. *Social Work, 19*(6): 714-723.

Christenson, C. V. & Gagnon, J. H. (1965). Sexual behavior in a group of older women. *Journal of Gerontology, 20*(3): 351-356.

Christenson, C. V. & Johnson, A. B. (1973). Sexual patterns in a group of older never married women. *Journal of Geriatric Psychiatry, VI*(1): 80-98.

Conner, K. A.; Powers, E. A. & Bultena, G. L.)(1979). Social interaction and life satisfaction: an empirical assessment of late-life patterns. *Journal of Gerontology, 34*:116-121.

DeMartino, M. F. (1974). *Sex and the intelligent woman.* New York: Springer.

Dillman, D. A. (1978). *Mail and telephone surveys: the total design method.* New York:: John Wiley and Sons.

Gagnon, J. H. & Simon, W. (1973). *Sexual conduct.* Chicago: Aldine.

Goldberg, G. S.; Kantro, R.; Kremen, E. & Lavter, L. (1986). Spouseless, childless elderly women and their social supports. *Social Work, 31*(2): 104-112.

Gorden, R. L. (1969). *Interviewing: strategies, techniques and tactics.* Homewood: Dorsey Press.

Greenberg, R. M. (1979). Women and aging: An exploratory study of the relation of involvement in support systems to adaptation to the experience of aging. (Doctoral dissertation, Columbia University Teacher's College).

Gundlach, R. H. (1967). Research project report. *The Ladder, 11*: 2-9.

Harris, L. & Associates, Inc. *The myth and reality of aging in America*. Washington, D.C.: National Council on Aging.

Kaye, H. et al., (1967). Homosexuality in women. *Archives of General Psychiatry, 17*(5): 626-634.

Kehoe, M. (1986). Lesbians over 65: A triply invisible minority. *Journal of Homosexuality, 12*(3/4): 139-152.

Kinsey, A. C.; Pomeroy, W.; Martin, C. & Gebhard, P. H. (1953). *Sexual behavior in the human female*. Philadelphia: Saunders. *The Ladder*, (1960). 4: 4-25.

Laner, M. (1979). Growing older female: heterosexual and homosexual. *Journal of Homosexuality, 4*(3): 267-275.

Lewis, M. I. (1980). The history of female sexuality in the United States. In M. Kirkpatrick (ed.), *Women's sexual development*. New York: Plenum Press: 19-38.

Lopata, H. Z. (1973). *Widowhood in an American city*. Cambridge: Shenkman.

Matthews, S. H. (1979). *The social world of old women: Management of self identity*. Beverly Hills: Sage.

Mendola, M. (1980). *The mendola report: A new look at gay couples*. New York: Crown.

Minnigerode, F. & Adelman, M. R. (1978). Elderly homosexual women and men: Report of a pilot study. *Family Coordinator, 27*(4): 451-456.

National Association of Social Workers (1981). Lesbian and gay task force pamphlet. Washington, D.C.: National Association of Social Workers.

Newman, G. & Nicholas, C. (1960). Sexual activities and attitudes in older persons. *Journal of the American Geriatrics Society, 20*(4): 151-158.

Pfeiffer, E. & Davis, G. (1972). Determinance of sexual behavior in middle and old age. *Journal of the American Geriatrics Society, 20*(4): 151-158.

Pfeiffer, E.; Verwoerdt, A. & Davis, G. (1972). Sexual behavior in middle life. *American Journal of Psychiatry, 128*(10): 1261, 1267.

Ponse, B. (1978). *Identities in the lesbian world*. Westport: Greenwood.

Poole, K. (1970). A sociological approach to the etiology of female homosexuality and the lesbian social scene. (Doctoral dissertation, University of Southern California).

Raphael, S. & Robinson, M. (1980). The older lesbian's love relations and friendship patterns. *Alternative Lifestyles, 3*(2): 207-229.

Rosen, D. H. (1974). *Lesbianism: A study of female homosexuality.* Springfield: Charles Thomas.

Soldo, B. J. (1980). *America's elderly in the early 1980's.* Washington, D.C.: Population Reference Bureau.

Tripp, C. A. (1976). *The homosexual matrix.* New York: Signet.

Tully, C. T. (1983). Social support systems of a selected sample of older women. (Doctoral dissertation, Virginia Commonwealth University).

PART VI

FIELD INSTRUCTION/INTERNSHIPS: TEACHING AND LEARNING

Introduction

Inasmuch as traditional agencies and service delivery systems frequently have not been receptive to working with lesbian and gay clients, alternative resources have been developed in many communities. However, these sources of care often are not utilized for training students. This section explores ways in which greater creativity can be exercised so as to broaden student and faculty learning and service.

Chapter 17 provides rationales for institution of non-traditional settings for field instruction. Woodman then provides models for learning goals, objectives, and activities at all levels of social work training. The assessment process at each step of the learning process is also included. Although comparisons can be made with learning in situations involving non-lesbian/gay client groups, this chapter emphasizes the need to expand our vision so as to include lesbian/gay populations.

In Chapter 18, Shattls and Shernoff describe the experiences of students and field instructors in two different settings involving persons with AIDS. Both are in the New York/New Jersey area, but each setting includes diverse populations. Although Gay Men's Health Crisis, Inc. serves primarily the New York gay male community, Hyacinth Foundation in New Jersey is a resource for all of that state's population, including women, pediatric referrals and I.V. transmission cases. The authors provide the historical backgrounds and descriptions of each of these settings. They then introduce the reader to the unique learning opportunities provided and to the students. Education has included the entire range of social work service at the direct practice, administrative, and community development levels. What has been of even greater significance has been the opportunity to deal with transference and counter-transference issues in the emotion laden arena of dealing with death and dying. The ecosystems approach with which this book began is continued in the field education in AIDS placements where such an approach is essential. Shattls and Shernoff also speak to selection of students in terms of the need for dealing with potential for homophobia from the non-lesbian/gay student or over-identification from lesbian/gay interns. However, regardless of orientation, the potential for learning in a nontraditional setting is vividly presented.

16

Implementing Nontraditional Field Placements for Services in Lesbian and Gay Communities

Natalie Jane Woodman, M.S.S.

Historical Background and Rationale for Placements

In the 1982 Delegate Assembly of the Council on Social Work Education, the Delegates approved a new Curriculum Policy Statement which included the following: "The curriculum (of schools of social work)...should include content on other special population groups...in particular...such groups (as) those distinguished by...sexual orientation." As described in other chapters, such curricula can be interwoven in theoretical learning of the various sequences. However, opportunities for implementing field instruction may be hampered by the fact that traditional agencies often do not serve lesbian/gay client populations. Homophobia within the social work profession and allied disciplines has deterred many individuals from seeking help from family service, mental health clinics, etc. (Katz, 1976; Hildalgo, Peterson & Woodman, 1984). Outreach from established mental health systems has been absent or minimal in most communities. Although knowledgeable and accepting private practitioners may be available, younger clients, women in transition, or those with major medical/ financial crises such as AIDS, often do not have financial resources for such services. Most large cities do have indigenous networks to provide some services and may utilize professional volunteers. However, schools of social work usually do not explore or use such non-traditional settings for field instruction placements. This is a loss to the community, students, and— most crucially— to clients. This author's practice experience and interviews with over 200 lesbians in suburban and metropolitan areas is corroborated by other authors (Baetz, 1979; Bell & Weinberg, 1978; Brooks, 1981) who also have noted the paucity of supportive social services for lesbian and gay clients.

Other facets of social work curricula are affected by the lack of such non-traditional field settings. Assessment, evaluation, and recommendations for implementing social services and policies which are non-homophobic rarely are a part of the practice experience of students. There is a definite potential for application of knowledge relative to community organization problem solving within this minority community. Finally, sharing experience gained from practice can result in further research in such areas as: myths and stereotypes regarding lesbian and gay populations; knowledge about the realities and diversities of gay lifestyles; understanding of and sensitivity to the ways in which lesbian women and gay men view themselves as different from and similar to the non-gay population.

In conclusion, the author would emphasize that lesbians and gays as a group are no more likely to be in need of social work or mental health services than the population at large (Hooker, 1957; Hammersmith & Weinberg, 1973; Freedman, 1971). However, oppression and social injustice are very real, and many within this minority group can and would benefit from the services which are a part of the student's field instruction experience. Also, students themselves will be impacted by observation of the school's commitment to serving all groups and ameliorating homophobic behaviors within communities.

Suggested Field Instruction Settings and Placements

At the direct practice level, a faculty based field instructor, agency based social worker, or private practitioner could initiate contacts and then provide instruction and supervision in a variety of settings. Many colleges and universities already have gay and lesbian student caucuses or coalitions. Within such groups, there is a frequent plea for hot line/crisis intervention, group leaders for varying levels of discussion/problem solving, and resource development. Larger cities (and some of smaller size) which have existing lesbian and gay assistance and information lines can benefit from the professionally trained student whose learning opportunities can be extensive. Also, there may be a number of indigenous groups and services where in-put from schools of social work would be valued. Included in this area would be a parents and friends of gays organization, lesbian/gay mothers and fathers groups, youth groups such as Chicago's Gay Horizons, resources for elders such as Seniors Active in the Gay Environment, alcoholism and substance abuse programs, and religious organizations.

Where such programs do not exist, there is significant opportunity for the student who is concerned with program and community development to work with a field instructor in originating needed services. Here, again, a starting place can be the college or university setting itself. Other possibilities would include: local church groups (this author has noted throughout the country that Unitarian Churches often are helpful in initiating out-reach and dialogue with lesbian women and gay men), women's centers and programs, human relations councils, and existing social service programs which are willing to assess needs and implement new services in new ways to reach this population. For example, health agencies may be helped in program development and counseling for persons with AIDS. Existing Information and Referral agencies may be enabled to identify resources in the lesbian and gay community not previously recognized and then utilize a social work student who will be available to provide assistance and empathy to those who call for help. Finally, development of in-service training for practitioners also can be a part of the student's learning experience. Using the state chapter of NASW in organizing a lesbian and gay task force/committee would be very reasonable entry point for the concerned field instructor and student.

In summary, flexibility of field instructor and student is obviously a key characteristic in moving into such placement opportunities. Another dimension that is crucial is the clarity of identified learning objectives and the continuing process of assessing learning. Integration of theoretical knowledge should be specified at the outset, as should the on-going process of values clarification. Both the student and field instructor can benefit from the interdisciplinary team work that would be involved in almost all communities. Roles and goals in working with other professionals and with para-professionals would involve continuing learning opportunities.

Learning Objectives and Activities

For purposes of clarity, this author has utilized the standard format for field instruction contracts developed by the Field Team at Arizona State University School of Social Work. This structure will provide for delineation of objectives and tasks congruent with social work knowledge, values and attitudes. Proceding from broad learning goals and specific objectives, the author has attempted to identify a spectrum of tasks. Many activities are predicated on the fact that there is an existing agency, indigenous group, or community resource available.

The outline format begins with those goals applicable to all levels of social work education (Goals I-III). The author then addresses the BSW level and MSW 1st Year (Goals IV-VI); 2nd Year MSW Direct Practice (Goal VI); 2nd Year MSW Community Practice (Goal VIII); and 2nd Year MSW in toto (Goals IX & X). In the process of writing this paper, more objectives and activities came to mind than could be included in this brief presentation. Therefore, the outlines which follow should be considered as a preliminary effort to explicate innovations in Field Instruction with lesbian and gay communities. It is hoped that the reader will eliminate, revise, add or create objectives and tasks appropriate for her/ his students and agency settings. This process should be continuous— most hopefully because of positive changes in our society and its social institutions resulting from social work teaching, learning, and doing.

PROGRAM LEVEL: All Students

LEARNING GOAL I: To increase the students' knowledge and value base relative to lesbian and gay life styles.

OBJECTIVES	ACTIVITIES
To identify historical perspectives which have had impact on lesbians/gays	Read (or re-read) *GAY AMERICAN HISTORY* and a minimum of one other historical book
To identify broad social work policy, practice and values issues.	Read NASW CODE OF ETHICS, Policy Statements on Lesbian and GayIssues, Historical Section of *NASW Manual on Lesbian and Gay Issues: A Resource Manual*
To identify evidence of homophobia and acceptance in the community	Research in local newspapers Discussion with local lesbian and gay groups Contact NGLTF
To identify evidences of homophobia and acceptance in social work as a profession and within agency	Read NASW Resource Manual Assess agency policies regarding intake, personnel decisions, etc. Assess school of social work policies regarding admission, retention, curriculum
To identify biases relative to lesbians and gays which may impede effective problem solving	Prepare a "think paper" regarding myths, positive/negative stereotypes, and how these can affect service delivery with lesbians and gays

LEARNING GOAL II: To increase the student's knowledge of community resources regarding lesbians/gays

OBJECTIVES	ACTIVITIES
To identify existing resources (traditional and non-traditional) in the community	Develop a resource file (with full identifying data) and prepare typed list of file contents
To identify needed resources/ social services	Formulate questionnaire Discuss with community agencies, indigenous groups, other contracts. Prioritize needs

To identify where resources   Identify linkages between prior
might be developed   two activities.

LEARNING GOAL III: To relate purposefully to interdisciplinary and
indigenous groups with which the student will work in facilitating self-
actualization of lesbians and gays.

OBJECTIVES	ACTIVITIES
To utilize communication skills and diverse knowledge in interacting with diverse professional persons/groups and with paraprofessionals	a. Read DSM I, II, III-R regarding changes in mental health attitudes/treatment of lesbians and gays. b. Identify terminology and other pertinent information regarding health issues c. Attend ___ meetings with interdisciplinary groups and paraprofessionals. Keep brief notes
To identify cultural diversities and implications of sexism and/or racism for lesbian and gay groups	a. Read assigned materials related to cultural factors, racism and sexism b. Discuss readings with groups who can provide feedback

---

**PROGRAM LEVEL: BSW and/or Foundation Year MSW
(Latter level would consider greater breadth/depth of learning)**

LEARNING GOAL IV: To implement the problem solving process with
individual lesbians and gays and with small groups

OBJECTIVES	ACTIVITIES
1. To identify specific knowledge in the area of human behavior in the social environment relative to development of a positive lesbian/gay identity	1. Read materials assigned by FI and HBSE faculty.
2. To identify problem areas which are unique to lesbian/gay clients	2a. Co-lead a rap group around a designated problem area (e.g. coming out to friends) b. Identify core group of individuals concerned with dealing with specific problem in depth c. Facilitate problem solving process with individuals, couples, small groups d. Evaluate outcome of intervention process
3. To engage clients in a problem solving process, utilizing skills appropriate to resolution of problem (with attention to unique needs of lesbian/gay clients)	3. See 2. c and d. above.

4. To mediate for/with/among lesbian and gay clients and significant social systems

4. Implement problem solving process with colleagues

5. To identify specific crisis needs and utilize crisis intervention skills with lesbians and gays

5a. Attend in-service training sessions regarding crisis intervention

b. With co-worker, take ___ crisis calls

c. Independently take ___ calls

d. Initiate and follow through on in-person interviews related to crisis counseling with ___ applicants.

PROGRAM LEVEL: MSW 1st Year

LEARNING GOAL V: To assess organizational problem solving with a lesbian or gay group

OBJECTIVES	ACTIVITIES
To identify leadership roles and styles	Attend ___ meetings
To identify organizational processes of the group	Write a systems analysis of the organizational structure and process
To identify alternative organizational strategies for effective attainment of group goals	Discuss with relevant organizational participants

LEARNING GOAL VI: To apply knowledge of research methodology to lesbian/gay issues.

OBJECTIVES	ACTIVITIES
To identify research problem areas specific to this population	Readings as assigned by Field Instructor and research faculty
To design a research proposal for study	Analyze an existing research study
To assess value issues in research	Prepare own written materials

---

PROGRAM LEVEL: 2nd Year MSW - Direct Practice

LEARNING GOAL VII: To increase social work knowledge and skill in problem solving with lesbian and gay clients who seek help with individual, family or group related problems

OBJECTIVES	ACTIVITIES
To identify populations at risk and identify particular inter-strategies which can be explored with clients/client groups	Assess agency intakes and outreach strategies in relationship to ventive client needs

Readings as assigned by FI and
campus faculty

Prepare contract for learning
activities for the semester/year

To implement diverse interven-   In recording, identify knowledge
tive strategies based on assess-   base utilized in problem solving
ment of client needs and inter-   process
vention outcomes
                                         Engage in problem solving with ___
                                         individuals, families and groups

                                         Design and utilize an evaluation
                                         instrument by which client's goal
                                         attainment can be assessed

---

PROGRAM LEVEL: 2nd Year MSW - Policy, Administration, Community Practice

LEARNING GOAL VIII: To utilize knowledge of policy, administration and
community organization for innovative service delivery to lesbian and gay
communities

OBJECTIVES	ACTIVITIES
To identify unmet needs desired by the community which can be implemented by social service delivery resources	Design and carry out needs assessment and analysis
To plan a program for new or changed social work service	Design program including budget, personnel needs, time deadlines, etc.
	Design evaluation instrument to assess program effectiveness
To initiate and evaluate a for agency or community implementation of service to lesbians and gays	Identify and secure needed program personnel to implement program
	Administer evaluation instrument and analyze effectiveness of service

---

PROGRAM LEVEL: 2nd Year MSW - All Concentrations

LEARNING GOAL IX: To utilize knowledge in education of others relative
to practice of social work with lesbian and gays

To identify theoretical know-   Design a program for in-service
ledge, attitudes and skills for   training with a community group,
other professionals who will work   agency staff or student(s)
with lesbian and gay clients

To identify and conceptualize   Initiate and carry through on a
learning objectives and outcomes   training program - including
designated learning publics   design and administration of
                                         evaluation process

                                         Where applicable, co-supervise BSW
                                         or 1st year MSW student or
                                         paraprofessional(s)

To identify, design and implement an empirical research project

Carry out research assignment in conjunction with research faculty

To enhance the state chapter of NASW or school of social work's implementation of programs, etc. on behalf of lesbian and gay communities

Assess state chapter goals, objectives, programs regarding lesbian and gay publics

Assess school policies, programs, etc.

If no existing Task Force/ Committee on Lesbian and Gay Issues exists, work with National NASW Committee/State Board regarding meeting need of colleagues and clients

Regarding school of social work, initiate contact with CSWE Commission on Lesbian and Gay Issues, identify a specific task and carry through to completion

If state chapter of NASW has an existing Task Force or Committee, initiate contact, identify a specific task for assignment and carry through to completion.

References

Baetz, Ruth. *Lesbian Crossroads: Personal Stories of Lesbian Struggles and Triumphs*. New York: William Morrow and Company, Inc., 1980.

Bell, Alan P. and Weinberger, Martin S. *Homosexualities: A Study of Diversity Among Men and Women*. New York: Simon and Schuster, 1978.

Brooks, Virginia. *Minority Stress and Lesbian Women*. Lexington, Mass.: D. C. Heath & Co., 1981.

Freedman, Mark. *Homosexuality and Psychological Functioning*. Belmont, Calif.: Brooks/Cole, 1971.

Hidalgo, Hilda, Peterson, Travis and Woodman, Natalie. *Resource Manual on Lesbian and Gay Issues*. New York: National Association of Social Workers, 1984 (in press).

Hooker, Evelyn. "The Adjustment of Male Homosexuality." *Journal of Projective Techniques*, 21, 1957, pp. 18-31.

Katz, Jonathon. *Gay American History*. New York: Avon, 1978.

Weinberg, Martin and Williams, Colins. *Male Homosexuals: Their Problems and Adaptions*. New York: Oxford University Press, 1984.

17

Field Placement in AIDS Service Provider Agencies

William D. Shattls, CSW, ACSW and Michael Shernoff, CSW, ACSW

> Everybody knows that pestilences have a way of recurring in the world; yet somehow we find it hard to believe in ones that crash down on our heads from a blue sky. There have been as many plagues as wars in history; yet always plagues and wars take us equally by surprise. (Camus, 1948, p.34)

It is no surprise, however, that social workers have assumed a leadership role in response to the health crisis precipitated by the sudden appearance of AIDS nor is it a surprise that social workers have been among the first to recognize the scope of the developing health crisis and the emerging need for psycho-social support services for people with AIDS (PWAs) and their loved ones (Lopez & Wein, 1982; Lopez & Getzel, 1984).

Social workers have been instrumental and actively involved in developing and organizing patient service programs in many of the AIDS service agencies springing up throughout the United States and Canada. It has been essential to conceptualize, design and implement services based on a comprehensive bio-psycho-social approach to meet the needs of people afflicted with AIDS and AIDS Related Conditions (ARC). Professional social work is oriented toward contextual perceptions of client and service delivery needs and is therefore uniquely qualified to serve on the front lines in combatting the ravages of this condition both in hospitals and outpatient settings (Baumgartner, 1985; Christ, Weiner, & Moynihan, 1986). If Lillian Wald were alive today, it is likely that she would have been involved in helping establish the new voluntary AIDS social service agencies that have been developed and mandated to provide services where none were available before.

New Agencies to Meet New Needs

The Gay Men's Health Crisis, Inc. (GMHC) was founded in August, 1981 by a small group of men whose friends were ill and dying of a then new and poorly understood condition. GMHC was the first organization created specifically to respond to the emerging AIDS crisis. Since then almost every major city in the U.S. has developed similar local AIDS service organizations that attempt to provide innovative services to an under-served client population. Historically, this has been the traditional response of professional social work to crisis.

In October, 1985 Hyacinth Foundation was formed to provide counseling and training and conduct research in the social work, health, and mental health fields, with a particular emphasis on issues related to human sexuality. Located in New Jersey where, at the time, there were no existing services for people with AIDS such as those provided in New York City by GMHC, the executive director began The New Jersey AIDS Project to meet the needs of people with AIDS and their loved ones. Hyacinth now has grown to be the major voluntary AIDS service provider in the state.

Gaps and voids in existing health care delivery systems have been filled in part by the emergence of new organizations and agencies in response to the needs of people affected by AIDS. Social workers have played vital roles as community organizers and planners establishing linkages and networks between social service and health care agencies and this new and increasingly large group of clients. This is social work in its most basic and fundamental form.

These newer community based agencies, organized to provide services to people with AIDS, are being required to develop innovative, creative, and dynamic programs. They represent not only a challenge to seasoned professionals but also a golden opportunity for learning and the training of social work students.

Effective service to people with AIDS and their significant others requires collaboration and a multi-disciplinary team approach - skills which are an intrinsic part of the traditional social work model. Like most agencies serving people with AIDS, Hyacinth and GMHC rely on these skills and this approach. Both agencies offer students exposure to a variety of professional situations and to professionals from various disciplines. The learning which occurs as students work in AIDS service agencies, service areas and organizations provides rich and diverse experiences which can be generalized and which will benefit the learner in whatever field of practice within the profession the student eventually may enter. For all these reasons, the authors believe that students in placement at any AIDS service organization have numerous opportunities for broad based and diversified training experiences. This chapter will describe the ways in which both GMHC and Hyacinth have functioned as field work placements and provided such opportunities.

GMHC is located in Manhattan in the heart of what has been referred to as "the gay ghetto". The majority of GMHC's clients are gay men with AIDS and those who care for them, geographically concentrated in this major urban center. Hyacinth serves people throughout the state of New Jersey. A substantial percentage of Hyacinth's clients are women with AIDS, pediatric cases, and I.V. drug use transmission-related cases in addition to gay men.

There are a number of issues which must be considered by both the agency and the school of social work when evaluating the viability of these new agencies as field placements for social work students. As new and rapidly expanding social service and educational organizations providing urgently needed services to an under-served population, GMHC and Hyacinth seem ideally suited to provide students with valuable learning opportunities. Naturally, it is the concern of social work schools and educators that students have appropriate learning opportunities and experiences while receiving high quality supervision from knowledgeable professionals. The agency requires placement of qualified and capable students sensitive to the requirements of the work to be done and the populations to be served. Where AIDS-related services are concerned, however, these issues may be more complex than usual.

Political, Ethical and Political Considerations Related to Field Placement in Gay Agencies

Students, especially second year students, often request placements they believe or have heard would be desirable—in part because of their particular interests and in part because of particular curricula requirements. It is not surprising, therefore, that the suggestion that GMHC be used as a field placement originated with students who wanted to be placed there. Both students described below had been volunteers at GMHC and, quite reasonably, recognized that the work they were doing as volunteers was often as rigorous and demanding with as much or more educational value as other placements to which they might be assigned by the school.

From the agency's point of view, given that GMHC is staffed to a large extent by social workers, there is a sense of responsibility to the profession as well as to the community to offer this invaluable educational service. Less obvious, perhaps, is the need to provide gay role models both for other professionals and all students regardless of sexual orientation. Social work, no less than other professions includes within its ranks many homophobic (i.e. unrealistically anxious, frightened and misinformed) "professionals". There is a danger inherent in placing only gay or already sympathetic "heterosexual" students in a gay agency. Nothing changes when a "stick to your own kind" approach is passively accepted as though it reflected real pluralism and a genuine acceptance of diversity instead of the mere appearance of it. There is little benefit derived when the already well informed or educated are the only recipients of information or education. It would be interesting to examine the policies of various schools to determine just how frequently gay field placements are offered or assigned regardless of the student's sexual orientation or request since, more often than not, students do not choose the agencies at which they are placed. In other words, it is quite easy to confuse conformity to the letter of non-discriminatory ethical codes and policies, such as NASW's, with the real spirit and intent of those codes and policies. That is, to identify and change the discriminatory attitudes and practices which are usually insidious and covert, especially where AIDS is concerned, represents efforts to eliminate the "epidemic" within an epidemic. One must wonder whose interests are being served when only gay students are placed in agencies which provide services to gay clients.

Conversely, all social work students, regardless of sexual orientation or any other characteristic, need to be educated and helped to develop their identities as professional social workers whose skills and knowledge are applicable and available to clients in any and all population groups. The line between affirmative action and reverse discrimination is not always clearly defined. (It should be noted that the administration and faculty at the Hunter College School of Social Work and Rutgers Graduate School of Social Work have been extremely supportive. Also, given the homophobic realities of society and the profession, especially in the face of the AIDS epidemic, they have been rather courageous and pioneering in support of GMHC and Hyacinth and the needs of the gay community in New York City and New Jersey.)

GMHC, Inc. and Hyacinth:
Unique Learning Opportunities

Two students began field placement at GMHC in the fall semesters of 1984 and 1985. Student placements at Hyacinth began one year later.

During the process of applying for approval as a field placement for the Hunter College School of Social Work, GMHC provided a description of the services it provides which include: Community education; direct support services to PWAs and collaterals including individual and group counseling, home care (through the "buddy" program), recreational services, financial aid advocacy, and legal services and counseling; fund raising for AIDS related program development including medical and psychosocial research; networking and inter-agency collaboration; and community AIDS program development. One could hardly hope for a more rich or diversified field placement for any student. Indeed, setting limits and structuring the fieldwork may be a greater challenge than finding opportunities for learning to occur.

Specific learning experiences made available to students at GMHC have included: Intake interviews and psychosocial assessments; individual counseling and psychotherapy; crisis intervention; experience in leading or co-leading AIDS support groups, groups for men with Kaposi's Sarcoma (a rare cancer that afflicts some people with AIDS), bereavement groups, support groups for care partners, parents' groups, therapeutic recreation groups; administrative and management experience in organizations; program development, implementation and evaluation; public and professional education; public speaking; community work; fund raising; patient advocacy in the areas of financial aid, legal counseling, and negotiating various entitlement programs at all levels of government; and collaboration with professionals from a wide variety of disciplines.

The field work program at Hyacinth operates under the auspices of Rutgers University Graduate School of Social Work. At the time Hyacinth was approved as a field placement the New Jersey AIDS Project was providing psychosocial and concrete support services to people with AIDS, ARC, their significant others, and to the so-called "worried well" (people who are healthy but highly anxious about contracting AIDS, sometimes to phobic proportions).

The learning experiences available to students at Hyacinth consist of many similar opportunities to those available to students at GMHC, including: staffing the telephone hotline; initial assessment interviews, co-facilitating support groups, individual crisis counseling, ongoing individual psychotherapy and supervision of volunteers.

There are numerous other opportunities for learning not addressed in official descriptions of agencies but which are equally important aspects of the learning and experiences required for "professionals-to-be." A new and rapidly expanding social service agency functioning in the midst of an unprecedented health crisis provides opportunities to learn perhaps more than is usual about "crises" and how these evolve, plus how organizations and individuals struggle to identify and manage the stresses and tensions these create. Other characteristics of such agencies which provide learning opportunities includes understanding and adapting to: the demand for services always exceeding availability; "staff" consisting primarily of dedicated and highly motivated volunteers with no formal training in the helping professions; both paid and volunteer staff frequently becoming clients of the very agency in which they are working as they, too, are diagnosed with AIDS; co-workers and friends suffering the same vicissitudes as one's clients, living - and dying - with AIDS.

The two students in placement at GMHC were gay men. Of the four students placed at Hyacinth, two were not gay. Thus, at Hyacinth, some of the issues described above concerning the sensitization of non-gay students to aspects of gay and lesbian lifestyles had to be explored during the initial stages of training. Similarly, all students, regardless of sex or sexual orientation, have to be sensitized to issues pertinent to intravenous drug using clients, women with AIDS, and other sub-groups within the PWA population. All need to be educated or, in some cases, re-educated about AIDS and to remain aware of new information and the rapidly unfolding events in medicine, social policy, treatment, research, experimental drug testing, etc.

Since the majority of staff and volunteers at Hyacinth and GMHC are lesbian or gay, non-gay students are immediately immersed in an environment where, as heterosexuals, they experience themselves as members of a minority. Exploration of the feelings raised in response to this novel situation provide many important discussions during supervision. This unique situation provides an opportunity for students to experience something of what it can mean to be a member of a sexual minority.

Basic AIDS-related information was provided for students when they attended the required three day training each agency mandated for all new staff and volunteers. These training sessions included an introduction to medical aspects of AIDS, current treatments, demographics, transmission, safer sex and risk reduction, psychosocial issues of people with AIDS, ARC, and Human Immunodeficiency Viral (HIV) infections (currently thought to cause AIDS), legal considerations for the person with AIDS, general counseling concerns, issues of death and dying, and particular concerns of I.V. drug using clients. As much time as possible was used for processing feelings raised during the training and was related to the information received and the work they will soon be asked to do. One way that feelings are surfaced is through the use of small discussion groups and through face-to-face interactions with persons with AIDS who are invited to come to the training and share aspects of their experiences as PWAs. Time is allowed for questions and discussion.

The Student Experience and Issues for Supervision

Joe, a second year student, candidly expressed his concerns about the sensitive and intense nature of work with terminally ill patients, those with long or protracted illnesses, the stigma of AIDS, the responses of significant others, and how these issues and others would both impact upon and be influenced by his personal attitudes, feelings, and experiences. These issues were monitored and explored continuously throughout his supervision.

When students in placement are self-identified gay men working with AIDS clients and their families there is a need to remain focused on the potential for over-identification with the client and on the student's feelings and reactions to the AIDS epidemic and its impact on the student's life. The countertransference issues raised are of necessity a constant theme in supervision.

Countertransference and identification with his clients were especially salient for Robert, a first year student who had been diagnosed with AIDS prior to his entering social work school. He had been a volunteer with an AIDS service agency for more than a year before he began his field work. As a volunteer he had worked in a recreational activities program in which opportunities for socialization and social activities were provided for PWAs. It was decided to use the broad range of social services available at his field placement as an opportunity for Robert to gain experience in other areas in order to enhance the development of varied social work skills and knowledge.

The responses and reactions of students and faculty at the schools and within the profession in general are among the issues that supervision needs to address. AIDS-related work bears many similarities to work in other social health care service areas but is at the same time unique, requiring many often subtle changes in the ways workers approach, manage and respond to the needs for and delivery of services to this population. In this regard all these students, but especially Robert as a self- identified gay man with AIDS, have been something of pioneers. Their courage, enthusiasm and dedication are laudable.

Since comprehensive assessment and needs evaluation represent a critical first step with AIDS clients and significant others, after completing the three day training, students in both agencies began to audit intake interviews conducted by more experienced staff or volunteers. This helped them become better acquainted with the variety of issues that people with AIDS present, as well as learn how the resources of each agency were able to meet, or failed to meet, the needs of a particular client.

Intake interviews provide students with exposure to clients of varying ages, ethnicity, and socio-economic backgrounds. Clients often present a variety of medical problems and conditions. Some are in the hospital at the time of intake while others are not. Many have psychological and emotional problems and coping difficulties related to the adjustment to life changes brought about by the disease or the diagnosis. Often there is difficulty making decisions about medical treatments and regimens, managing anxiety about mortality issues, the impact of their condition on significant others, employment concerns, financial problems and needs, the impact on sexual activities and functioning, internalized homophobia and homophobic responses from other individuals and institutions, and more. In the process of making assessments at intake interviews, before referrals are made or other services are provided, students gain exposure to a broad range of professional social work issues and some of the challenges present in AIDS-related work.

The diagnosis of AIDS often precipitates a crisis not only for the individual who is ill but also for his or her family and significant others. There are instances in which the originally identified client requires relatively few services and the client's significant others need many.

One way that AIDS service agencies attempt to meet the needs of PWAs and their significant others is by providing short term peer counseling. GMHC calls the people who do this work "crisis intervention workers" (CIWs). Both GMHC and Hyacinth train "buddies", volunteers who provide various concrete services like grocery shopping, cooking, driving the client to medical appointments, and even baby sitting in addition to supportive listening, companionship, and counseling.

CIWs and buddies work as advocates for their clients, providing liaison services between the client and all departments of GMHC or Hyacinth as well as basic counseling services which facilitate the client's better adaptation to the difficulties he/she is encountering in coping with issues and stressors which often, though not always, are related to the AIDS diagnosis.

A bio-psycho-social approach to evaluation and service provision is absolutely essential if the needs of the AIDS client population are to be met. Work with clients who are hospitalized requires that students learn how to confer and consult with professionals from a variety of disciplines; work as client advocates and learn to negotiate large bureaucratic systems; and develop expertise in the areas of discharge and aftercare planning and follow-up services.

Examples of Students' Experiences in the Field

Brief case summaries provide excellent examples of the learning experiences students are offered. Annabelle was a fifty five year old black woman whose daughter was in prison, pregnant, and had AIDS. The strains of pregnancy on her daughter's body resulted in rapid deterioration following the birth of Annabelle's granddaughter. In her initial call to Hyacinth, Annabelle asked for help in provision of concrete services. The newborn was placed with Annabelle who had no furniture for an infant. As a result, the child was sleeping in a dresser drawer. The student helped obtain a crib for the infant and drove Annabelle to and from the prison hospital to see her dying daughter. The student also arranged for rides to and from a support group. Annabelle was forbidden to touch her daughter by prison hospital officials. Her daughter died shortly after the birth. The student provided an empathetic ear and counseling to Annabelle during their drives to visit her daughter, and after her daughter's death. The child was born sero-positive for HIV antibodies and soon manifested symptoms of pediatric AIDS, adding a new dimension to the need for services and the role of the student.

Sarah was a 36 year old former I.V. drug-using heterosexual woman with AIDS. The woman's husband had died a

year an a half before her request for services. She had two
children, aged seven and two, and was socially isolated. The
student successfully engaged this initially resistant client in
an ongoing CIW-PWA relationship, offering her the opportunity to ventilate concerns and work toward the resolution
of problems that had seemed to her to be overwhelming.
Helping a client to partialize issues and difficulties often
increases the client's sense of control and ability to cope.

Miguel was a 24 year old Hispanic gay male living with his
mother. The student helped Miguel secure financial aid by
serving as liaison between the agency's Financial Service's
Department and the Department of Social Services. Initially
the client had been provocative and irresponsible in his
approach to making and keeping appointments with the
student. The student successfully worked through his own
anger and resentment so that he could focus on the needs of
the client in relation to the client's struggle with independence and autonomy issues, confused and contradictory
messages from the client for the student to intervene on his
behalf with the client's mother, and massive denial regarding
the client's very real medical problems. When this client went
into crisis, the student was confronted with an extremely
difficult situation. The client decompensated, having what
might best be described as an acute psychotic break requiring emergency hospitalization and medication. The
client's behavior had become suddenly violent and bizarre,
precipitating a general crisis involving the whole family and
requiring active and intensive involvement with a NYC hospital. There was much resistance on the part of the hospital
staff to provide what the student, supervisor and others at
student's agency felt were necessary and responsible services.

The student had to work with the family in ways which
required sensitive handling of issues pertaining to the client's
homosexuality, a fact which the client's brother in particular
had trouble accepting and with which the rest of the family
was also struggling. Also there were a number of issues
concerning the hospital staff's paranoid and inappropriate
response to the client's medical condition. The Emergency

Room staff refused to let the client use the ER bathroom and insisted he wear a mask for fear he might contaminate them. All this occurred, despite the well documented fact that such "precautions" are generally unnecessary. The student handled these difficulties with tact and sensitivity, and always with the client's welfare clearly in mind. The student's facility managing the rapidly unfolding events was laudable and demonstrated skills one might expect, perhaps, from a seasoned and experienced professional but not, ordinarily, from a student.

At most agencies serving PWAs and their collaterals, group work is the treatment of choice. However, such groups often present unique problems and challenges. Persons with AIDS, most of whom are relatively young, are forced to confront and struggle through the issues and problems which follow from the perception that AIDS is a terminal illness. To complicate matters, AIDS is largely a sexually transmitted disease which has affected a disproportionally large number of gay and bisexual men. Confronting the issues which pertain to AIDS, therefore, forces these clients to deal with many psychodynamic and social conflicts related both to sexuality and mortality in ways which are usually not required of young people in the prime of life. This situation forces both group members and leaders alike to confront very emotionally charged material - a challenge even to the most experienced clinical social workers and psychotherapists.

Group work experiences present a rich opportunity for the student to help clients explore the impact of an AIDS diagnosis and the resulting medical realities and life changes on intrapsychic functioning, interpersonal relations, family dynamics, issues of sexuality, and conflicts related to the issues of death and dying. As medical and psychological conditions of group members or their loved ones variously improve and deteriorate, students are required to join with their clients in coping with emerging and changing problems.

When students sense that significant issues are being avoided, denied or resisted, or that necessary treatments are being compromised by fear or denial, they are required to learn techniques and to make determinations about appropriate interventions. It is necessary to find ways in which to gently encourage clients to reveal more of their feelings while, at the same time, avoid attacking defenses the clients often need.

It is worth noting that issues of termination are even more sensitive than usual with this population and these field assignments. Saying "goodbye" to an AIDS patient is, for all intents and purposes, saying "goodbye" to a terminally ill person. During one meeting to discuss discharge plans, a student, the client's mother and a physician at the hospital found themselves discussing the inevitable death of the patient. The mother acknowledged her acceptance of the inevitable concerning her son. During a supervisory session following that meeting late in the spring semester the student expressed feeling badly about termination. Everyone's focus, including the student's, was on the loss to the client and family precipitated by the student being required to leave. No one seemed to be addressing the loss to the student. This was highlighted by the recent and untimely AIDS-related death of a close personal friend of the student. Not surprisingly, the termination process proved even more difficult because the student was somewhat reluctant to raise termination issues with his long term clients. There is a potential for guilt and a strong sense of loss for the student. Through discussions between the supervisor and student the various aspects of the issues involved need to be clarified and worked through.

Conclusions

The "innovative" quality of AIDS-related work and some of the problem situations which may arise in work with clients, families, hospitals and other bureaucratic organizations, and within the AIDS service provider organizations have been briefly described. Since many of the social service agencies serving populations impacted by AIDS are themselves relatively new, doing work, developing programs and attempting to provide urgently needed services in the context of an ongoing community crisis, the organizations themselves and all of their operations and service areas represent innovative attempts to meet newly identified client needs in imaginative ways. Students placed in these agencies have the opportunity to participate in and contribute to this organizational development as colleagues within the agencies. At the same time, students learn to assess individual and community needs and to plan, implement, and evaluate programs and services designed to meet these needs and resolve the problems that continually surface.

Obviously, any field placement could be said to offer unique opportunities and difficulties for a particular student. However, there are a number of special issues involved in work with AIDS clients, their families and significant others within an AIDS service provider organization. For example, many agencies devoted exclusively to serving persons with AIDS and their significant others, because they are relatively new, often struggle through intense growing pains as they attempt to provide a broad range of social and educational services in the midst of a terrible, frightening and expanding crisis. Also, it is often impossible for the most experienced professionals to achieve an adequate balance between professional distance and personal involvement when doing this work. Students need a great deal of support and help as they encounter all of these issues. It is difficult to remain objective with an AIDS client when one's friends are dying and one's own health could be in personal jeopardy. It is a tribute to these particular students' developing professionalism, maturity and dedication that they performed so excellently.

Placement at an AIDS service agency is not for every student. The opportunities for learning are so emotionally laden and the challenges so numerous that even second year students need to be at an exceptional level of maturity and professional skill development in order not to be overwhelmed by the demands of the work at such a placement. Using an AIDS service agency as a placement for a first year graduate student is not recommended unless, like Robert, the student has had prior experience as a volunteer for an AIDS organization.

There are valuable rewards inherent in the learning

which occurs when one is part of the AIDS services delivery system. Students choosing to train on the front lines in this war on AIDS through the provision of high quality and dignified social work services for all people with AIDS will come away from the experience with more than the development of social work skills and the acquisition of a body of knowledge that will sustain them throughout their professional lives. They will have contributed to the quality of life - and death - of PWAs and provided support to those who must suffer the loss of lovers, friends, children, or parents. But, they also will have challenged themselves in ways that offer unique opportunities for personal growth and development and which make lasting contributions to the student's self-confidence and self-worth.

References

Baumgartner, G. H. (1985) *AIDS: Psychosocial factors in the Acquired Immune Deficiency syndrome.* Springfield, IL: Charles C. Thomas.

Camus, A. (1948) *The plague.* New York: Random House

Christ, G., Wiener, L., & Moynihan, R. (1986) Psychosocial Issues in AIDS. *Psychiatric Annals*, March.

Lopez, D. & Wein, K. (1982) Psychosocial issues of people with AIDS. In *Volunteer Training Manual*. New York: Gay Men's Health Crisis, Inc.

Lopez, D. & Getzel, G. (1984) Helping gay AIDS patients in crisis. *Social Casework, 65*(7), 387-394.

Index